Ms. Helen MacDonald
5030 Blenheim St
Vancouver BC V6N 1N5

Victorian Sisters

Victorian Sisters

Ina Taylor

ADLER&ADLER

Published in the United States in 1987 by
Adler & Adler, Publishers, Inc.
4550 Montgomery Avenue
Bethesda, Maryland 20814

First published in Great Britain in 1987 by
George Weidenfeld & Nicolson Limited

Library of Congress Cataloging-in-Publication Data

Taylor, Ina.
    Victorian sisters.

    Bibliography: p.
    Includes index.
    1. Women—Great Britain—Biography. 2. Baldwin,
Louisa, 1845–1925. 3. Burne-Jones, Georgina, Lady,
1840–1920. 4. Kipling, Alice, 1837–1910. 5. Poynter,
Agnes, 1843–1906. 6. Sisters—Great Britain—Biography.
7. McDonald family. 8. Great Britain—Biography
I. Title.
CT3320.T38   1987   941'.0088042   [B]   86–28766
ISBN 0–917561–34–1

Printed in the United States of America

FOR COLIN AND HEIDI

Contents

Acknowledgements

I am grateful to the following people for their generous help and, in many cases, hospitality: Mrs Julia Atkins, the Revd A. R. Ankers, Mrs Meryl Macdonald Bendle, Miss Ida Callow, Mr John Cory, Mrs J. Dietholm, Mrs J. Dowson, Mrs Edna Drake, Mr and Mrs Peter Drury, Penelope Fitzgerald, Miss Norah Hebden, Mrs Hollamby at the Red House, Mrs Barbara Hurst, Miss Alison Inglis, the late Mr Ralph H. Jackson, the Misses Helen and Betty Macdonald, Dr Jan Marsh, Mrs Hazel Pettifor, the Revd W. C. A. Povey, Mr Colin Thornton, Mr Lance Thirkell and Mrs Young at The Gables; and to the staff of the following institutions, I am also grateful for their assistance: the Art Gallery of New South Wales; the Art Gallery, York; Batemans and the National Trust; Bewdley Museum; Birmingham Reference Library; Bodleian Library; the British Dental Archives; British Library, Department of Manuscripts; Castle Howard Archives; East Sussex Record Office; Arthur Findlay College Library; Fitzwilliam Museum Manuscripts Department; India Office Library; Kipling Society Library; Kidderminster Library; William Morris Gallery; Preston Manor (Brighton Museums); Salisbury Central Library; Sheffield Central Library; Southwark Local Studies Library; University of Sussex Library Manuscripts Department; Victoria and Albert Museum Library; Wellington Library, Shropshire (for cheerfully finding the archaic and the obscure); Wightwick Manor; Wolverhampton Central Library; and Worcester Record Office.

The following have kindly given permission for quotations from their material to be used: the Beinecke Rare Book and Manuscript Library, Yale University for extracts from the George Eliot letters; Mrs Meryl Macdonald Bendle for extracts from family papers; the Bodleian Library, Oxford for extracts from the letters of F.G. Stephens and the

Gilbert Murray papers; the British Library for extracts from the Burne-Jones letters; Castle Howard Archives, York for extracts from the correspondence of Georgiana and Edward Burne-Jones with George and Rosalind Howard, 9th Earl and Countess of Carlisle; Penelope Fitzgerald for extracts from her book *Burne-Jones: a biography*; the Fitzwilliam Museum, Cambridge for extracts from the Burne-Jones papers; the estate of Philip Henderson for extracts from *William Morris: His Life, Work and Friends* and from *Letters of William Morris to His Family and Friends* (Longmans); Dorothy Henley and the Hogarth Press for extracts from *Rosalind Howard, Countess of Carlisle*; the Houghton Library, Harvard University for extracts from the letter of C.E. Norton to G.W. Curtis, 1869; Professor Norman Kelvin for extracts from his *Collected Letters of William Morris*, Vol. 1; the Kipling Society for extracts from their Journals; the Misses Helen and Betty Macdonald for extracts from family papers; Dr Jan Marsh for extracts from *Pre-Raphaelite Sisterhood*; Mr Lance Thirkell for extracts from family papers; the Trustees of the Victoria and Albert Museum for extracts from the letters of Lady Burne-Jones with Sir Sidney Cockerell; A.P. Watt Ltd on behalf of the National Trust for Places of Historic Interest or Natural Beauty, for extracts from the Kipling Papers.

The Illustrations are reproduced by kind permission of the Misses Helen and Betty Macdonald with the exception of: the photograph of Rosalind and George Howard, by kind permission of Castle Howard, York; the photographs of Edward Burne-Jones and Edward Poynter by kind permission of Jeremy Maas; the photographs of George Eliot and John Ruskin by kind permission of the National Portrait Gallery; the woodcut by Georgie Burne-Jones by kind permission of the Trustees of the Victoria and Albert Museum; '*Kings' Daughters*' by kind permission of the Earl of Shelburne.

On a personal level thanks are due to my daughter Heidi who happily assisted in all manner of tasks and to my husband Colin who acted throughout as a researcher, first reader and editor and whose constant encouragement brought me through.

Illustrations

ILLUSTRATIONS

Rudyard Kipling
Trix Kipling
A room at Bikaner Lodge, the Kiplings' home in India
Alice and Rudyard Kipling
John Ruskin
A woodcut by Georgie Burne-Jones
Rosalind and George Howard
George Eliot
Philip Burne-Jones
Margaret Burne-Jones Mackail
John William Mackail
Agnes Poynter
Edward Poynter
Hugh Poynter
Ambrose Poynter
Alfred Baldwin
Louisa Baldwin
Edith Macdonald
Stanley Baldwin

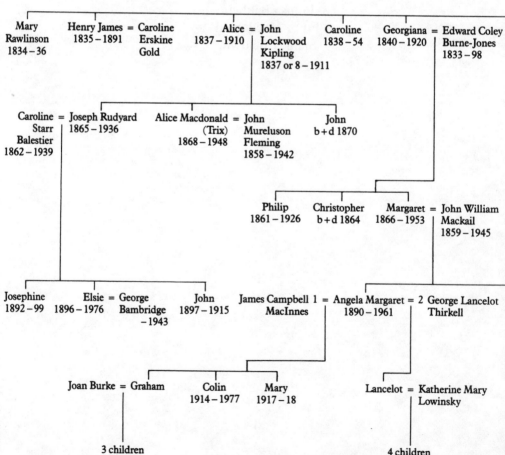

John

Allan = Flora Macdonald

| Mary Rawlinson 1834 – 36 | Henry James 1835 – 1891 = Caroline Erskine Gold | Alice 1837 – 1910 = John Lockwood Kipling 1837 or 8 – 1911 | Caroline 1838 – 54 | Georgiana 1840 – 1920 = Edward Coley Burne-Jones 1833 – 98 |

Caroline Starr Balestier 1862 – 1939 = Joseph Rudyard 1865 – 1936

Alice Macdonald (Trix) 1868 – 1948 = John Mureluson Fleming 1858 – 1942

John b + d 1870

Philip 1861 – 1926

Christopher b + d 1864

Margaret 1866 – 1953 = John William Mackail 1859 – 1945

Josephine 1892 – 99

Elsie 1896 – 1976 = George Bambridge – 1943

John 1897 – 1915

James Campbell MacInnes 1 = Angela Margaret 1890 – 1961 = 2 George Lancelot Thirkell

Joan Burke = Graham

Colin 1914 – 1977

Mary 1917 – 18

Lancelot = Katherine Mary Lowinsky

3 children

4 children

Macdonald Family Tree

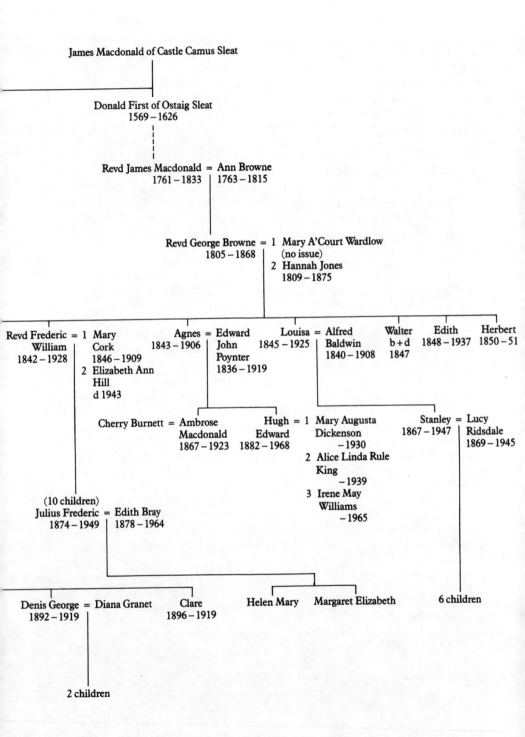

James Macdonald of Castle Camus Sleat

Donald First of Ostaig Sleat
1569 – 1626

Revd James Macdonald = Ann Browne
1761 – 1833 | 1763 – 1815

Revd George Browne = 1 Mary A'Court Wardlow
1805 – 1868 | (no issue)
2 Hannah Jones
1809 – 1875

Revd Frederic = 1 Mary   Agnes = Edward   Louisa = Alfred   Walter   Edith   Herbert
William   Cork   1843 – 1906   John   1845 – 1925   Baldwin   b + d   1848 – 1937   1850 – 51
1842 – 1928   1846 – 1909   Poynter   1840 – 1908   1847
           2 Elizabeth Ann   1836 – 1919
             Hill
             d 1943

Cherry Burnett = Ambrose   Hugh = 1 Mary Augusta   Stanley = Lucy
            Macdonald   Edward   Dickenson   1867 – 1947 | Ridsdale
            1867 – 1923   1882 – 1968   – 1930   1869 – 1945
                                   2 Alice Linda Rule
                                    King
                                      – 1939
                                 3 Irene May
                                    Williams
                                      – 1965

(10 children)
Julius Frederic = Edith Bray
1874 – 1949 | 1878 – 1964

Denis George = Diana Granet   Clare   Helen Mary   Margaret Elizabeth   6 children
1892 – 1919 | 1896 – 1919

2 children

Introduction

My interest in the Macdonald sisters was first aroused by the apparent coincidence of four girls from the same family marrying into families which became famous: they were allied in marriage with the Kiplings, Burne-Joneses, Poynters and Baldwins. I therefore expected that the progress of these girls had been manoeuvred either by a mother possessing the head-hunting instinct of one of Jane Austen's Mamas or by a socially well-connected father. It was a surprise to find that their origins were humble, for as the daughters of an itinerant Methodist preacher they belonged firmly to the lower middle class, and their early years were spent in grim industrial towns of the North and Midlands.

It was equally surprising to discover that these four women had been overlooked by historians despite their status as wives and mothers of famous men. The only study made of their lives was an excellent compilation of their correspondence by A. W. Baldwin in 1960, based largely on his family's papers with little critical assessment, but such a book inevitably raises more questions than it answers. Biographies of Rudyard Kipling, Stanley Baldwin and Edward Burne-Jones have tended to dismiss the women in their lives as mere ciphers.

The characteristics generally assigned to these women were wit and delicacy, which conclusions seemed meaningful until further reading revealed that most middle-class Victorian women were said to be similarly endowed. Wittiness, it transpired, was merely a euphemism for intelligence, and because few nineteenth-century men wanted clever wives, the more acceptable drawing-room attainment of 'wit' was substituted. In the same way no middle-class woman would be flattered to be described as robustly healthy. This attribute was expected in female servants, but not in their employers, for it was widely believed that physical strength accompanied a deficiency in the spirit; thus the more delicate the body, the more sensitive the nature.

Despite the anonymity shrouding these sisters, it seemed unlikely that four women who rose from a humble background, two to become the titled wives of major artists, one the mother of a prime minister and another the mother of a leading literary figure, could be of no account. Similarly the interrelation between the apparently unconnected worlds of the Methodist manse, the artist's studio, India under the Raj, parliamentary politics and the London literary scene promised to be spellbinding.

I began with four names, Alice, Georgiana, Agnes and Louisa Macdonald, but no faces, no personalities and an equal sympathy and interest in them all. What emerged were four distinct individuals with whom I identified to varying degrees. A study of four people will always differ from a biography of a single person – and indeed the story of no one Macdonald sister would warrant an exclusive telling – but this was a rare opportunity to study four women sharing the same inheritance and childhood environment and to see how their personalities and lives developed. Inevitably in such a study some characters demanded more detailed treatment than others, and in the same way the qualities of some were easier to appreciate than others. Although a biographer tries to identify with the subject, with four subjects an order of favouritism inevitably emerges, reflecting the writer's personal interests and prejudices.

I could not help but admire the eldest sister Alice, who married John Lockwood Kipling and shocked her family by disappearing off to India, where Rudyard was born. She emerged as a curiously modern woman in outlook, despite being born just before Victoria came to the throne. Her immense determination and strength of character would have taken her far in twentieth-century life had she not lacked the educational opportunities and social freedoms we take for granted. Given these, Alice Macdonald could have had a spectacular career in her own right, most likely as a writer, but equally the sort of forcefulness with which she promoted her family in Anglo-Indian society could have had wider application. Alice accepted that an independent life for a woman in mid-Victorian society was extremely difficult, and so directed her energies into fostering the careers of both husband and son. The role Alice was forced to adopt in the late nineteenth century has changed little since. Many intelligent middle-class women are still prevented from having their own career by husbands who see a working wife as a slur on their own status. All that is left to such wives, as it was to Alice Kipling, is to use their intelligence to entertain and intrigue in the promotion of their husband's career. It was a job Alice was admirably suited to, and when her son returned to India in his late teens she did all in her power to advance him, with even greater success.

Because Rudyard's early literary progress owed much to his mother, she more than any of the sisters could be termed the power behind the throne. The origins of Rudyard Kipling's literary talent seemed hard to distinguish at first, even though both parents wrote and published articles. His father's work was of a higher standard than his mother's, but neither contained much of the perception and humour which characterized Rudyard's early writings. The answer appeared unexpectedly in Alice Kipling's private correspondence, which of course has never been published. Here she revealed a sharp eye for and a caustic commentary on the paradoxes and pretentiousness of life in British India. Her observations are clever and viciously funny. Had she been permitted to write in that vein for publication, the world would have seen a brilliant female satirist, but society was not ready for such an innovation. It is a pity that the published works of Alice Kipling are turgid, consciously literary efforts which bear no comparison with the letter writer.

Although Alice had my admiration, she did not engage my sympathy as much as the next sister in age. I have to admit that for me Georgie Burne-Jones was the heroine amongst the Macdonald sisters. As one of the present-day members of the family told me, despite her diminutive stature Georgie stood head and shoulders above the others. It was also interesting to observe that she was the only sister the family universally adored, a circumstance which continued into the next generation. This was surprising because she maintained the most exacting personal standards and was animated more by the dictates of conscience than any of her sisters, an intimidating feature of her character for outsiders. Consequently few got to know her well, but those who did discovered a genuinely selfless individual. She was the one to whom people instinctively turned in time of trouble because she could be relied upon to give sympathy and practical help. Her loyalty was unswerving both to the friends of her youth and to her family. Even in the face of her husband's infidelity she remained constant, a virtue little admired perhaps by present-day observers, but which was vindicated by the ultimately successful career of her husband, the artist Sir Edward Burne-Jones, and by the repair of their marriage. Georgie was certainly another sister who could be said to be the power behind a famous man, but in an altogether quieter and more supportive manner than her elder sister. Edward Burne-Jones could not have succeeded without his wife, for although he had the artistic ability, it needed someone to organize him, his life and his business in order for that ability to be converted into solid achievement. Someone so meek and unassuming as Georgie was hardly the type of person to be seen as a heroine. But once she felt her husband's career was assured, and after years of dazzle from the light of other suns, Georgie Burne-Jones acquired sufficient confidence to pursue her own interests, and a different character emerged.

The life of her younger sister Agnes was the hardest to elucidate. She was the extrovert social butterfly of the family, who experienced a swift transition in fortune, for in a matter of a few years she moved from being a simple Methodist minister's daughter into a world of continental travel and glittering balls attended by such as the Prince of Wales and Lillie Langtry. The essential Lady Agnes Poynter remained elusive because at the time of her death much of her correspondence was destroyed or passed to her favourite sister Louisa Baldwin, whose descendants have sadly not felt able to allow the material to be seen. Ironically Sir Edward Poynter, although a doyen of the Victorian art world, so totally lost favour in his final years that no biographies and few articles have been written about him. There were two children of the Poynter marriage, but the line ended with their deaths, one of which took place in Australia. Agnes Poynter's life was the least satisfactory of the sisters' both from the biographer's point of view and probably her own. She started out with the same advantages as her sisters, plus the most attractive looks and personality of the four, but ultimately achieved little in her own right. She began by supporting her husband socially, but he was never a likeable character and his dour influence ultimately sapped her energy and charm.

Louisa, the youngest of the four Macdonald women, was a difficult person to understand or sympathize with, because she affected severe ill-health immediately after the birth of her son Stanley and nurtured this condition to the exclusion of everything else for the rest of her life. It was a method of seeking attention and compensated for a marriage and way of life she found disappointing. Indeed, life with a morbidly religious industrialist deep in the Worcestershire countryside could not compare with the experiences of the other three sisters. Yet, despite her apparent infirmity, Louisa Baldwin went on to write and publish poetry, novels and children's stories and, more significantly, gave her son the impetus to reach the highest political office.

Events and people of the past are often viewed in the light of current standards and obsessions. If so judged, the Macdonald sisters under-achieved. All were able, intelligent women, but none possessed the ultimate decisiveness to attack the restraints of their age. Yet this is an easy criticism to make from a distance of a hundred years and shows little understanding of their lives. These women were brought up to limit their horizons to being supporters of their husbands; the extent to which they explored these boundaries varied from Alice Kipling – who was very much the instigator of success – to Louisa Baldwin, whose influence on her husband was almost negligible.

Amongst the sisters themselves there was a strong sense of family unity, and no matter whom they married, they regarded themselves essentially as Macdonalds. The sisterly bonds which were so vital in childhood loosened in early marriage, but strengthened again towards the end of their lives, providing great comfort and support in their final years. Talented the women most certainly were and as such appealed to exceptional men, but theirs was not the sort of talent to beget a line of great names. Nevertheless, the Macdonald sisters remain a unique and fascinating group of women who, from the hallowed portals of the manse, were propelled into the more public arenas of art, politics and literature.

Chapter One

Venerated Ancestors

From their earliest years the Macdonald girls knew they were descended from 'a galaxy of brilliant kinsfolk', which they believed made them superior to other families. The precise details of their ancestry were unknown to them, but they were confident that the Highland blood of that great Scottish clan, the Macdonalds, conferred all manner of gifts on them.

Alice, the eldest girl, was the one most aware of her Celtic origins, from which she claimed mystic, creative powers and which she believed were passed in turn to her children. Indeed her son Rudyard told an audience in Edinburgh in 1922 that his literary skills were of Scottish origin, for 'there's ink in the blood of the Macdonalds'.[1] Similarly his sister Trix, who had Macdonald as her middle name, was convinced that the supernatural powers of the Highland clan had passed down to her and enabled her to communicate with the spirit world. To Alice, the Macdonald lineage was so vital that her final request was that the legend on her tombstone should read 'Alice Macdonald wife of John Lockwood Kipling'. Such matters were of little concern to Georgie, who lived essentially in the present and the future. As a child it had pleased her to think the Macdonald family might have behaved like Walter Scott characters, and the idea of ancestors prepared to lay down their lives for their beliefs drew her admiration. Agnes too was a girl who lived for the present. Only when confronted by her husband's impressive Huguenot ancestry did she trouble to revive her noble past and insist that her eldest son have the middle name Macdonald. For Louisa, the Macdonald connection was a romantic idea around which she could weave stories; one humorous epic was entitled 'The Macdonald Bratton' and purported to trace the family's descent via such obscure ancestors as the Loch Ness monster and the Old Man of

1

the Isles. Georgie drew a suitable cover showing a chubby Macdonald baby or 'brat' cutting his teeth on a huge key, whilst being carried aloft on the shields of bearded chieftains. This was naturally intended as a joke, but Louisa took her Scottish forefathers quite seriously enough to request that her honeymoon be spent in the Macdonald homeland, and she was delighted when her new husband saw fit to buy her a shawl of the correct dress tartan and a silver brooch with the clan's coat of arms. Although Louisa had no intention of taking anything but her husband's name on her tombstone, it is no coincidence that the design she chose for her memorial window was Saint Margaret of Scotland. Her son Stanley Baldwin, brought up in the knowledge that he was of the Macdonald line, publicly acknowledged a Celtic strain in his character which he said was typified by a 'love of an almost divine individualism coupled with the ambition to get learning, not for the sake of money, but for its own sake'.[2]

The idea of a glorious Scottish past was a convenient peg on which to hang anything and provided a much needed mark of status for the generation to which the four girls belonged. As a consequence of their father's profession, the girls grew up as members of the Wesleyan Methodist Society, an essentially middle-class movement drawing heavily for support on those prosperous families engaged in commerce or industry in the new industrial towns. Although Methodism preached equality, it was quite obvious to observers that the Reverend George Macdonald and his family were not as affluent as most members of the congregation; in the opinion of the Macdonalds a noble ancestry hidden in Highland mists, in alliance with an impeccable Methodist pedigree where Wesley had personally called one of their number to preach, helped to redress the balance. The girls' father instituted this ancestor-worship when he declared that his lineage was godly and more prized than anything the Heralds' College could offer, but in reality he could only have vouched for his father's behaviour, since most of his predecessors' activities were anything but godly.

The family's knowledge of their forbears was limited to the fact that they originally came from the Isle of Skye and that sometime after the 1745 Rebellion one couple emigrated to Canada and another set out for America. This latter branch failed dismally in their objective, for the ship's captain, using one imagines the charts of Columbus, mistakenly put them down in Ireland; it was a story which lost nothing in the retelling, for speaking at a dinner Rudyard Kipling waxed eloquent

2

about his ancestors fighting alongside Bonnie Prince Charlie and being shipwrecked off Ireland. A scholar of clan history has since worked out that the branch of the Macdonalds who did settle in Ireland were descended from the great Macdonald clan of Ostaig and Capstill on Skye, and whilst John Macdonald was landing in Ireland, shipwrecked or otherwise, another kinswoman, Flora Macdonald, was whisking Bonnie Prince Charlie to safety – a romantic association the four Macdonald girls would have revelled in had they but known.

It was to James Macdonald, the girls' grandfather, that the family looked with admiration. He was born in 1761 in Ballinamallard, near Enniskillen in Ireland, the son of the John Macdonald who originally emigrated from Skye. The family were devout members of the established church and as such attended open-air meetings held by John Wesley, engaging in one of his Irish missions at that time. The young James Macdonald was so inspired by the great preacher that he joined the Methodist Society. This was in no way incompatible with the family's beliefs, because Wesley taught that his was a movement within the Church and strongly resisted attempts to form a separate sect.

At the age of twenty-three James Macdonald accepted Wesley's invitation to become an itinerant preacher. It was a very hard life demanding, in addition to deep religious conviction, tremendous physical stamina to take the word of God around Ireland on foot and horseback. There is no doubt that Wesley's recognition of James Macdonald as an exceptional man was justified, for during his arduous travels Macdonald found time to teach himself Hebrew, Latin and Greek to a standard sufficient to read the Scriptures.

During his ministry in Newry in 1789, he married another Irish Methodist, Ann Browne, who subsequently bore him six children. The two born in Ireland also died there before attaining their third birthdays, but the other four born to the family in England reached adulthood. After eleven years preaching in the Irish countryside between Londonderry and Dublin, the Methodist Society transferred James Macdonald to England, where for thirty years he carried the Word around many of the industrial towns of the north – places such as Rochdale, Bolton and Liverpool. During his one-year ministry in Stockport in 1805 the last child, George Browne Macdonald, was born on 2 October, only weeks before the battle of Trafalgar.

The Reverend James Macdonald was described by his grandson as 'essentially an intellectual man and a student, refined in his tastes, and

3

disliking everything that was hasty, crude and unbalanced in thought or irreverent in spirit'.[3] He was the first member of the family to display literary skills, initially as a contributor to the Methodist magazine, later as its assistant editor, and then as the author of four theological books. His reading was extensive and not restricted to religious works, so the large library he amassed and which was handed down the family was appreciated by his granddaughters when they sought to widen their education.

Languages were his fascination, and in later years he learnt Italian, Spanish and Portuguese, ostensibly to read commentaries on the Scriptures, but in reality for sheer pleasure. This Macdonald flair for languages reappeared in subsequent generations, most markedly in his granddaughters. Alice learned Hindi with ease within a short time of her arrival in India, whilst her sisters voluntarily undertook lessons in French after their marriages and became competent enough to read and converse in the language. Being of a more academic disposition, Georgie worked at literary translations with her friend, the novelist George Eliot, then progressed to the study of Latin.

James Macdonald's intellectual prowess first manifested itself in his elder son, an able scholar, who with financial sponsorship was able to attend Queens' College, Cambridge to read Divinity, from whence he intended to enter the Methodist Society as a preacher. His career was tragically brought to a close at the age of twenty-five when tuberculosis killed him, as it had his mother and sister.

Since it was James Macdonald's dearest wish that the teachings of John Wesley be handed down the Macdonald line, he turned to his remaining son George. This boy had been educated at the newly-opened Woodhouse Grove Wesleyan Boarding School near Bradford, where his attendance coincided with a very significant marriage, that of the headmaster's niece Maria Branwell to the local curate Patrick Brontë. It was a marriage which produced a better known set of sisters – Charlotte, Anne and Emily Brontë.

With little choice in the matter, George Macdonald joined the Methodist Society whilst at Woodhouse Grove, but his membership finished with his education, and after leaving school he took a commercial post in London. The temptations of life in the big city caused his sister great concern, and her letters contained dire warnings of the dangers of becoming entangled with gay, thoughtless young men, whose only intention was to extract hellish pleasure from corrupting others. Both sister and father were determined that George should enter the ministry and began to tighten the moral screw with wistful remarks from Mary Ann Macdonald about the joy and honour there might be in the family if they had a brother as well as a father preaching the gospel. In case the hints had been too discreet, Mary Ann finished off by requesting that they be told as soon as George had made up his mind to join the Methodist Society. His father followed this up with useful, though quite unsolicited, advice about becoming a full-blooded preacher:

> Whenever you begin to preach . . . accustom yourself to speak with ease and propriety in private, and it will become habitual to you to do so in public. A strong devotional spirit, free from enthusiasm, is an admirable requisite for the pulpit. Let your heart be filled with your subject, take sufficient time in delivering your discourse, and then you will speak to purpose. Be calm and cool in the beginning of your address, and more than ordinarily deliberate; your auditors will then be easy, and disposed to accompany you. After some time your passions will begin to work, and you will find them too eloquent. But care must be taken lest they rise to such a height as to produce extravagance of language, or too great loudness of voice.[4]

Continual pressure of this nature was hard to resist, especially when bolstered with the power of religion, and by the time he was twenty George Macdonald had succumbed, and to his family's delight and immense relief was received into the Methodist Church as a junior minister to his father, then preaching in the Devonport circuit. Sometime during his early ministry, George Macdonald married Mary A'Court Wardlow from Dorset, but tuberculosis deprived him of this wife, and no children survived the marriage.

His marriage to Hannah Jones took place on 2 May 1833 in Manchester. She was twenty-four and thus four years younger than her husband. As her maiden name suggests, on her father's side the family originated from Wales, more precisely from the Vale of Clwyd, but her mother was English. Thus the children of George and Hannah Macdonald received an equal blend of Scottish, Irish, Welsh and English blood, although it was always the Scottish contribution they chose to acknowledge.

Hannah Jones's background was typical Wesleyan Methodist, in that her father was a partner in a wholesale grocery business in Canon Street, Manchester, which enabled the family to enjoy a comfortable standard of living. They lived in a large house close by the warehouse, employed

5

a bevy of servants, and were well-known for their entertaining, with fine porcelain and silver utensils much in evidence. The six Jones children grew up accustomed to holidays away from the unhealthy Manchester air, either in the country or by the sea at Southport. Little has been recorded about Hannah's father, save that he was an amiable gentleman, but her mother, formerly the widow Mrs Rawlinson, made a stronger impression on all who knew her. In this lady can be seen some of the personality traits which her granddaughters inherited. Mrs Jones was a formidable woman with a 'strongly marked character sure to make itself felt wherever she was', one of them recalled.[5] Once she embraced a cause, her commitment was total. It was said that she gave up all hope of worldly advancement to join the Methodist Society, and expounded its virtues with all the zeal of a proselyte: 'A pillar of the congregation', her granddaughters called her.[6] The other issue which she so passionately believed in was education, both for her sons and her daughters, which in the early nineteenth century was unusual. The two Jones boys attended school, but the four girls were educated at home by a tutor who gave instruction in all the basic subjects and some less common ones like Latin, Italian and musical theory.

Alongside Grandmother Jones's admirable qualities there existed some of more dubious value. She was not a happy person: the religion which she observed so rigorously gave her all the satisfaction of martyrdom. Her granddaughters, who of course only knew her as an old lady, noticed she had 'a certain tendency to bitterness and anger when provoked which is not attractive' and felt that most of their aunts 'seemed framed neither to be happy nor to make happy', although their mother and Aunt Pullein they were sure had escaped that characteristic.[7] This was not really true, for Mrs Jones was the origin of that distinct strand of melancholy which troubled first her daughter Hannah and later the Macdonald sisters themselves and their descendants.

Hannah Jones was brought up in a devout Methodist home, but unfortunately this did nothing to prepare her for life as the wife of an itinerant preacher. Marriage to George Macdonald was a step downward in social terms, though full of moral virtue. Questions of status, however, rarely troubled Hannah Macdonald; it was her husband's complete dedication to his work which she found really hard to accept. This work took him away from home for days on end to preach, and demanded that every three years the family pack up their possessions and move to any town the Wesleyan Conference cared to nominate.

Added to that, the minister's stipend was so low compared with her father's income that instead of the disciplined body of servants she had grown up with she could only afford two menials. Their standards never accorded with her own, and the Macdonald household lurched from one domestic crisis to another as new servants were engaged and others sacked.

In Mrs Macdonald's opinion, influences combined to ensure she did not enjoy a happy life: more truly it could be said she *did* enjoy an unhappy one, and her diary reads, as she herself forecast it would, as a catalogue of complaints. Admittedly her life was difficult. She inherited a full measure of her mother's pessimism and 'the early Methodist training which had been hers encouraged introspection, which was not a healthy influence in her sensitive disposition. Looking within, she did not find the confident spiritual experiences which she was led to expect in a "believer", and this saddened her', one of her daughters recalled.[8] Even the intense love Hannah felt for her husband was a source of pain, because when he left home on his all-too-frequent preaching expeditions, she felt herself to be as lonely as a widow and became absorbed in self-pity, sitting up until the early hours to await his return, only to find that the Lord's work had taken longer than anticipated and he did not appear until breakfast the following day. Her diary is full of woe about being married to an absent husband, and the attendant household problems, and when the self-control slipped, the writer was wont to scrawl with passion how sick she was of their itinerancy.

Despite her husband's never-ending absences, Hannah Macdonald experienced nineteen years of perpetual childbearing, beginning nine months after her marriage. In her children's opinion there never was a mother who so delighted in babies, but this conclusion was completely wrong. Mrs Macdonald had no particular maternal feelings and resented the demands which little children continually made upon her. Since there was never enough money to employ a nursemaid, unlike most middle-class women she had to look after the ever increasing number of offspring herself, which tried her patience to the limit. She found the constant pregnancies drained her strength, and babyminding, to her way of thinking, was an unrewarding occupation. Guiltily she noted in her diary that she was fighting the self-will that demanded she use her time more profitably. At other times she recorded her disinclination towards nursing and child-rearing, because the babies were fractious and the young children boisterous and all but overpowered her. 'She possessed a caustic tongue when she chose to use it', one of her children recalled, but added loyally: 'Her self-control seemed perfect.'[9] Only when her family reached their teenage years did she appreciate their company, for they were then able to share in the intellectual pursuits she so enjoyed.

With limited finances, Hannah Macdonald attempted to make a home for her husband and children from the various houses assigned to them by the Methodist connexion. It was a disheartening process because no sooner had she got one house together than her husband's three-year ministry was finished and the family were on the move to yet another town and dirty, broken-down house. If the Macdonald experiences were anything to go by, local Methodist societies did not trouble greatly about the accommodation they provided for their ministers. Furnishings were frequently inadequate, and so Mrs Macdonald found herself compelled to go in search of sufficient beds or chairs soon after the family's arrival. The house they were given in Marylebone demonstrates other problems. She wrote:

> If you can imagine a house in a state of utter confusion and disorder, many degrees transcending anything you ever saw, you may perhaps form some conception of things here. Whitewashing, papering, joinering, blacksmith's work and glazier's repairs mingle with washing, sweeping, rubbing, scrubbing, arranging and disarranging, and form a whole so discordant that order and decorum seem to have taken flight in terror. This is a very old house, and it has evidently suffered an amount of neglect sufficient to break the heart of anything but an old house.[10]

Triennial house-moving continued for most of her married life and did nothing to raise her spirits: 'This removing is a growing (I was going to say "evil") burden, and I think sometimes I shall sink under it . . . unless, indeed, I never find time to do so', she confided in her sister.[11]

Mrs Macdonald's tragedy was that she was an intelligent woman, but felt herself trapped by the constraints of her sex, the times and lack of money. She tried to participate in her husband's interests and enjoyed philosophical, literary or theological discussions with him, because hers was an alert mind, well-informed on many subjects. Whenever possible she attended the classes and lectures organized by the local chapel on subjects as diverse as the virtues of emigrating to Natal, national education, magnetism and, naturally, religion in various guises. She welcomed any chance to learn about things at first hand, so when Methodist business moved her around the country she turned it to her advantage, visiting places like Worcester Cathedral, a silver-plating factory, an iron foundry and Wedgwood's potteries. Too often though, pregnancies or nursing restricted her activities, and her knowledge had to be derived from reading. Religious books with titles like Godwin's *Redemption* and *Zeal without Innovation* loomed large in her choice, but there was also space for poetry, Shakespeare and travel books. In later years she was an avid reader of the novels of Mrs Gaskell and the Brontës and encouraged her daughters to follow suit.

Religion was important to Mrs Macdonald in her personal life as well as in her role as the minister's wife, but it yielded her no comfort. She saw only high ideals she failed to attain, which reinforced her innate sense of guilt and spiritual depression. Following the strict guidelines laid down in her childhood, she suppressed any feelings of rebellion or self-will, but this only exacerbated her problem. Hannah Macdonald became prey to all manner of psychosomatic ailments. She herself admitted they were the result of mental exercise and anxieties, but the pain was real enough and produced further misery. Since she sub-scribed to the idea that sensitive intelligent minds were housed in delicate bodies, she looked for proof of her own and her daughters' abilities in this way. The Macdonald girls grew up therefore in an environment where hypochondria was a normal part of life.

Their father, however, was a totally different character. He himself admitted trouble rolled off him like water off a duck's back, but his complete disregard for his own well-being and the family's placed an additional burden on his wife. He remained quite oblivious to the domestic crises occurring around him and would either go quietly into his study to prepare a sermon or leave for the railway station bound for another preaching engagement.

The Reverend George Macdonald might have been pressured into becoming a preacher against his will, but once ordained he treated it as his vocation in life and lived exclusively for his work. It occupied him seven days a week for most of his waking hours, and in accordance with usual Victorian attitudes, family matters were his wife's domain. He may not have had the same academic abilities as his father, but he was acknowledged to be a very fiery speaker and consequently received many invitations to preach away from his own circuit at special Methodist gatherings. He travelled enormous distances, mainly by rail, and it was not unusual for his itinerary to take in such places as Birmingham, St Neots, Grimsby and Oxford, all within the space of ten days. This meant that the time he spent at home was severely circumscribed, and much of that spent out amongst his flock or closeted in his study preparing sermons. He was by temperament a man of restless energy, well-suited to the strict precepts of Methodism which made a virtue of early rising. He required little sleep, went to bed late and always rose to pray before six o'clock in the morning. The amount of sleep he required was so minimal that his night-time activities resembled those of an insomniac, but he had little patience with members of the family who did not share this inclination: when he was resident at home, all were likely to find themselves roused at hours they regarded as less than godly.

His children were brought up to regard idleness as one of the greatest sins they could commit, so it behoved them to ensure that they were never caught wasting a moment. The punishment for being found idle was to have to endure a spontaneous prayer-meeting, which the minister immediately instigated for everyone. Not surprisingly his children soon learnt the art of instant busyness, with sewing or reading ready to hand. Some, like Georgie and Alice, retained this early training for life and could never completely relax without feeling the need to be engaged in some worthwhile activity. George Macdonald's restlessness proved an embarrassment at mealtimes, for once he had finished his own small portion he could not bear to wait for slower eaters and was quite likely to go off for a walk until the next course arrived. For him and his daughter Alice, eating was no pleasure, merely a necessity, and both consumed the minimum to sustain them. In practice the children only saw their father for the main midday meal when he was home, because he did not trouble with breakfast and preferred to take tea (two minute pieces of buttered toast and a cup of tea) alone in his study so that God's work could continue uninterrupted.

Methodists were not teetotal at that time, but George Macdonald imposed the strictest standards on himself and did not partake of alcohol. In 1841 he published a pamphlet entitled 'An Apology for the Disuse of Alcoholic Drink', in which he urged all Christians to abstain, but it was noticeable that his wife, brought up in a sociable household, did not share his views, and beer was regularly brewed at the manse. In the same way the gifts of wine, sherry and port which appeared at Christmas from the congregation were always gratefully accepted. His daughters, on marriage, varied in their response to alcohol: Alice, though requesting that only tea and coffee be drunk at her wedding reception, soon discovered it was more acceptable in Anglo-Indian society to indulge in alcohol, whereas Georgie, who regularly kept the inebriated company of artists, quietly sipped at water; Agnes happily adopted the habits of the society she moved in with her husband, and Louisa discovered that champagne provided a most efficacious cure for some of her illnesses.

Although the Reverend George Macdonald eschewed drink, he was a heavy smoker, rarely seen without the long clay Broseley pipe he favoured. No one regarded this as a vice, merely the normal habit of a learned man, but heavy smoking combined with hard work and sparse food and rest put an immense strain on his health. In total contrast to his wife and daughters he paid scant attention to himself, regarding this as a needless distraction from his work, but his punishing regime pushed his body to the limits of its endurance, forced early retirement on him at the peak of his career and shortly after brought him to an early grave.

Whilst respecting their father's dedication, few of his children were inspired to be so single-minded. He had not only set a difficult example to follow but also shown the price to be paid. If anything, the opposite lesson was learned, and his children grew up at pains to show they were not narrow-minded. Only his daughter Georgie, appropriately called after her father, had a similar attitude to personal morality, imposing on herself the most exacting standards, yet not demanding them of others: 'At all events I have obeyed my conscience – which is always something', she remarked late in her life after taking what she knew would be an unpopular decision.[12] For her as for her father, personal integrity was of the essence.

Outside the field of religion, George Macdonald was surprisingly liberal in his views, being both concerned and well-informed about the issues of the day. Scientific discoveries particularly fascinated him, and so absolute was his faith in God that he never regarded them as a threat to religion, rather as a further proof of the omnipotence of the Creator. Although he was a daily reader of *The Times* and well aware of events in Parliament, party politics held no interest for him. Like most Wesleyan Methodists, he voted Liberal, but like them also his inclinations more accurately accorded with the Conservative Party. Perhaps because of this lack of enthusiasm for politics on the part of both parents, the Macdonald girls developed an especial interest in and awareness of the subject, though they diverged widely in the parties they supported.

To the Macdonald children their father was a distant figure who came and went, and even during his time at home was so preoccupied that he often did not notice them. Nevertheless he was the ultimate authority: his rules were laid down in firm and often dramatic ways, such as the time when he sombrely called them into his study and read aloud a newly-written entry from his diary: 'Ruth Scott dismissed for telling lies.'[13] Nothing else was said. The lesson was understood, and the housework shared round again until a new servant could be found. He also had a hatred of malicious gossip and would quell it by the simple expedient of asking some irrelevant question, so that the girls might find their chatter interrupted by the apparently innocent enquiry: 'What is the price of potatoes?'[14] In the ensuing silence they would understand the sin they had committed.

George Macdonald was a much more cheerful and good-humoured person than his wife, and his children prized the small amount of attention he paid them. Significantly the saying of his they remembered best was the one he would use when a small child stayed too long on his lap: 'Offspring, spring off!'[15] Without further ado the infant would be set down and the minister return to the Lord's work. But for the Macdonald girls it was their melancholic mother who was the beloved linch-pin of their lives.

Chapter Two

An Introspective Childhood

There were no rolling Scottish mists surrounding the birthplaces of the Macdonald girls, rather the smog-filled air of industrial towns where parliamentary acts had made little impression; children struggled to survive in disease-ridden slums and endure the horrors of mine and machinery. Although the girls were born in the heart of social problems, they were cocooned from knowledge of such deprivation. The Wesleyan movement, whilst encouraging philanthropy, avoided direct contact with the poorest elements of society, and any subsequent ideas the girls had of urban poverty owed more to the novels of Charles Dickens than to personal experience.

Alice Macdonald was born in Sheffield, a town whose fortunes rested on the cutlery trade. Her birth on 4 April 1837 came in the final months of William IV's reign, when the Great Reform Bill was still fresh in people's minds and there was agitation for the franchise to be widened. She was the third child of George and Hannah Macdonald and never knew her elder sister Mary, who died at the age of two-and-a-half from a disease which caused blindness. Henry James, always known as Harry, then became the eldest, for he was born in October 1835.

Soon after Queen Victoria's coronation, which the family celebrated by watching the spectacular fireworks display in Sheffield, the Methodist Conference moved the Reverend George Macdonald to a circuit in Birmingham. It was hardly an auspicious time to arrive in that town because the supporters of the Chartists were becoming very impatient. Formed around a six-point plan they called 'The People's Charter', they wanted greater representation for the lower classes in Parliament. What began as a respectable working-class movement changed when the militant Birmingham Political Union joined in. In the late summer of 1838 the Macdonalds came to a restless Birmingham. There had been a large meeting addressed by the powerful demagogue Feargus O'Connor, at which he urged his supporters to use force to obtain their objectives; with no shortage of discontent it was a potentially explosive situation.

Mrs Macdonald was apprehensive in the extreme; she was eight months pregnant with her fourth baby (Caroline, who was always called Carrie, and was born in October 1838), had two young children to look after, a husband who was frequently absent, and to make matters worse knew no one in the town. The atmosphere of unease got worse the following year when the authorities brought in soldiers and constables from London to disperse gatherings. Mrs Macdonald, who had previously only dared to venture out of her house in the afternoons for fear of encountering a riot, was terrified by the new development. One hot July night a crowd of five hundred stormed the town's prison before burning and looting at will. Next morning, one eyewitness said, 'Birmingham appeared like a town in a state of siege . . . the shells of the burnt houses looked as if the place had been attacked by an enemy.'[1] Mrs Macdonald did not wait to see: grabbing her children she fled to Manchester and the security of her mother and sisters. Conditions there and in most other industrial towns were only marginally safer as the Chartist unrest spread and angry scenes flared up wherever crowds collected. Even in Manchester the family were obliged to keep inside the house, but Hannah was relieved to have her family round her.

By the time Georgiana, known to the family as Georgie, was born in Birmingham on 21 July 1840, peace had returned to the town. Sporadic outbreaks of violence continued in the North for the next ten years, which were 'the hungry forties' when many families had no choice but to send even their small children into the mines and factories to ensure survival.

In 1841 Mr Macdonald's next circuit took the family to Leeds. This town was also experiencing chronic poverty. Another visitor there that year was horrified at 'the swarms of meanly-clad women and children, and the dingy, smoky, wretched-looking dwellings of the poor', where 'hundreds of thousands of human beings huddled together in attics and cellars or [were] crawling over the earth as if they did not belong to it'.[2] If Mrs Macdonald thought their accommodation left much to be desired, a contemporary report on housing conditions in Leeds indicated that most of the population lived in far worse conditions. In one area only three out of ninety-three streets had any system of drainage, and the overcrowding was such that government inspectors calculated each room in some houses averaged four occupants, whilst ten persons appeared to occupy each bed in one lodging house! It was hardly surprising disease was rife. The town had suffered a severe epidemic of cholera ten years before the Macdonalds arrived, with regular outbreaks of typhoid since.

Frederic William and Agnes, born in Leeds in February 1842 and on 25 September 1843 respectively, entered the world in circumstances far superior to those the government inspectors found, and consequently stood a greater chance of survival than most babies in the town. Louisa, known as Louie, was the next child in the family, born on 25 August 1845 during their sojourn in the textile town of Wakefield, and Edith, the last one, born in another Yorkshire town, Huddersfield, in September 1848. There were also the infant deaths of two boys, yet Mrs Macdonald was more fortunate than most of her contemporaries because out of her eleven confinements seven children reached adulthood, whereas for those living in the slums two survivors from five pregnancies would be considered good.

For the Macdonald children the most memorable feature of their childhood was not the poverty they saw, but the continual itinerancy. Every third year there was a different town, a different house, even different furniture. There was nowhere they could call home; they merely possessed 'a moving tent', and Georgie thought her lot as a Methodist preacher's daughter 'might be reckoned as a wandering gypsy'.[3] Because they were always on the move, the girls made few friends and were forced to rely on each other to an exceptional degree. Mrs Macdonald said proudly that there were few families as united as theirs, but Frederic, with the benefit of hindsight, thought problems were created as a result. The Macdonald children tried to form a protective shell around themselves, which outsiders were not encouraged to penetrate. The family lauded their own virtues and talents, but were highly critical of those they thought inferior. It was an exclusiveness which was promoted by a partiality for in-jokes and 'Macdonald' expressions, so that they earned a reputation for aloofness. In rather pharisaic tones, Agnes announced she was grateful to have been born a Macdonald because there were characteristics to be found amongst her brothers and sisters which were lacking in others. This sort of comment did little to win them friends, but the heightened sense of family bond brought them through a difficult childhood and became a source of much comfort to them in adult life. Paradoxically, Frederic, although experiencing the traumas at first hand, subjected his own family to a similar nomadic existence, for he too became a preacher.

As young Methodists, the Macdonald girls' upbringing centred on two fundamentals: salvation and education. The first was naturally well catered for, but it was education which made the greatest impact. Wesley taught that salvation could only be achieved through a personal understanding of the scriptures. Thus, at a time when female education was generally neglected, the Methodist Society actively encouraged girls to read, debate and evaluate the Bible for themselves. Educational opportunities were not restricted to theological matters, for, believing that all knowledge enriched life, Wesley encouraged the cultural as much as the sacred. Not only were Sunday schools set up to educate the working classes, but local chapels organized regular meetings and lectures to extend the horizons of their members. The Macdonald girls were therefore exceedingly fortunate to have received a Methodist upbringing because it gave them a far wider education than almost any other would have done.

Lessons took place under the guidance of mother, herself well-taught and convinced of the value of female education. When space permitted, she set one room aside as the school-room and, using whatever books of instruction she could obtain, conducted formal lessons in reading, writing and arithmetic. The older girls fared better than the younger ones because, as the family grew in size, lessons often had to take second place to domestic duties, leaving Louisa at the age of nine still obliged to dictate her correspondence through an elder sister. Mother liked to give the first lessons to a child herself, but relied on the older girls to teach the younger ones thereafter. Education in the home was augmented by meetings in the room behind the chapel where they attended lectures illustrated by magic lantern slides and various social gatherings designed both to entertain and inform. Opportunities for educational advancement certainly existed, which all Methodists were exhorted to pursue, yet the Macdonald girls regarded their tuition as mere crumbs of learning, for only a proper school such as their brothers attended would have satisfied their desires.

Pastimes in the home were frequently of an instructive nature, taking the form of literary or musical activities. 'Versifying' was a particular favourite and required each member of the family to compose a parody of a poem, then read it back for the rest of the family to try and identify.

It was a source of great merriment because the efforts were invariably humorous, but it was a game which encouraged careful study of literature. Prose writing was treated more seriously in the family, as one of George Macdonald's letters to his daughter Louisa indicated:

> I am anxious for your improvement in English composition. I do not mean letter writing merely in which you will be sure to excel. I mean composition which will show how much of what you have read and thought is producible in writing. You have read very extensively for a child, but in a very desultory manner. I have been thinking of giving a subject for a short essay on which I should like you and Agnes and Fred to write your thoughts . . . on 'the greatness of little things'. You may illustrate this by examples very readily. . . . History – Science – Biography – Religion will all supply you with facts – the moral and rational inferences will readily suggest themselves to your minds. Now will you all try – Mamma in the chair, each writer of the essay to read his or her production.[4]

Tedious though such an exercise sounds, there is little doubt that it was excellent grounding for anybody with literary or political aspirations.

Despite the seemingly heavy religious and educational atmosphere in the home, the Macdonald children, like most others, were resourceful when it came to playing. Birthdays particularly offered scope for improvisation, and Alice devised ever more daring surprises for her younger sisters. For Louisa's seventh birthday, some branches from an apple tree laden with fruit were dragged into the house and used as the framework for a bower to be erected in the bedroom Louisa shared with Agnes. The real *pièce de résistance* was the trampoline created by turning the bed over and stretching some sacking across the frame as tightly as possible to make a springy surface for the little ones to bounce on.

Toys also had to be manufactured at home rather than purchased, although the older girls were fortunate enough to be given dolls by their more affluent aunts. This generosity was not extended to Agnes and Louisa, who, once the wax-faced dolls were broken, had to content themselves with making their own grotesque figures out of stuffed pillows tied with string in appropriate places. The splendid set of five hundred wooden building blocks which the older ones had been given survived in a depleted state, but Agnes lamented that there were not enough blocks to build the sort of Tower of Babel Alice and Carrie had constructed, which had tripped up one of their domestics and broken her ribs. But it was playthings they made up out of discarded objects which ultimately provided the most amusement. An old brown ringleted wig from years gone by supplied the inspiration for endless amateur dramatics, and an old pair of yellow slippers with sharp pointed toes and smooth worn soles was easily transformed into parlour skates for sliding round the floor. Other games – involving a sound effect of thunder, achieved by rolling blocks of wood on bare floorboards or throwing bunches of keys around – did not meet with their mother's approval and were destined to be short-lived.

There were other less seemly games the minister's children engaged in, involving lighting a fire in the wooden toolshed and sending the smallest of their number into the larder to steal food for them to cook. Louisa recalled how she dashed on one occasion into the pantry and grabbed the first thing she saw. It proved to be a joint of veal reserved for the family's midday meal, but realizing it was too large to fit into their cooking pot she took one of the cook's sharpest knives and butchered the joint up into manageable proportions. Her return to the toolshed was greeted with great jubilation, and the meat was wedged into a pan to boil, but the game came to a dramatic end when the shed caught fire.

Animals both dead and alive fascinated the girls, from the more usual stray dogs and cats to tadpoles kept on the bedroom mantelpiece. At one time they were given some silkworms, which lived in a box also on the mantelpiece and fed on lettuce. Probably their most bizarre pet was a lizard, a present one of their brothers brought back from a visit to Jersey. The girls were somewhat apprehensive about this creature, but overcame their fears sufficiently to let the reptile nestle inside the sleeve of a dress one of them was wearing. Lizzie Green, as it was called, came to a dusty end after escaping into the room and vanishing. A month later its desiccated corpse was found behind a book and provided them with material for the next game of funerals. Two black cats which perished were buried under some gooseberry bushes, and the younger children were convinced the bushes bore particularly hairy gooseberries as a consequence.

Louisa had a strange fascination for mice and would try to acquire the dead ones from traps to keep in her pocket and stroke. One mouse that looked prettier than the others was selected for the more permanent fate of being stuffed. Without the slightest hint of squeamishness, she stole a chopping board and knife from the kitchen, then locked herself away in the bedroom to begin the task. Writing about the incident many years later, she recalled that she was as keen to learn about the inner workings of the animal as she was to preserve it. Once the dissection was complete, the carcase was filled with cotton-wool soaked in turpentine, which to her mind would ensure it did not smell, and the whole sewn up with two black beads stitched in place to give the eyes an added sparkle. So pleased was Louisa by her handiwork that she could not resist teasing Charles Erasmus, the cat. He was given tantalizing glimpses of the rodent through the glass lid of its box; but with potentially fatal results. The cat, eager to get at a meal, leapt up, smashed the glass lid and to Louisa's horror ate the mouse, turpentine and all. The whole episode left her with a terribly guilty conscience lest Charles Erasmus be poisoned: but all turned out well.

Their father preferred to believe that his children spent any spare moments augmenting their education, to which end he provided many books spread around the house. It was a particular point with him that every book in the house was kept on an open shelf, never behind glass or a locked door, for this he believed would encourage the habit of reading. Nevertheless, the books which the children most wanted to read were the forbidden ones residing on a shelf in father's study and known to include the highly unsuitable plays of Shakespeare. Parts of Grandfather Macdonald's extensive library could also be found in most rooms as a further inducement to the children to read. Their diet of reading contained a preponderance of religious books, with some Kingsley and Scott for light relief. Few periodicals found their way into the house, apart from Methodist journals and the *Quarterly Review*, so that the odd copies of *Blackwood's Magazine* and *Chambers's Journal* which did appear were much prized. Books specifically for children were uncommon, and beyond a copy of the *Ballads of Robin Hood* and *Gammer Grethel's Fairy Tales* there were none at the manse. These two books came to them by courtesy of their mother's sister Aunt Martha Jones, whose talents extended to reviewing for *Blackwood's Magazine*.

Music was the pastime the Macdonald girls enjoyed most and was one their father heartily approved of, because music was a central part of chapel life as well as being an entertainment. 'Methodism was born in song', the Wesleyan hymnal proclaimed, and all their gatherings whether sacred or social were opened with two or three hymns sung with great gusto. Musical evenings also formed an important part of the family's social life; these events were held at the homes of prominent members of the congregation, with lavish suppers of the kind Mrs Macdonald's family had been accustomed to provide in her childhood.

The minister and his older children were always invited to such events, and it was therefore imperative that the girls in particular should be able to acquit themselves well musically. Their mother's wide education had ensured she was an able pianist, and she delighted in teaching her daughters, although only Alice and Georgie received lessons directly from her: the younger three girls were taught by Georgie, who was more patient than Alice.

Singing was something all the family enjoyed because it demonstrated family harmony in all senses as well as being a pleasurable pursuit. Throughout their lives, the Macdonald girls retained a great love of music both as performers and as listeners. It is noticeable that whenever they met together as adults there would be music-making. Agnes was recognized as the most competent pianist in the family, and after her marriage took professional piano lessons for many years, so that at soirées she regularly entertained the gathering. The other girls were generally held to be better at singing, and Alice found her vocal talents were an asset in Anglo-Indian drawing-rooms, where it was reported she 'sang in duets and choruses like a bird', whilst Georgie's rendering of old French songs was a great favourite with artists like William Morris and Gabriel Rossetti.[5]

Culture also extended to occasional visits to art galleries but never included theatres, which were considered by Methodists to be evil places. Despite the seemingly liberal approach to education, the Macdonald girls' upbringing could be termed a narrow one, being spent exclusively in the company of Methodists. The family were attended by Methodist doctors, bought their provisions from the shops of leading members of the congregation, and even had their photographs taken by fellow-believers; yet this situation arose as much from expediency as from deliberate policy. As newcomers to a town, the family were dependent upon the local Methodist connexion to recommend a good doctor, school or haberdasher, and it followed that those recommended to the minister's wife would also be regular worshippers at chapel.

The family's social life centred on the activities of the Methodist Society, because the family usually knew no one else in the locality. This meant that the girls were expected to contribute sewing to bazaars and charity collections, and attend book, missionary and tea meetings, to name but a few of the chapel events. As she grew older, Agnes was observed to be attending an ever-increasing number of tea meetings, which prompted Louisa to offer her sister the full measure of her own share if she found them that good. But Agnes, never one to be lost for an answer, was swift to retort. She said she only went to them to get out of the house and meet people, not because she enjoyed them. Since even Alice had attended such a gathering the previous night, Louie was advised to get her facts right. As a parting shot, Agnes added she was also going to a Bible Society meeting at the Manchester Free Trade Hall later.

Opportunities to 'see life' were severely restricted in the Macdonald home, for there was not enough money to entertain more than was absolutely necessary, namely other itinerant preachers who required overnight accommodation. The children found these visitors a trial because they arrived full of missionary zeal and bombarded the younger members of the household with texts and religious instruction. Frederic recalled one particular young cleric partial to didactic conversation at breakfast, who launched into yet another account of a dream in which he had seen his heart black and full of stones. Louisa interrupted him with the helpful advice that it was not his heart but his gizzard, effectively silencing the impromptu sermon.

The girls naturally received a full measure of religious instruction, but not from their father, who was too taken up with the needs of his congregation to worry about his own family's spiritual welfare. From the girls' point of view it was unfortunate that their mother, with her melancholic view of religion, should have been their spiritual teacher; as Alice's husband wrote many years later: 'You know, all of them – bar Aggie – have a decided touch of the elegaic in their nature and are just a little prone to what a poor but pious Yorkshire poet, James Montgomery, called "the joy of grief".'[6] It also ensured that once they were old enough to choose, all the girls left the Methodist Society.

For all his single-minded attitude to the ministry, their father was more liberal in his view of religion than his wife: he always maintained that he cared more that his daughters grew up good Christians than that they should necessarily be Methodists. He was not insistent upon their attendance at every service either, saying only that he 'hoped' to see them at chapel. Their mother, however, preferred adherence to the letter of the creed, and all the children were taken to chapel regularly from babyhood, spending the service sitting on her lap, if necessary in the vestry. In her opinion, ill-health was the only acceptable reason for non-attendance at chapel, and in that case she would hold her own service at home, reading aloud to the children from their father's sermons and leading them in religious discussion. All the children were assigned a book specifically for Sunday reading, which for the younger ones would be the life of a saint, and for the older ones, a personal religious testimony. On Sunday no other activity was permitted, as Georgie recalled: '. . . nor did we as a rule go anywhere on that day except chapel: I remember thinking it a very bold measure when my brother in vacation time took a walk in the afternoon.'[7] But the Macdonald family's sabbath day observances were similar to those of many families in the middle years of the nineteenth century. The extra dose of religion which finally turned the girls against the chapel came not from their parents but from their elder brother Harry.

As soon as he was born, Harry was marked out by his father to carry on the Macdonald tradition of Methodist ministry. He had an elevated position in the family as 'the apple of his father's eye, the son of his right hand',[8] and Mrs Macdonald made no attempt to hide the fact that he was her favourite child. She spoke of Harry and herself being the very closest of friends, trusting that such intimacy would save the boy from any snares the devil might set. Within the family Harry's needs were paramount. Whatever he requested was done and any discipline he chose to mete out to his brothers and sisters had to be accepted gratefully. It was a strange and lonely position for a child to be in but one which Harry exploited to the full, becoming sanctimonious and overbearing towards his sisters. He told his mother to insist on earlier bedtimes, lectured the girls on good behaviour and religious matters as well as insisting on petty demonstrations of his power by a ritualistic inspection of hands before every meal. Mrs Macdonald was delighted by what she regarded as proof of Harry's growing powers of leadership, whilst his sisters seethed with anger. The only respite came when Harry returned to his Wesleyan boarding school, but even then 'improving' letters arrived for the girls, containing lists of books they must read and demands to know what texts they were studying, as well as complaints about the slovenly standard of their letters. Frederic received a letter containing the promise: 'When I come home you will be put through your drill, that I may see what progress you have made. If it is satisfactory we shall both be pleased; if not, why. . . .'[9]

Frederic described Harry's exercise of power as 'a quasi-feudal supremacy', an apt description since Harry was under tremendous pressure from above to become not just a Wesleyan preacher, but an outstanding one, 'as becomes a cadet of the noble house of the Macdonalds of the Isles'.[10] It was something he had never been consulted about nor given any choice in, and ultimately it ruined his life. He was permanently haunted by a fear of failure, which would let down not just his father, but also his grandfather and John Wesley himself, as well as add to the misery of the mother who adored him. He struggled through school, pushed on by letters from his father ('could you not in some thoughtful and studious hour write out a short prayer to be used daily before your private studies'[11]) and during vacations he spent most of his time closeted with his father in the study receiving extra tuition. At this time his only safety-valve was to make his brother and sisters suffer as much as he could – in the name of religion, of course.

Harry possessed less spirit than his sisters, for his had been curbed at an early age, yet significantly neither he nor they ever rebelled against the enforced religion. The girls were given to muttered complaints amongst themselves, and Alice once made a bold gesture of defiance: during one of the regular house-packing operations, she discovered a yellowing envelope containing a carefully wrapped lock of John Wesley's hair. Scornfully she held it before her sisters, then, with the words 'See! A hair of the dog that bit us!' tossed it in the fire.[12] The incident caused more than a spark. Her mother was furious at such blatant disobedience, whilst her sisters waited awestruck, expecting the hand of God to strike. Beneath the superficial consent displayed by all the girls, there was plenty of self-will. Their narrow upbringing did nothing to stifle their spirit: if anything, it made them all the more receptive once outside influences came to bear.

Chapter Three

Widening Horizons
(1850–56)

The Birmingham to which the Macdonald family returned in September 1850 had improved little during their nine-year absence. Although the riots had died down, the appalling conditions which had prompted them remained. Despite a terrible infant mortality rate, the population continued to rise rapidly as people flocked to the town seeking employment in various industries such as railway carriage building, armaments and chemical manufacture. A splendid town hall had been opened in the Macdonalds' absence, but the workers continued to live in the fifty thousand back-to-back slum buildings, lacking proper sewerage systems or water supplies and crammed around the centre of the town. No improvement in their lot came about until Joseph Chamberlain arrived in Birmingham in 1854 and John Bright became their Member of Parliament soon after.

The lower classes could purchase education from the People's Instruction Society, where for a penny a week a workman could be taught to read, play chess and debate, and for tuppence, he might also learn writing and singing. Ironically, education at the King Edward vi Grammar School was free, for the school had such a wealthy endowment its 450 pupils need only pay for their books. Equally significant to Mr Macdonald was the fact that the school was famed for its scholarships. Its endowment stretched to funding numerous places at university, and whilst Cambridge was the traditional favourite, there were many ex-pupils at Pembroke College, Oxford, who formed a so-called 'Birmingham Set' around Dr Jeune, a former King Edward's headmaster. In the Reverend George Macdonald's eyes, the Birmingham appointment was divine intervention, enabling Harry to attend the excellent grammar school and have the opportunity of a university education which otherwise could not have been afforded. But it was equally a 'godsend' from the girls' point of view because events in Birmingham were to transform their lives. Writing with fifty years' hindsight, Frederic said that this was the place where the family felt the effect of new influences which were to reach their peak in London three years later.

The girls did not in fact relish the prospect of returning to Birmingham, and the knowledge that Harry would be coming home from the Wesleyan college in Sheffield where he boarded was further cause for depression. Privately they detested this sanctimonious brother who analysed their every action, but they were careful not to air such heretical views. The mention of visits from Wilfred Heeley, son of their mother's closest friend and Harry's childhood playfellow, did nothing to alleviate the feeling of despair. Alice confidently predicted that this eighteen-year-old, in his final term before taking up a scholarship at Trinity College, Cambridge, would be another supercilious academic like Harry. It therefore came as a complete surprise to discover that he was a kindly, somewhat awkward adolescent, who arrived very much in awe of these girls. Once the barriers were broken, he opened up a completely new world for the three older sisters. They found it possible to enjoy a friendship with him on reasonably equal terms, and there followed much good-humoured banter, serious discussion, reading aloud and music-making, from all of which, of course, Harry remained aloof, as befitted his special vocation.

Wilfred Heeley, normally a shy, quiet young man, basked in the girls' attention, and Georgie felt 'his talk was always witty and always kind, but a certain shyness and big-boy clumsiness made him occasionally the victim of the little girls to whom he was so indulgent. He could at all times express himself best in writing, and, as he found we enjoyed it, used to amuse himself and please us with writing notes at school and sending them by our brother as postman to one or other of the sisters.'[1] The girls' efforts to compose witty replies had a more beneficial effect on their writing skills than all Harry's destructive criticism.

Fond though she was of Wilfred, Alice felt the need to establish a position of superiority over him, as she tried to do with people throughout her life. An opportunity came when their talk hinged on what a person could eat if forced to and Wilfred maintained that it would be no problem for him to eat a mouse. Alice seized upon his boast, challenging him to eat the animal if she could first catch and cook it. Never one to be squeamish, she trapped a mouse and baked it in a pastry case before issuing the invitation to lunch. When Wilfred failed to turn up, Alice was jubilant: she had called his bluff and won. Wilfred took it in good part, and the friendship continued.

Although Wilfred's attention was mainly directed towards Alice, Carrie and Georgie, he was kind enough not to neglect the little ones and accompanied them on walks in the Birmingham Botanical Gardens, or took them to tea with his family. Writing of the Heeley family a few years later, Agnes commented: 'They are repulsively numerous, being thirteen in number and legion their name, so that their house is, one might say, a hutch or a warren', but at the time she and Louisa were more than grateful to Wilfred for these outings.[2] Alice and Georgie soon realized that his presence offered them something more than a diversion. 'Wilfred's talk was different from anything we had known before, and our intelligence was stimulated by his taking it for granted that we should understand him,' Georgie recalled. 'What he said and wrote lit up a world for us who, as girls, in those days had small chances of education.'[3] It was an injustice which both girls felt keenly, particularly when Harry flaunted his learning.

After considerable agitation, the eldest three sisters succeeded in their aim of being sent to a 'young ladies' school'. Naturally it was run by a Methodist, a Miss Howell, whose brother ran the boys' school next door which Frederic attended. However, it was soon apparent that there was little academic content in the education, so their schooling was terminated and they returned to their mother's instruction. There still remained the longing for that which was denied them, and in Wilfred they found a method of acquiring a vicarious schooling. They pleaded with him to pass on to them all he had learned at school, to loan them his textbooks and generally guide their studies, to all of which Mrs Macdonald gave her wholehearted approval.

If Wilfred Heeley 'schooled them', then his great friend William Fulford took them on to university. Fulford was a fascinating character, reputedly the cleverest pupil at King Edward's in his time, and reading Divinity at Oxford with the aid of yet another scholarship. He was a very short person with a prodigious energy of mind which would soon dominate any gathering. At first the Macdonald family were stunned by his ebullient personality, then totally captivated by his charm; any expectation of theological argument there might have been was swept away as Fulford launched into his two main interests, literature and music. There was nothing the girls liked better, and since Fulford thrived on an audience, it was natural he should supersede the quiet Heeley as teacher and entertainer of the elder Macdonald girls. Georgie described how he had

an endless interest in expounding the poets, and naturally found his readiest disciples amongst the girls whom he knew. Towards us he shewed a judgement for which I can never be thankful enough, for he fed us with Longfellow first of all, as food suitable for our years, and so brought us gradually into a condition more or less fit for the revelation . . . Tennyson. It seemed quite natural to us that he should write poetry himself. He loved music, also, and taught us names of the works of Beethoven and Mendelssohn

– a refreshing change from the repertoire of sacred music they had learned from their mother.[4]

Through Fulford they acquired a flavour of Oxford, which for Georgie meant an affection for the city for the remainder of her life. She said it was 'a centre for many thoughts and imaginings of women, who make themselves pictures of it according to the degree of their respect or admiration for the men they know'.[5] Both girls became absorbed in the new literature which flooded into the manse with Fulford – the poetry of Keats, Shelley and Meredith, along with the writings of Carlyle and Dickens, all of whom enjoyed popularity amongst the undergraduates of the 'set' at Oxford. Alice's own writing skills flourished under Fulford's guidance and ultimately reappeared in her son Rudyard. It was perhaps predictable that the fifteen-year-old Alice should be bowled over by such a dynamic person as William Fulford; though Georgie's discreet comment was that 'we little girls liked and admired him very much, and he was very kind to us'; for Alice it was a case of love at first sight.[6] Everything about him was so daring, so exciting and such a contrast to the life she had known. From the beginning she accepted him as her superior, which she had never done with Wilfred Heeley, but it did not stop her pitting her wits against him in thrusts of sparkling repartee.

Fulford's advent had another, almost imperceptible effect on both girls, in that the hold of Methodism over them began to loosen. For in him they saw a successful combination of hard work and fun, which seemed to contradict one of the basic Methodist premises, that work was everything and pleasure could not exist alongside. From then on, as their experiences widened, they drew further away from the church in which they had been brought up, but the void was not filled by High Church doctrines which attracted so many young men at Oxford, including Fulford himself.

Fulford returned Alice's affection. After his cloistered existence at school and university, he found this impulsive, intelligent girl refreshing company and a kindred spirit. There was never a formal announcement of their engagement (nor indeed did Alice ever seek her parents' permission for her various engagements, preferring, it seems, to present them with a *fait accompli*), but soon after the family moved to London in 1853, Mrs Macdonald took Fulford on one side and asked about his exact intentions. From then on it was accepted that the two would marry after Fulford was ordained. Amazingly, the family did not regard Fulford's religious beliefs as a stumbling block. To Mrs Macdonald's credit, she accepted both Fulford, and later Edward Jones, as suitors for her daughters purely on their own merits. 'Looking back I feel the deepest respect for my parents,' Georgie wrote, 'because they never discussed with me the "prospects" of my marriage; my father . . . so far as my judgement goes, acted as a minister of the Christian religion should do, seeking nothing but character and leaving the question of fortune altogether on one side.'[7] This open-mindedness was a trait which Georgie inherited to a far greater degree than her sisters, and enabled her to move between the manse and Bohemia with some ease. For all that, Georgie's reaction to Fulford might have baffled an observer, for her diminutive figure could be seen sitting quietly at the edge of the family group just watching; nevertheless she welcomed his presence and throughout her life found pleasure in the company of those who could combine the intellectual with a sense of fun. Unlike Alice, Georgie did not seek to be at the centre of attention: for her it was enough just to absorb the atmosphere and occasionally deliver the *mot juste*.

Meanwhile Carrie, who had participated in Wilfred Heeley's earlier visits, was forced by ill-health to retire from many of her sisters' activities. Consumption was not officially diagnosed until the end of 1852, but Carrie said that from the moment she felt the first pains in her chest she feared the worst. Alone of the girls, she found her religion a great comfort in the difficult final years. At the time of Fulford's visits, Mrs Macdonald's journal recorded the gradual decline in Carrie's health, starting as the occasional indisposition but leading later to her virtual exclusion from the family circle. She could no longer sit down at table with the family, and it saddened her mother's heart to see how easily the others accepted this. It seemed they had almost forgotten the existence of the pale little figure in the bedroom, and as time passed there were clear indications that Carrie would never resume her place in the family.

Fulford's hyperactivity was exhausting to someone in Carrie's frail condition, so she remained in her room where the quieter Heeley visited her and tried to keep her spirits up with conversation and reading aloud. Even back at Cambridge he continued the correspondence, and his last letter contained plans to take her to the Royal Academy Summer Exhibition, though he admitted he found it very difficult to write something which would amuse her. He thought the best thing would be to write the letter as if she were perfectly well and just the same lively Carrie of three years before. Then attempting to shut his mind to the inevitable, he reminded her of the fun and laughter of the past, which he said was not far below the surface, even if outward things looked different. Sadly, as he wrote, the sixteen-year-old girl lay dying in her mother's arms. In true Victorian deathbed tradition she bade farewell to her brothers and sisters, reaffirmed her trust in God and expired. The five-year-old Edith was present and noted many years later that her sister's last words were: '*I am* so comfy.'[8]

Her death did not leave her sisters as distraught as might be expected, because they had watched the illness wearing her down and accepted that death was a merciful release for their tortured sister. Harry explained to them that if a person was ready for heaven, particularly when still young and unmarried, it was impossible to feel regret. So successful was Harry in getting his message through to Louisa that when she wrote to her parents, who had gone to Oxford to be with Harry immediately after Carrie's funeral, she was at pains to tell them that whilst she hoped her Papa was well she would quite understand if he were dead and God had called him to pass into the life immortal like poor dear Carrie. It is hard to judge whether the Reverend George Macdonald, who had been suffering from a cold, was heartened by this sign of faith or not.

Alice and Georgie had participated in séances a few years before Carrie's death, but they made no attempt to use them to contact her. These experiments began just before they left Birmingham, when Fulford drew the two girls' attention to an article in the *Quarterly Review* about table-turning and mesmerism, which were enjoying a vogue as parlour entertainment. Georgie recalled that they established a code of rapping with a very communicative tea urn and contacted spirits through an ouija board. The real *pièce de résistance* lay in table-turning, achieved by kneeling up on the back of the dining-room chairs and using the powers of concentration.

> We children had heard of it and tried it, with what are still to me astonishing results. The power, whatever it might be, was discovered whilst our parents were from home, and duly reported to them on their return as treasure-trove. Our father said something like, 'Well, well, my children, if it ever does it again, call me'; so one day, when he was safely within the double doors of his study, we set to work. We had no theory about it, and were only curious each time to see what would happen. The table, a large round one, did not fail us now, but seemed to awaken just as usual, turning at first with slow heaviness and then gradually quickening its pace till it spun quite easily and set us running to keep up with it. 'Call Papa!' was the word, and a scout flew to the study. He was with us at once, not even waiting to lay down his long Broseley pipe. Incredulity gave place to excitement at the first glance, but, to convince us of our self-deception, he cried out, 'Don't stop children' and leapt between us pipe in hand, upon the middle of the table, thinking to stop it in a second. His weight, however, made no difference – the table turned as swiftly and easily as before, and we ran round and round with it laughing at our amazed father.[9]

Even Mrs Macdonald, not one given to superlatives, was impressed by the phenomenon and recorded with great excitement in her journal how she watched the table move for the first time, and then went on to note that Harry brought boys from King Edward's on subsequent evenings to watch the spectacle. Alice was very pleased to learn that her fame had spread to Oxford when Fulford took the technique back with him after the weekend. In a letter to the Macdonalds, he complained that Faulkner (later of Morris, Marshall, Faulkner and Company) 'has been moving tables, books, papers (whatever he can lay his hands on) in a surprising manner since Monday, when we initiated him into the mystery'.[10]

Amongst the Macdonald visitors at this time was one who was to feature prominently in all their lives – Edward Jones. Although a few years older than Harry, the two had become friendly at school, and at the time of Jones's first visit to the house in October 1852, he was waiting to take up a university place, which like so many consisted of a scholarship to read Divinity at Oxford. His visit with school fellow

Cormell Price was not felt to be a success by anyone. He arrived looking exceptionally pale from an illness and was very uneasy in the female company. His well-meaning attempts to amuse the four-year-old Edith were disastrous: taking the young girl between his knees he pulled the sort of grotesque faces which amused schoolboys, but the little girl was petrified, and the family stared in shocked disbelief at his behaviour. After that, Jones's visits were few and far between because Harry said Jones was a mysogynist. That was an overstatement, for it would be truer to say that Jones, whose mother and only sister had died when he was a baby, was embarrassed in the company of girls. Admittedly at Oxford he was to talk of forming a monastic community, but his later celebration of female beauty in art shows that these were only transitory feelings. His real opinion of the Macdonald girls was heard muttered under his breath during one visit: 'Hear the ladies as they talk; tittle tattle, tittle tattle, Like their pattens when they walk; pittle pattle, pittle pattle,' and they were not flattered![11]

Alone of the girls, Georgie saw beyond the awkward exterior and was intrigued by the young man. Her impression on that first ill-fated visit was of someone

rather tall and very thin, though not especially slender, straightly built and with wide shoulders. Extremely pale he was, with the paleness that belongs to fair-haired people, and looked delicate, but not ill. His hair was perfectly straight, and of a colourless kind. His eyes were light grey (if their colour could be defined in words), and the space that their setting took up under his brow was extraordinary: the nose quite right in proportion, but very individual in outline, and a mouth large and well moulded, the lips meeting with absolute sweetness and repose. The shape of his head was domed, and noticeable for its even balance; his forehead, wide and rather high, was smooth and calm, and the line of the brow over the eyes was a fine one. From the eyes themselves power simply radiated, and as he talked and listened, if anything moved him, not only his eyes but his whole face seemed lit up from within. I learned afterwards that he had an immoveable conviction that he was hopelessly plain. His ordinary manner was shy, but not self-conscious, for it gave the impression that he noticed everything. At that time he sat as many men do who are not very strong, sunk down rather low in his chair with an appearance of the whole spine seeking for rest. At once his power of words struck me and his vehemence. He was easily stirred, and then his speech was as swift and clear as possible, yet well ordered and going straight to the mark. He had a beautiful voice. . . . Epithets he always used wonderfully.[12]

Jones's quiet strength appealed to Georgie far more than Fulford's extrovert manner, for in her judgement Jones had the greater depth.

Her interest went unnoticed by the rest of the family, who soon found themselves caught up in another move. The new circuit was Chelsea, and there was suppressed rejoicing when Harry came home with the news that the headmaster of King Edward's advised him to remain a further year at school before trying for a Corpus College scholarship. Mrs Macdonald, however, was devastated, confiding to her journal that it felt like tearing a part from herself and leaving it behind, so that in the future she would be only half-hearted. It was, she felt, yet another example of the harsh reality of life. The girls had mixed feelings about London. Alice was excited, because she regarded it as a place with unlimited opportunities for education through art galleries, concerts and the company of fascinating people. Fulford was living in London as well having left Oxford after graduating. He had taken a teaching post in Wimbledon, being in two minds about proceeding to ordination. Georgie also welcomed the thought of a more stimulating life in the capital, but as the train pulled out through the tunnel from Birmingham, she 'grieved in the darkness . . . leaving the place where he lived'.[13] The little girls generally feared any move which overturned the world they had grown accustomed to, and consequently were miserable.

Once installed in the house in Sloane Square, their doubts were forgotten. In a letter to Harry a few days after their arrival, Louisa admitted that London was turning out better than she had expected because there was so much happening. The Crystal Palace was in the process of being re-erected on Sydenham Hill, Big Ben had just been completed, the Houses of Parliament were not yet finished and Buckingham Palace was being enlarged. The visit to the latter was a big disappointment to the girls because there was so much scaffolding round the building and tents in front to house the soldiers that Louisa said she could hardly see the stonework. Nevertheless she was impressed by the guards and decided the Queen probably was lucky enough to have a good view of the swans from her bedroom window. The house assigned to the family was too small, so Mrs Macdonald set about finding more suitable accommodation for them as her husband rushed about the Lord's work, unaware of the problems. Sloane Square at that time had many dilapidated cottages and no properly-made roads. Across one end of it passed the busy King's Road thoroughfare, regularly used by the Queen and Prince Albert between Buckingham Palace and Kew. There was also intense interest in the visit of the French Emperor and Empress to London in 1855. Fred fell wildly in love with the beautiful Empress and spent every moment he could snatch from school rushing from place to place in the hope that he might catch a glimpse of her. He recalled:

A boy who can push his way through a crowd may see many things if he will, and so I had a sight of the Emperor and Empress of the French . . . and a good view of the illuminations and fireworks which marked the close of the Crimean War the following year. When the shattered remnant of the Brigade of Guards returned from Crimea, and half London was in the streets to give them welcome, I kept up with the gallant fellows all the way from Waterloo Bridge to Buckingham Palace, the tears running down my face as I pushed along through all obstacles, cheering with such a voice as I had.[14]

They were heady days to be in the capital city.

London emphasized the division between those of the sisters who were almost young women and those who were still little girls. Into the latter category fell ten-year-old Agnes, eight-year-old Louisa and five-year-old Edith, whose chief concerns were making dolls from stuffed pillows, scrabbling in the soil to create a garden and keeping tadpoles. London made a special impression on them, reared on the romantic tales of Walter Scott and the poetry which Fulford and Jones brought into the house, so that even the dingiest London street was alive with some historical association. Old Chelsea Church took on a special significance when they learned that the headless body of the great Sir Thomas More was supposed to rest there; parts of West Brompton that were then fields and parks had once, they were told, been as familiar to Oliver Cromwell as they were to them. One of the houses they passed regularly on their walks was where Lord Byron was born, and they fantasized about the likelihood of Dr Johnson walking down the streets they had got to know well. Georgie recalled how a special ray of light fell on their shabby home when Fulford told them it was not far from Elizabeth Barrett Browning's home, and another gloomy building was revealed to them as the place where Turner, the great painter, had lived. Red Lion Square, Holborn, caught their imagination because the girls were told of a legend that the body of Oliver Cromwell had been buried in its derelict gardens. True or not, such stories were a source of great fascination to the younger Macdonald girls especially, who listened wide-eyed to Alice's young man.

For the youngest too, one of the greatest pleasures of the winter was to spend an afternoon at the German Fair in Regent Street. To them it was like a visit to fairyland, because this bazaar was only open in the darkest season of the year, and they entered from the gloomy street into a brightly gaslit interior. As far as Louisa could remember there were three or four rooms devoted to every imaginable variety of pretty toy or mechanical wonder. A brass band played lively marches, and the air was filled with a strong smell of wax dolls. The children progressed excitedly through all the rooms, for though the first ones contained the newest and most spectacular toys, it was the smaller room towards the back of the bazaar they really wanted to see. This also contained toys, but all purchasable for a penny. Whatever money came the girls' way during the year had to be saved for a spree in this room.

Alice and Georgie, then aged sixteen and thirteen respectively, considered themselves young ladies and had little interest in such things; they were intent on exploring London in the company of Fulford and his friends or with their aunts. Their mother's sister Mrs Alice Pullein had moved from Manchester to a house in Islington, at which time Edmund Pullein entered into a partnership with another accountant in the city. The Pulleins were also strict Methodists, but enjoyed a higher standard of living than the Macdonalds, entertaining a great deal and attending concerts. Aunt Alice was a great favourite with the girls, being one of the more light-hearted of the aunts, whereas Martha Jones, their maiden aunt who had moved to London with the Pulleins, but kept her own establishment in Great Coram Street, Bloomsbury, was oppressively religious and unpopular with the young female Macdonalds – going to stay with her was never anticipated with enthusiasm.

Not only did the older girls go out more, but they also received more visitors when they lived in London. Wilfred Heeley and Fulford appeared the day after the family were installed at Sloane Square, but more remarkably, two days afterwards Mr Edward Jones appeared in the back parlour of the manse, to the great astonishment of the family. Jones, on his way back to Oxford via his Aunt Catherwood's in Camberwell, had been moved to call on the Macdonalds. This visit was more successful than the previous ones and inspired him to call regularly when he was in London, sometimes with Fulford or Heeley, at other times on his own. The young men began taking the two eldest girls to the Beast Gardens in Regent's Park, to exhibitions at the Royal Academy and for walks in the Chelsea Hospital gardens.

Another significant set of visitors at the manse were the Baldwins. These ironmasters from Stourport in Worcestershire were good Methodists and delighted in entertaining the Reverend George Macdonald in their home when he preached in their area. In December 1853, it was Mr George, Mr Stanley (both uncles to the future prime minister) and their sister Miss Sarah Baldwin who went to make the acquaintance of Mrs Macdonald and her daughters for the first time. The visit was deemed a success, with the Baldwins returning to take several meals with the family and inviting Alice and Georgie to accompany them to the oratorios *Samson* and *Elijah* at the Exeter Hall. Louisa and Agnes were of course too young to be considered. Whenever any of the Baldwin family came up to London thereafter, the friendships were resumed.

Once Harry had gained his Oxford place, many young men called at the house during vacations. Some were old friends from Birmingham days like Cormell Price, known to all as Crom, and others new ones like Charlie Faulkner and William Morris, who came with Jones. The girls revelled in such stimulating company: 'They all made upon us the impression of being gifted, interesting, and amusing beyond words. That we thought them good, goes without saying. Some of us chose Fulford, some Edward, some Cormell Price for lode-star. . . . They had no conquering airs with women, but were either frank and pleased in their society or shy and humble . . . all ardent, all filled with enthusiasm about something or someone.'[15] The two girls involved themselves in the tide of medievalism which was sweeping 'the set' (as these young men liked to be known). Talk was of Malory's *Morte D'Arthur*, Fouqué's *Sintram* and *Sidonia*, with which the older girls made themselves conversant.

Alice became involved with plans to produce an Oxford and Cambridge magazine, but though she contributed ideas, she had no chance of writing for it, whereas Harry, whose literary skills she despised, was able to have accepted a 'Notice on the Song of Hiawatha'. Alice drew comfort, however, from Fulford's assurance that 'Macdonald is at present a complement. When we have filled our staff to completion he will retire.'[16] The idea of writing for magazines appealed to Alice, but she decided to use pseudonyms to prevent her work being rejected on grounds of sex, and although she began writing at this time, success eluded her for several years.

Whilst Alice and Fulford's relationship seemed to flourish, the object of Georgie's affection was in a quandary. Jones had reached a turning-point in his life, unsure whether he should pursue his studies at Oxford and make a career in the Church, or, along with William Morris, give it all up for the precarious world of art. In the background were the delightful Macdonald girls in Chelsea, who were always pleased to see him and enchanted him with their singing, their knowledge of literature and their cosy home life, which he had never experienced and was a total contrast to the essentially masculine nature of life at Oxford. In her *Memorials of Edward Burne-Jones* Georgie was somewhat coy about her courtship, suggesting that Jones called at her house on a few occasions purely to see Harry and that this was followed by her parents springing Edward's proposal upon her. The reality was rather different. From Mrs Macdonald's diary, it is clear that Jones's visits became increasingly frequent as he grew more disillusioned with Oxford. As Fulford helped Alice with her writing, so Edward began to help Georgie with her drawing. By the beginning of 1856 she was ready to attend the Government School of Design at Gore House in Kensington. As she explained: 'I had a certain deftness of hand, but I did not learn anything vital' – but she revealed: 'Often on the way back Edward met me with flowers and we walked home together. I had no precise idea of what the profession of an artist meant, but felt that it was well to be amongst those who painted pictures and wrote poetry.'[17]

Edward decided to finish with Oxford, and arrived in London in May 1856 full of determination for an career in art. 'The house in Sloane Terrace where Edward lodged was almost exactly opposite the chapel of which my father was a minister, and sometimes after service, as the congregation filed out, the eyes of a girl amongst the slowly moving crowd were lifted and saw for a moment his face watching at a window.'[18] Jones was swept along in a romantic haze of art, medievalism and courtly love, into which Georgie fitted easily. Her affection for Edward had grown steadily and solidly over the years, so that she was quite content to be seen against this landscape. Even Edward's proposal on 19 May 1856, in front of Arthur Hughes's painting *April Love*, which Edward had gone to purchase for Morris, seemed totally in keeping: the mood of the painting echoed their own feelings. On her return from the Royal Academy, Georgie unburdened herself to Alice, for although she knew her own feelings, she was far less sure of her parents' reaction to this match between a fifteen and a twenty-two-year-old. Alice was quite unable to keep such an exciting piece of news

to herself and despite vows of silence to Georgie could not resist telling
her mother. In her journal Mrs Macdonald asked for divine wisdom to
direct their decision, but she also noted that she went on to seek Harry's
opinion. In a formal fashion, a marked contrast to Alice's betrothal,

> my mother called me into her room and told me that Edward had been to see
> my father and herself: and then she went on with what seemed to me to have
> been written from the beginning of the world, and ended by saying that they
> left the answer they should give him entirely to my decision. There was no
> difficulty in her seeing what that was, and we knelt down together to ask for
> the blessing of God upon it. I was not quite sixteen. . . . Neither he (Papa)
> nor my mother had at that time any idea of Edward's genius, but they liked
> him very much and trusted him completely,

for which Georgie was eternally grateful.[19]

With both Alice and Georgie's engagements, the Macdonald parents
respected their daughters' judgement to a surprising degree, but they
took into account the youth of the two girls, which made their marriages
distant prospects. Mrs Macdonald had the wisdom to realize that time
would correct any impulsive decisions.

Chapter Four

Pre-Raphaelite Experience
(1856–60)

Georgie's euphoria following her engagement was tinged with concern that within three months she might find herself on a train heading away from Edward again, for her father's ministry in Chelsea was due to end in September 1856. None of the family wanted to leave London, so the news that the Wesleyan Conference had appointed the Reverend George Macdonald to Hinde Street Chapel in Marylebone was greeted with intense relief.

Life in that part of London was different from Chelsea, but Edith, the youngest in the family, thought it far more entertaining. For one thing there was a mews behind their house in Beaumont Street, where she and Louisa were able to watch the grooms fetching horses out to wash, then schooling them in their street. Other diversions included organ grinders with monkeys, Punch and Judy shows and street tumblers, and on 5 November, with the Crimean War fresh in people's minds, a group of masked figures were carried through on chairs, chanting a contemporary version of the old rhyme:

> Please to remember the fifth of November,
> Sebastopol, powder and shot,
> When General Leprandy charged Jack, Pat and Sandy
> And a jolly good licking he got.[1]

Italians carrying plaster casts of kneeling figures, called 'praying Samuels' by the girls, begged for money, and someone, with a show called *A Happy Family*, pushed around a cart with a cage containing a real cat sitting next to a rat and tried to collect money, but it was Edith's opinion that both animals were drugged. Two beggars particularly attracted the girls' attention. Edith recalled one morning, when they were sitting indoors reading, the cry of 'Kind Christian friends look out of the window, my wife has nothing on!' sent them scurrying to see, but to their disappointment there was only a scantily clad female beggar shuffling down the road with a man.

Edward moved lodgings at the same time as the Macdonalds, sharing rooms in a house in Red Lion Square, Holborn, with his Oxford friend William Morris. Once the Macdonalds were installed in 17 Beaumont Street, both young men became regular visitors. The Macdonald family accepted Edward within their ranks with surprising alacrity, considering his uncertain career, his High Church views and his involvement with Bohemian artists. 'His sweetness of temper endeared him to them at once, and as they came to know him better his endless sense of fun and treasures of knowledge that he was ready to share with them in ways portioned to their understanding made them adore him.'[2] This gentle, kindly person brought with him the aura of a world that the family could only imagine. Within a short time he was known by his Christian name, included in visits to Mrs Macdonald's sisters and accompanied the family to many Methodist social events. Fulford, whose moods tended to fluctuate, never achieved this position with the Macdonalds; he was always treated as a visitor rather than a future son-in-law, whereas Edward, though never compromising his beliefs, delighted in the female company and the sense of belonging to a family, and was therefore even willing to attend chapel with them. As Georgie sagely summed up: 'The advent of "Mr Edward", as the children called him, was of infinite importance to more than one of them.'[3]

It was Mrs Macdonald's opinion that Edward would gradually be absorbed into their way of life and any wayward tendencies deriving from the art world thus curbed. In the event her predictions were totally inaccurate, for the family were secretly intrigued by Edward's activities and only too willing to be part of them. Thus it comes as no surprise to find that a little over a year after Georgie and Edward became engaged, Mrs Macdonald and the two elder daughters were being entertained to supper at Red Lion Square by Edward, in the illustrious company of William Morris, Gabriel Rossetti, Arthur Hughes and Ford Madox Brown. What was more remarkable was the presence of the Reverend George Macdonald. At first glance it is hard to comprehend how a minister could reconcile the strict Methodist way of life with the unconventional behaviour of the Pre-Raphaelites. Fortunately Mr Macdonald was blessed with a 'live and let live' attitude as well as a genuine interest in the arts. In any case there was probably more common ground between the two sides than might at first be realized. The cult of medievalism which so preoccupied these artists stressed the virtues of a simple life close to nature, a craftsman's pride in his work and the nobleness of chivalry, all of which would strike a sympathetic chord in a Christian. The young men's burning zeal to transform the world was also quite familiar to a follower of Wesley, and therefore Mr Macdonald, usually so absorbed in his ministry, happily found time to talk with these artists. There was no problem in Mrs Macdonald's mind either. She shared Georgie's view that 'the young men were as good as they were gifted', and since many of them were known personally to Harry through the Oxford connection, she considered they were acceptable company for her daughters.[4] Added to that she trusted Edward completely, and if he proposed to take Alice and Georgie to visit a particular artist, no objections were raised.

The girls were not slow to sense this new atmosphere of freedom and determined to take full advantage of it. One of their early visits was to Rossetti's studio in Blackfriars where Edward was studying painting. Rossetti's flamboyant life-style included a succession of female models (and rumour had it mistresses), but Alice and Georgie's innocence kept them ignorant, and they looked forward to the meeting eagerly. Edward carefully prepared the ground beforehand lest Rossetti's language or behaviour should shock the girls. Only a few nights before, Rossetti had attempted to widen his pupil's experience by paying a woman five shillings to follow Edward home. 'She came after me and I couldn't get rid of her. I said, "No my dear, I'm just going home" – I'm never haughty with these poor things, but it was no use, she wouldn't go and there we marched arm in arm down Regent Street – I don't know what my friends would have thought,' he reported, though not to Georgie.[5]

Despite Edward's qualms, the girls' visit was deemed successful. Rossetti behaved like a paragon of virtue and continued painting at his easel without uttering a word. This disappointed Alice, who had hoped for some discussion with the poet-painter about the scraps of his verses that Edward salvaged for them to read. In the end, it was the studio rather than the painter which astonished the girls, because they had never expected anything so untidy. Broken furniture mingled with bits of musical instruments and half-finished paintings, and books – those most hallowed of Macdonald possessions – were relegated to propping up easels or were simply thrown out of the window into the Thames as 'things which obstructed life'. Alice found the whole experience exhilarating, whereas sixteen-year-old Georgie felt completely over-awed. 'I wish it were possible to explain the impression made upon me as a young girl whose experience so far had been quite remote from art, by sudden and close intercourse with those to whom it was the breath of life,' she wrote. 'I felt in the presence of a new religion. Their love of beauty did not seem to me unbalanced, but as if it included the whole world and raised the point from which they regarded everything.'[6]

Georgie tried to explain her feelings to William Morris. She first met him at the Royal Academy exhibition in 1855, at which time Morris was more interested in studying a Millais painting than talking to this slip of a girl whom Heeley had introduced. Once in London permanently, though, Morris fell into Edward's habit of spending several evenings a week at the manse. Georgie did not find Morris an easy person to get to know because his manner towards women seemed too brusque, but gradually both came to appreciate the other's character, and a friendship began which lasted throughout their lives. It was a relationship which amounted to love in later years – albeit a chaste love – and has prompted some of Morris's biographers to speculate that Morris always wished he had married Georgiana Macdonald. It is unlikely that Georgie ever regretted marrying Edward, but she had an affection for Morris which was only transcended by her love for her husband.

Georgie's impression of Morris appeared in one of her letters: 'I am sure you would like Morris so much if you came to know him well, he is altogether *the* most remarkable man I ever saw – I don't say the greatest, though I think him great, but certainly the most remarkable, and I often call myself names for not quietly putting down for the delight of our old age, if we see it, some of his doings and sayings, which are more amusing and interesting than words can tell. He is so comfortingly far from the "bard" in daily life, and yet so remote from the commonplace man.'[7] Mrs Macdonald, too, thought Morris was excellent company since he would discuss literature with her endlessly: anything from Mrs Gaskell's recent biography of Charlotte Brontë to the works of Fouqué. She did have words with Morris about keeping Georgie out talking on the balcony until eleven o'clock at night, but once the family's standards were understood, he was always very welcome at the house.

For Alice it was a marvellous opportunity to study poetry with someone she regarded as a real poet, and she listened with rapture to Morris reading aloud from his own works. In return she expected to be given the chance to read hers, but Morris tended to overlook that courtesy. He gave her the nickname 'my lady Alice de la Barde' to the family's amusement, and Alice was rather flattered to discover their private joke appearing in his collection of poems *The Defence of Guenevere* published in 1858.[8] The younger girls Agnes and Louisa found Morris's long poetic orations a real trial because his noisy delivery, gasping breaths and sing-song intonation gave them the giggles. Even his most ardent disciple Georgie recalled 'with shame often falling asleep to the steady rhythms of the reading voice and biting my fingers and stabbing myself with pins in order to keep awake'.[9] Nevertheless, the girls did not want to lose Morris's company, for he had the same sense of humour as Edward, and when both were present, things came alive.

Morris's standing as a poet rose in Louisa's estimation when she found herself included along with her sisters in another of Morris's poems. A watercolour he bought from Rossetti in 1857 portrayed four young girls in a medieval setting playing a keyboard instrument and bore the title *The Blue Closet*. To Morris the four damozels in the picture were the Macdonald sisters imprisoned in their manse and making music:

> Four lone ladies dwelling here
> From day to day and year to year.

He began the poem to the evident delight of two girls:

> Lady Alice, Lady Louise,
> Between the wash of the tumbling seas
> We are ready to sing, if so ye please;
> So lay your long hands on the keys;
> Sing 'Laudate pueri'.[10]

Following the family's curiosity about art, Morris and Jones began to involve them actively. Agnes and Louisa, who had previously been regarded as too young, were now aged fourteen and twelve respectively and eager to be involved in evening discussions or art lessons. Even Frederic was drawn in: as the boy in the midst of many girls, he was frequently overlooked, but Edward went out of his way to include him. Like his sisters, he was invited to Red Lion Square, not only to watch the artists at work, but to experiment with paints himself. He was sometimes given the additional treat – denied his sisters – of being allowed to stay overnight and indulge in the general horseplay and antics, which were quite alien to his home life. Sessions of horror-story-telling in the darkened studio, where each tried to outdo the other with more grisly and gruesome tales, were followed by 'Mexican Duel', which was a sort of hide-and-seek played around the unlit rooms until the early hours.

The studio at Red Lion Square was just as untidy as Rossetti's had been: 'a noble confusion', Frederic called it,[11] for it contained all the flotsam of the artists – canvases, pieces of tapestry and drapery, sketch books, bits of Flemish and Italian earthenware, old pieces of metalwork and lay figures were all muddled in with a pair of Morris's boots or one of Jones's hats. If Mrs Macdonald or her daughters were to be entertained, an open space was created, which Frederic said resembled a clearing in a jungle, so that the ladies could be seated at a table near the fireplace. The furniture in the rooms was always a source of amusement because Morris had designed much of it himself and the proportions sometimes got out of hand. The settle he planned was so large when it arrived that it blocked the passageway and had to be dismembered. 'I think the measurements had perhaps been given a little wrongly,' Jones conceded, 'and that it was bigger altogether than he ever meant, but set up it was finally, and our studio was one third less in size.'[12]

Errors like that seemed of no consequence to Alice and Georgie, who, impressed that anyone could design and decorate such an item, felt it an honour to be associated with him. These were memorable days for the two girls, and indeed the whole family: 'I am surprised on employing the ruthless measure of weeks and months to find how short a time the brilliant days of Red Lion Square really lasted,' Georgie mused, 'for on looking back it seems so much longer. But I believe that it made the same impression upon many of us and that every minute then contained the life of an hour.'[13]

From their time there, they gained a clear understanding of art, for Edward proved a particularly good teacher, able to combine serious concepts with a sense of enjoyment. He showed them pictures, prints and engravings of various sculptures and tried to explain what was good and why, and conversely what was bad and why. None of them got bored because the lessons were accompanied by jests, parodies, caricatures and exaggerations; indeed Frederic frankly admitted that Edward became his hero.

Georgie continued to work at her drawing under Edward's tuition, and the younger girls, who were impatient to be doing something positive, began learning woodcuts with Morris. It proved so popular that they saved up to buy their own sets of tools and blocks, and Louisa designed a monogram to be printed on her writing paper, comprising a Gothic L and M intertwined. For her birthday Morris gave her a copy of Albrecht Dürer's engravings, in addition to taking her to the Beast Gardens in Regent's Park, and Edward encouraged her art work with talk of jointly producing an illustrated book.

It was a delight to the girls to find themselves appearing in Edward's pictures as well as in Morris's poetry. During the evenings when Edward sat with them, if he was not actively involved in demonstrating something to them, he would quietly get on with his pen-and-ink sketching. Many of the Burne-Jones drawings produced at this time show the Macdonald sisters in such medieval guises as *Kings' Daughters*, *Wise and Foolish Virgins*, *Going to the Battle* and *Buondelmonte's Wedding*. Mrs Macdonald recorded in her diary that the sketches for *The Blessed Damozel*, Edward's first commission, were drawn from Georgie on two evenings in February 1857, whilst she sat working at her drawings for Edward. She was naturally his favourite model, but the fourteen-year-old Agnes came a very close second. According to Georgie, Agnes had the sort of symmetrical features which Edward so admired, but it can also be seen from the way he depicted her that he regarded her heavy-lidded eyes as similar to those of Lizzie Siddal, Rossetti's mistress and favourite model. Agnes was at an age when she was very conscious of her looks, and requests to pose flattered her greatly, so that her vanity became a family joke. Edward would tease her gently by pretending that she was really the plainest of the sisters, who needed encouragement to prevent her being overwhelmed by a sense of her own inadequacies. The resultant wheedling and pleading for her to take up a particular stance for him reduced the rest of them to helpless laughter.

Louisa, then aged twelve, was drawn occasionally, as was Alice, though she developed a complex about her looks. Her face was much rounder than the other sisters' and not the type Edward usually liked to draw. She was never a willing subject of the artist or the photographer, put off perhaps by the typically tactless comments of Agnes, who told Alice on one occasion that though it was a good idea to have her photograph taken again, the chances were that it would not be any better, because her face never came out right. In any case Alice was far more interested in Pre-Raphaelite poetry than art, and whilst being prepared to accompany Georgie to any art studio rather than stay at home, she infinitely preferred the long conversations she had with Rossetti about poetry. Her own writing began to flourish. She always felt she was inspired by the ideas of Morris and Rossetti, but a reading of her work would suggest a much greater debt to the melancholy ideas of her mother than anyone else. With a true sense of Victorian melodrama, Alice's verses concentrated on the idea of the lover lamenting the death of his beloved – as in the poem written in 1856:

> Once I wished to live,
> Now what matters it?
> Life had worn that dream
> And death scatters it.
> Nay, you must not weep, love,
> Nothing is amiss,
> Press on my pale forehead
> One last kiss
> So all here is ended –
> Is this bliss?[14]

Other efforts contain harrowing descriptions of dying:

> The pale lips drink, deep soul disturbing draughts,
> A deadly sickness fills the sinking heart

until after throbbing pulses and painful breathing:

> One pang, one groan and the whole thing is done.

It seems likely that the last painful days of her sister Carrie provided copy for her. These poems, written at the drawing-room table in the manse and read out to artists at Red Lion Square, were then sent on to the *Temple Bar* and *Cornhill* magazines in the hope of publication. Although rejected in the late 1850s, some of this material did get into print early in the next decade.

Whilst Alice occupied her mind with love poetry, her personal romance was falling apart. It was quite obvious to her family that although nominally engaged to Fulford, Alice showed far more interest in an evening at Red Lion Square (described by Jones as 'a stunner or two to make melody – victuals and squalor at all hours'; scarcely Mrs Macdonald's impression of events![15]), than in remaining at home quietly sewing in case Fulford should call. The love affair began to disintegrate once Fulford made up his mind to enter the church, gave up his teaching and resumed serious studies. Alice went with her family to his ordination in St Paul's in December 1856, but felt the net closing round her. She was nearly twenty, and once the Reverend William Fulford was settled in as the curate of Camden Town, with sufficient income to support a wife, she knew that he would expect them to be married. But having entered into the life of Red Lion Square, she realized she could never contemplate the role of a curate's wife, and in any event the vivacious Fulford of former years had disappeared. Some time in 1857 Alice broke off her engagement, but for a while Fulford continued to call at the house, hoping she might change her mind and consoling himself by taking Agnes and Louisa to visit the same art galleries and concert halls he had attended with the two older girls. Then to everyone's relief he ceased calling; William Fulford vanished from their lives and those of his Oxford friends.

Heartened by the freedom their mother now allowed them, Georgie determined to visit Oxford, about which she had heard so much. At first Mrs Macdonald had doubts about the enterprise, but as Alice quickly pointed out, Harry was studying theology there and would value a visit from his sisters. Thus, on the first anniversary of her engagement, Georgie found herself again standing in front of another painting, this time Holman Hunt's *Light of the World*, which was being shown in Mr Combe's house in Oxford. Here was a situation which twelve months before would have been inconceivable. Oxford had become the city of Georgie's dreams from the time Fulford first described it to her. In her imagination it took on legendary proportions as the fount of intellect and inspiration: Oxford was essentially her spiritual home. Even in later years, when her travel experience included the glories of Italy, she could still say that Oxford was her favourite place in the world. She took holidays there, but more significantly turned to this ancient city in time of trouble, when, once more ensconced in undergraduate rooms, she would try to recapture the sense of mysticism and enchantment felt on that first visit.

Georgie approached Oxford in June 1857 much in the manner of a pilgrim entering a holy place, leaving behind her all the petty irritations and jealousies recently encountered on a visit to Edward's old nanny in Birmingham, and instead opening her soul to the beauties of this seat of learning. With her went Alice, not as awestruck, for she was far more down-to-earth. For her, Oxford provided an opportunity to meet some dashing young men, and for a brief time learn something about the world that had been denied her. Edward and Morris naturally went to Oxford with them, and the university held Crom Price and Charlie Faulkner, both known to the girls, as well as brother Harry.

The first few days were spent viewing the city, visiting Edward's old haunts, admiring colleges and chapels and punting on the River Cherwell in idyllic June weather with various undergraduates all eager to entertain. An invitation soon arrived for the girls to stay with the Maclaren family at Summertown, a village outside Oxford. Georgie had corresponded with Mrs Maclaren the previous year to thank her for an opal ring given as an engagement present. The friendship between Edward and the Maclarens grew out of his frequent attendance at Archibald Maclaren's gymnasium in Oriel Lane. Invitations followed for Edward and Morris to call on the family at home, and there Mr Maclaren sought the young man's help. A fairy-story book was being planned for the Maclarens' little daughter Mabel, and Maclaren asked Edward to illustrate it. There was a further reason why Mrs Maclaren wanted to meet the Macdonald girls. Her sister Peggy Talboys had fallen in love with Harry Macdonald, and it seemed that the two families might well become related shortly. Oxford had wrought changes in Harry unbeknown to his family!

Romantic days spent at Summertown in 1857 and again in 1858 seemed to belong to another world. During the hot weather the girls sat in the garden laughing, talking and sketching, or safe in the shade of the orchard eating cherries and telling tales. Evenings passed listening to Edward reading from Malory or Morris reading from his 'Guenevere' poems, with general music-making and merriment. There was no compulsory attendance at chapel, no evening prayers or sensible subdued behaviour, instead the romance of the Arthurian legends dominated their conversation, their writing and their art. As they wandered to the legendary burial site of the fair Rosamund, the two girls felt they were reliving the noble past. But a sudden jolt into the present came with the arrival of the Reverend Macdonald at Summertown, hot-foot from a preaching mission in the county, and bearing a message from their mother that they had been ten weeks from home and were expected back. Georgie reluctantly returned, her head full of Edward's ideas: 'I came back in a delirium of joy. . . . In my mind pictures of the old days, the abbey and long processions of the faithful, banners of the cross, copes and crosiers, gay knights and ladies by the river banks, hawking parties and all the pageantry of the golden age.'[16]

Back in Beaumont Street, the two girls were plunged into the usual domestic problems: Elizabeth Townley, the housemaid, had just been sacked. She had apparently spent the day complaining about her health, but in the evening got very drunk and rampaged noisily around the house. The quest for the holy grail was set aside in favour of the washing, which had begun to mount up. Set against such mundane chores, the company at Red Lion Square became even more magnetic, and the two elder girls sought distraction there. They immersed themselves in the plans under discussion to decorate the Oxford Union building with scenes from the *Morte D'Arthur*. It was especially interesting to them now that they had a personal knowledge of the building, but within a couple of weeks they found themselves alone, as the young men disappeared to Oxford and Mrs Macdonald refused to let her daughters go back barely a month after their return. It remained a disappointment to Georgie that she never had the opportunity to see the Union painting in pristine condition. Her mother saw it in February 1858 when Harry took her into the building, but by then work was at a standstill. Many of the artists had left, and Edward too had packed up, disillusioned with the way the painting had dragged on. He missed Georgie's company, and his health was poor.

The true purpose of Mrs Macdonald's journey to Oxford was to discover the extent of Harry's attachment to Peggy Talboys and to put pressure on him to make sure he passed his final exams with distinction. The time spent with him seemed to do nothing to prepare her for future developments, for several months after her return home a letter arrived from Oxford which stunned the family. Instead of sending news of the anticipated results, Harry admitted that he had never even taken the exams because he had become petrified of failing and bringing disgrace to the family. Instead he proposed to take Civil Service entrance papers, marry Peggy and go to India, as Wilfred Heeley had recently done. His mother was devastated, declaring with great melodrama that on that day she buried all her hopes and was not likely to survive them herself. His father, taking as his text 'I reckon that the sufferings of the present are not worthy to be compared', collapsed during the evening service and was obliged to retire to his bed. Thereafter his health gradually declined, a fact which weighed heavily on Harry's conscience all his life.

The episode with Harry was a powerful lesson for Alice and Georgie, although the conclusions they reached were not the ones their parents would have wished. The girls observed it was possible to rebel against parents and chapel and still survive. Although considerably changed, Harry emerged from the affair without being struck down by a thunderbolt. Gone was the self-righteous brother and in his place was a humble, even abject, figure. Both girls saw the misery that compulsory religion had caused and vowed that when they had children of their own there would be complete freedom of religious choice. This they were to adhere to, but paradoxically both Rudyard Kipling and Philip Burne-Jones were later to bemoan the lack of religious guidance in their childhood.

In the short term, one good thing did come out of Harry's misfortune – Alice and Georgie were dispatched to Oxford to discover what had happened and to persuade their errant brother to come home and face his parents. Although their mission was accomplished in a matter of days, they gratefully accepted the Maclarens' hospitality for a further month, whilst the soul-searching continued at the manse. The carefree atmosphere of the previous year was gone: the problems of Harry cast a cloud, as did the ever-present worry about Edward's health. He did manage to join them for a short time, but was obliged to spend much of it lying on the sofa. Earlier in the year, when he returned to Red Lion Square after the Oxford Union painting, he had been confined to bed, receiving daily visits from Mrs Macdonald and her daughters, who attempted to nurse him. But the sudden shock Harry's news caused brought that arrangement to an end, and Mrs Prinsep, the rich, sympathetic mother of one of the Union painters, came to Edward's rescue and carried him off to Little Holland House to be cared for. Georgie lamented not being able to see him, but contented herself that in this opulent house at the centre of fashionable culture Edward would improve. His recovery was such that he was able to join the two Macdonald girls for a few days at Summertown and revive something of the previous summer's charm.

During their absence, Harry decided to postpone his wedding to Peggy Talboys. He had achieved excellent results in the Indian Civil Service exam, coming sixteenth out of sixty-nine, so preparations began for him to go to Asia, establish a home there and then return to collect his bride. Shortly before he was due to sail, as horror stories of the Indian Mutiny outraged England, Harry changed his passage to New York. Within six days he had gone. Peggy remained behind awaiting his return for several years, then, hearing he had taken an American wife, she deemed the betrothal over and married someone else.

Georgie was very unsettled: she could neither take her place quietly in the family, nor resume the lively activities of Red Lion Square. The doors there had closed when Edward stayed on at Little Holland House and Morris became preoccupied with his impending marriage and designs for his home. None of this dampened Alice's spirits; she turned instead to the company of Aunt Pullein in Lonsdale Square. Ostensibly it was to help with her little cousin Kitty, but Alice quickly discovered that the Pulleins led a more exciting social life than the Macdonalds and were quite willing to incorporate her into their social round. She was a welcome guest on account of her singing and witty remarks, but this life was brought to a painful conclusion when she became plagued by toothache. Several weeks of agony followed, and despite liberal doses of wine and morphine, her face became so swollen she could not be seen in public. Eventually she was forced to consult a dental surgeon. Like her father, Alice was always willing to try something new and agreed to have her tooth drawn under the influence of electricity, a recently-mooted form of anaesthetic. A letter to *The Times* in September 1858 claimed the merits of this method over the use of chloroform, which had caused several deaths. Alice's treatment by Mr Olive one month later must therefore have been in the nature of an experiment. She sat in the chair holding on to a metal arm-rest. Forceps were attached to the offending tooth and at the precise moment of extraction, an electrical circuit was made. It was an excruciating experience, for in addition to the pain of the tooth being pulled, Alice received an electric shock – suffice it to say this type of 'anaesthetic' never became popular!

The year 1859 was enjoyed by none of the sisters. There was a general concern about Harry and a feeling of anticlimax now that the stimulating company of Morris and Jones was less in evidence. The three-yearly move loomed again, and with two consecutive circuits in London they felt sure they would be sent away from the capital. Some of the general malaise affected Georgie. Normally cheerful and uncomplaining, she became rebellious and miserable. The holiday her mother planned for the first time ever was greeted by a refusal on Georgie's part. There were only two months of the family's time left in London, and Georgie intended to spend them as near to Edward as possible. However, after several full-scale family arguments, Georgie had to obey her mother. Her minor victory was the invitation issued to

Edward to join them in Kent for a few days on Georgie's nineteenth birthday.

When the family packed up for Manchester that September, Alice and Georgie persuaded Aunt Pullein to let them stay on at Lonsdale Square for a little longer. Listlessly, Georgie moved on to Birmingham for a while and thence to Manchester. Alice remained in London and threw herself wholeheartedly into the Methodist social life in Islington. Within a month she was engaged to an anonymous schoolmaster, then returned to tell her parents the glad tidings. They were not impressed by this whirlwind romance, and her father lectured her on the evils of being a flirt. Her pert reply was to spell out the letters 'P-H-L-U-R-T'. 'What is that?' she asked, with seeming innocence.[17] Although now twenty-two, she was kept under her parents' eyes for several months until they considered that love had gone cold.

Georgie's long engagement drew to a close the following year. Emma Madox Brown, the wife of the artist, felt sorry for Georgie isolated from them all in Manchester and invited her to stay at Fortress Terrace in Kentish Town. She also extended a welcome to Edward. On their arrival, Emma pointed out that they might as well be happily married and penniless as unhappily apart and still penniless. Georgie and Edward needed no further encouragement. In a letter sent to Mrs Macdonald Georgie said that so much of her had already left her mother's kind hands: 'I prayed her now to set the rest free, and she and my father consented, asking Edward no questions, but committing us both to the care of God.'[18] In the year 1860, on 9 June, a day they had always intended should be their wedding date, being the anniversary of the death of Dante's Beatrice, Georgiana Macdonald married Edward Coley Burne Jones in Manchester Cathedral. She was a month short of her twentieth birthday, and he was aged twenty-six.

Chapter Five

The Marriage Stakes
(1860–66)

Manchester society did not come up to Mrs Macdonald's standards: she thought it offered only entertainment of an animal nature, which left her family's more sensitive spirits starved of sustenance, with any cultural activity arising through what they provided for themselves. But this was not completely true, for she later admitted to enjoying some concerts at the Free Trade Hall, where with her daughters she heard the pianist Carl Hallé and his newly founded orchestra. Agnes remained unaffected by this snobbery and participated happily in the gatherings organized by local Methodists. Alone of the girls she inherited her father's untroubled, optimistic nature and was therefore quite adaptable. In London she had enjoyed the company of poets and artists, taking up drawing or writing on their suggestion, but once they vanished so did her work, whereas Louisa plodded on, patiently cutting blocks for engraving and sending them to Edward for approval, believing she would one day make her mark on the art world. Agnes was perfectly content to practise the piano, embroider a little and enjoy life.

At seventeen, and for many years to come, she was acknowledged to be a beauty. 'Tyrannously pretty', was John Kipling's verdict, whilst another admirer drooled that she looked as beautiful as an exquisite piece of sculpture, with her delicately chiselled features, her beautiful blue eyes and her neat little figure, like a model stepping out of one of the finest canvases in the Royal Academy Exhibition, as in a vision or a dream rather than living flesh and blood. Agnes was aware of her assets and capable of using them to advantage. She came equipped with all the accomplishments for drawing-room success: in addition to looks and musical ability, she displayed a nimble wit (her conversation sparkled like champagne, one person remarked). She had a predilection for anecdotes and repartee, and though lacking the sarcasm of Alice, could hold her own in any company.

There were no brothers available to escort Agnes. Harry continued to languish in New York, from whence he sent dismal letters back to his family, upsetting his mother for days after. His post as a correspondence clerk on Wall Street he considered only fit for horse or devil, and lamented that he was pinned like an insect specimen to his desk. Fred, by contrast, thoroughly enjoyed his work, because after an uncertain beginning he decided to take up the challenge which had defeated Harry, namely to continue the family tradition of preaching. Following school, Fred had been set against his will to work in the offices of his Uncle Pullein in Lincoln's Inn, although his own career plans had ranged from going to sea, being called to the Bar and, after Rossetti predicted Fred was 'destined to raise the fortunes of the British stage', even to becoming an actor.[1] That idea was destined to be stillborn, because as Methodists none of the Macdonalds had ever entered such iniquitious places as theatres. Finally he decided to put his extrovert character to more worthy causes, and entered the ministry. His father showed no enthusiasm for the idea; instead he would have nothing to do with it, owing to the guilt he felt about Harry's wasted life. Fred therefore struggled to finance his own progress in the Church. When the family departed to Manchester, he remained in lodgings with a sympathetic and devout family in London who guided his progress, and his own family only saw him on short visits thereafter.

Agnes pleased her parents with regular attendance at chapel and keen interest in Methodist class meetings, but this spiritual rectitude sprang from a desire for companionship rather than salvation and led to invitations and even proposals of marriage. One suitor, referred to enigmatically as JBJ, fell so hopelessly in love with her at chapel that he wrote offering his hand. This amused most of the family and flattered Agnes. Still unmarried at twenty-three, Alice found her sister's easy success with men irritating, and took it upon herself to counsel Agnes about the evils of leading young men on, a lecture Agnes did not think Alice was qualified to give! Without the calming influence of Georgie, tempers frequently became frayed. Alice and Agnes tried to score points off each other, leading Agnes cheerfully to report to Louisa that she spent her time teasing Alice, and at long last had worked out the vital difference between them: Alice had no looks to speak of but a thousand vanities, whereas she, Agnes, had all the good looks and none of the vanity. Alice was not amused.

Quarrels like this washed over Louisa, who at fifteen felt she was in the shadow of her elder sisters. She did not wish to be classified with the twelve-year-old Edith, but it was also obvious that she was not part of the same social scene as Agnes. Marriage and men barely entered Louisa's head; instead she enjoyed the company of her Manchester cousins and spent time on her art in order to draw praise from Edward and Morris when she next met them. Georgie promised to invite each of the sisters to London, and Edward once spoke of taking a house large enough for Louisa to share with them.

It was the same prospect of visiting London which sustained Alice. Eleven months were to elapse before the longed-for invitation was issued, whilst the Burne-Joneses seemed to enjoy a protracted honeymoon.* In the intervening time Alice occupied herself with housework and poetry, lamenting in her verses: 'Oh strange pathetic power of days gone by . . . how we laughed a year ago.'[2] Poetry poured from her pen, concerned as ever with the beloved dying, but one poem showed that Alice was having qualms about her treatment of Fulford. In 'Changed' she considered the plight of the lover wasting his life on a girl who ultimately jilted him:

> And they say who heard the story told
> (Tho' they heard it not from me)
> 'Since the girl was heartless and false and cold
> 'Tis the best thing that could be.
>
> But I know a better that might have been
> 'Tho 'tis sad to write it down,
> Of her fair face I had never seen
> With its change from smile to frown.
>
> Well, God bless her, I think she meant me truth
> When she promised my wife to be
> I pardon the sin of her needless youth
> And I pray God to comfort me.[3]

When the summons to London came, Alice went, aglow with the triumph of her first publication, a poem called 'Three Times', in which she described the three occasions when a young man saw his love: the first as a maiden dressed in white and clutching a bunch of roses, then as a corpse shrouded in white with roses on her breast, and finally as an angel clad in white with a palm of victory exchanged for her roses. It

*Although Edward did not add Burne to his surname until a few years later, and did not use a hyphen until 1885, to avoid confusion Burne-Jones is used from now on.

appeared in *Temple Bar* in May 1861, the same month as she returned to the capital. Now Alice had received public recognition for her poetry, she felt confident of her place in the group who met regularly in the Burne-Joneses' rooms in Russell Place and included people new to her like Swinburne, an artist called Simeon Solomon, Philip Webb, an architect friend of Morris's and William De Morgan who later became a celebrated ceramic designer, as well as the familiar faces of Crom Price, Morris, Faulkner and Rossetti. Georgie was pleased to see her favourite sister again, at least during the day: the Burne-Joneses' flat was so small Alice had to sleep at Aunt Pullein's.

Morris, now married and living out at Upton near Bexleyheath in Kent, had always enjoyed Alice's company, so urged her to spend some weekends at his home, the Red House, with Edward and Georgie. The riotous undergraduate atmosphere was on the wane now that Janey Morris had a baby daughter and Georgie was pregnant. But after the tedious months in Manchester it all seemed idyllic to Alice, who patiently worked at the new type of embroidery Morris wanted the women to execute. Once more in the presence of Morris, it was natural that her verse should flourish, although the opening lines of the poem written during her stay at the Red House on 7 June 1861 give no hint of the carefree nature of those days:

> I had prayed as the dying prayed for life,
> With outstretched hands and bitter groans;
> I had cried as the starving cry for bread,
> With wailing tears and with hungry moans,
> That once again 'ere life closed for me,
> I might see her face whom I pined to see.[4]

Yet this, along with other poems published the following year, shows that Alice's choice of themes was finding favour with editors.

The London holiday was stretched out for as long as possible, and only the imminence of Georgie's baby forced Alice home. Mrs Macdonald had promised to be with her daughter for the birth, and it was necessary for Alice to exchange places with Mama to run the house in Manchester and attend to her ailing father. In the event, Alice delayed her departure so long that Mrs Macdonald arrived twenty minutes after her first grandson.

Back in Manchester there was great interest in Alice's latest exploits because, as Edith remarked, whenever Alice went on a visit she usually became engaged to some strange cad or another, but on this occasion she disappointed them all, declaring there had not been so much as a cloud in the sky. Edith, fast becoming a match for her sister, expressed feigned surprise that there had not even been a cloud the size of a man's hand.

Alice provided something far better for them to gossip about the following year when she left for London on 7 October 1862 and by the 23rd was able to write and announce her engagement to William Allingham. At thirty-eight, this Irish poet was thirteen years her senior and a popular member of the group that met at the Burne-Joneses' rooms. Georgie considered him 'a great addition to our circle for he liked and was liked by so many different people. And he brought with him a breath of the wild Irish loughs and mountains.' These qualities obviously captivated Alice.[5] He was essentially a quiet person, but one easily moved to conversation or laughter. He was reputedly good-looking with 'eyes of celtic glamour' and was certainly very fond of 'Mrs Ned', as he called Georgie. The more animated version of Georgie, with a particular knowledge of poetry and a beautiful singing voice, he found irresistible. Alice delighted Allingham by setting some of his poetry to music, then performing it with Georgie.

This poet had hovered around the Pre-Raphaelite circle for ten years, although employed as a customs officer in his native Ireland and only infrequently in London. His verses 'The Music Master' and 'Day and Night Songs' had been illustrated by Millais, Arthur Hughes and Rossetti. They were published in 1855 and were so popular they were reissued in the 1860s. Now this poet's work is almost forgotten except for the opening lines of a fairy poem:

> Up the airy mountain,
> Down the rushy glen
> We daren't go a-hunting
> For fear of little men,

which most people can recite, without knowing who the author was.

Allingham believed his poetry would never prosper in Ireland and arranged a transfer to the London customs the month before he met Alice. Details of their romance were edited out of existence by the woman Allingham ultimately married, the water-colourist Helen Allingham. He was a great diarist as well as a shameless cultivator of famous names, so it is unlikely that it would have escaped his notice that the girl he was engaged to in 1862 later became the mother of Rudyard Kipling. However, the diary edited and published by his wife omitted any reference to Alice Macdonald. For reasons which can only be guessed at, the engagement was terminated, and Mrs Macdonald expressed no surprise that the bubble had burst before the month was up. Having lived on his own for many years, Allingham was set in his ways and had developed some strange idiosyncrasies which would have tried Alice's limited patience. With the engagement over Allingham was plunged into the depths of despair and returned to Ireland. Alice herself was hardly euphoric and certainly had no intention of meeting the gibes of Agnes, who was collecting proposals like visiting cards. The stay in London continued into the following year until the complaints of Agnes and Louisa could not be ignored: they too wanted the opportunity of a holiday.

This time Alice returned to a different town, as her father's latest circuit had brought the family to Wolverhampton. Those closest to him were of the opinion that this would be his last circuit because he was fifty-eight and his health very poor. He was troubled by severe pains in his back, so that walking was only possible with crutches, and sleep now eluded him. In Alice's absence, her sisters had found their way into the upper echelons of local society by way of the mayor and his family, who were members of the chapel. This was of no consequence to Alice, for once home she barely had time to raise her head from the ironing board. With her father ill and her mother at the end of her tether, Alice ran the household. It alarmed her to see how, at twenty-five, she fitted neatly into the role of an unmarried daughter/housekeeper, and all were keen to point out that the house ran far more smoothly under her supervision than it had ever done with mother. Fearful of the outcome, Alice became very depressed and took refuge in 'delicacy', despite having always enjoyed good health.

The way out of her predicament appeared in the unexpected guise of Frederic, who had been ordained in September 1862 – an event his mother celebrated with some feeling: 'God help the poor boy!' Fred himself had not been so sure about his appointment to the Potteries, where there was rather a large working-class population; as he remarked: 'Perhaps I am not as well fitted by temperament as some of my brethren to gain easy access to working people.'[6] However, he seems to have managed well enough, making friends with the owners of various factories, and once settled was keen for his sisters to come and visit. Agnes and Louisa were always eager to go somewhere different, and both went, but Alice expressed no interest in anywhere outside London. Burslem, she said, would be even worse than Manchester, but by April 1863 it sounded more attractive than another round of housework, and she willingly accepted.

There she met John Lockwood Kipling, an acquaintance of Fred's and also the son of a Methodist minister. But it was their mutual interest in literature and arts and crafts which brought them together, rather than religion, for Kipling's Methodism was fast becoming a thing of the past. He was employed as an art workman for the Department of Science and Arts at South Kensington and as such was responsible for interpreting in stone the ideas of an architect or artist. (Earlier in 1863 Kipling had been awarded a prize for a design for the projected Wedgwood Institute.) Details of Alice and John's first meeting have been blurred by legend, but some time between 21 April and 15 May 1863, Alice joined Fred, John and others on a picnic beside Rudyard Lake, near Leek in Staffordshire. The event was organized by the Misses Pinder, daughters of a leading pottery manufacturer, who being hospitable Methodists invited the Wesleyan minister and his sister who was staying with him, though it might be added that the Reverend Frederic Macdonald was at that time paying court to one of the Miss Pinders. Also included in the invitation was Kipling, who was working on designs for the Pinder Bourne Pottery.

An understanding tantamount to an engagement was reached between John and Alice during her stay in the Potteries, but after the previous disastrous affairs Alice had learnt discretion. The first anyone in Wolverhampton knew of John's existence was when he appeared one evening *en route* for London. A popular story in the family was that as the Reverend George Macdonald was conducting family prayers, he reached a point in his text where he read: 'There came a man sent from God, whose name was John', and in Kipling walked. True or not, he was heaven-sent from Alice's point of view, and her health promptly took a turn for the better. Agnes reported to Louisa, then enjoying herself in London, that Alice was in good spirits and good health, though, she added hastily, that did not mean to imply the strength of a navvy, but as well as could be and quite cheerful. In fact, Agnes declared, Alice was better than she had been for years, and they were both getting on more sweetly than usual.

Alice continued to keep her own counsel until shortly before John's next appearance in Wolverhampton on 1 August. She said she did not want to tell anyone in the family until they had met John and could judge for themselves. With her reputation in the family for flightiness, it was probably a wise move, for her parents declared they had never liked a young man so well as Mr Kipling on first acquaintance. He even seems to have charmed Agnes, for she reported to Louisa, then staying with Georgie in London, that she had studied John Kipling profoundly and believed in him, and in her opinion this match would really work out because he was aware of Alice's previous alliances. John's arrival on the scene had apparently done so much to lift Alice's spirits that Agnes said it did everyone's heart good to see them. All her previous talk of being an old maid and a burden to people had disappeared. John proved a perfect foil for Alice because he had a quiet, calm and essentially good-humoured nature and was someone who respected his future wife's right to hold her own opinions. Fred said, 'Mentally they had much in common, though with certain obvious differences of temperament. She was keen, quick and versatile beyond anyone I have known, saw things at a glance and dispatched them in a word. His mind moved more slowly and was patient and meditative.'[7] This last characteristic, although mentioned in an approving manner from the distance of fifty years, was received at the time in a less complimentary way by the Macdonalds.

Only five feet three inches tall, John was a shy person, and, despite the initially favourable impression, the family generally felt themselves superior to Alice's fiancé. Closer acquaintance taught them a lesson, as Fred continued:

> John was one who seemed to know something about everything, as well as everything about something. He was widely read, and what he read he remembered and had at his disposal. He made no show of his knowledge, or oppressed one with it, but it would come out quietly in the course of conversation, or reveal itself easily and naturally in unexpected ways. Sometimes with gentle scepticism he would abate the confidence of those who were too sure of what they knew, or would supplement what he had modestly advanced in a way that showed he had more at his disposal if it were called for.[8]

The Macdonalds never again underestimated John Kipling, for in many ways he was more than a match for the family. He possessed uncomfortably accurate powers of perception and was not one to tolerate pretensions of an intellectual or a religious kind. The comments which John made about members of the family in later years are refreshingly honest. Unlike Alice, whose 'wit was for the most part humorous and genial, but on occasions . . . was a weapon of whose keenness of point there could be no doubt and foolish or mischievous people were made to feel it', John never willingly caused offence.[9]

His artistic ambitions were not as lofty as those of the set that gathered in Georgie's rooms, but Alice adored him and had every confidence in his abilities. Aspects of his character such as forgetfulness and lateness, which she found infuriating in others, were indulgently overlooked. Alice had celebrated her twenty-sixth birthday and yet seemed reluctant to tie the knot, perhaps because previous abortive love affairs had made her cautious. Even as early as July 1863, when their engagement was first known to the family, Agnes could see no obstacle to a swift marriage, for Kipling was willing and, unlike Edward Burne-Jones, did have regular employment. Nevertheless, Alice persisted in a long engagement, to her mother's irritation. A year after John Kipling's advent, there was no indication of a wedding date, and Mrs Macdonald, who continually met a stone wall whenever she asked Alice about her plans, declared that she would take no further interest in the matter; the following month, October 1864, Alice announced that she and John were going to Bombay, not a plan Mrs Macdonald welcomed. She had grown used to Alice's impulsiveness and believed that as in Harry's case this Indian folly would pass. The sudden illness of Georgie in London took Mrs Macdonald away and curtailed further argument. In fact John Kipling had already applied for a post at the Jeejeebhoy School of Art in Bombay, advertised as an architectural sculptor, and in December 1864 was offered a three-year contract. Plans for the wedding were hurried through once the contract was signed. Though losing the baby she had borne, Georgie recovered, whilst her father became very ill and was forced into premature retirement, making a wedding in London the easiest solution. Alice wanted the wedding dispatched with the least fuss, and with her Aunt Pullein's assistance she was married on 18 March 1865.

Alice's removal from the family circle did not affect her sisters as much as might be expected because she had become a transient figure, alternately appearing to take charge of the house and then disappearing for months on end to London. Her absence caused Agnes and Louisa to draw closer, once Louisa entered the ranks of womanhood. At the time of Alice's marriage, Louisa was twenty and Agnes twenty-two, and both were much in demand in provincial society. In reality it was Agnes who attracted the invitations with Louisa added as a polite after-thought, for the younger girl did not have the same magnetism as her sister. John Kipling said that Louisa's conversation lacked any spark, and it was another artist's impression that Louisa was sweet, gentle and religious. Her reserved manner in company arose from very poor eyesight. She tended to wander around in a haze most of the time, unable to distinguish faces even at close quarters and not wishing to wear spectacles, which hardly flattered a young lady. Dining with others often proved a trial, but as she observed to Agnes, she had to wear her glasses on some occasions because she was quite unable to eat her dinner with her head off the plate. Once the meal was over though, the accursed spectacles were removed so that Louie could feel herself again, enveloped in the usual misty blur. A family tendency to poor vision showed itself later in her nephew Rudyard Kipling, whose eyesight deteriorated at a very young age.

Louisa secretly believed she was inferior to Agnes. Initially it manifested itself in a strong desire to gain favour, and Louisa would willingly carry out small tasks for her pretty sister, such as trimming a bonnet or getting rid of persistent admirers. One Henry Brookes followed Agnes from Manchester and visited so regularly that he jokingly offered to contribute to the rent. Agnes was quick to counter that if he was that keen he could get down on his knees and clean the step for them, but it took the even blunter comments of Louisa finally to send him packing.

Wolverhampton society was felt to be most congenial. Mrs Macdonald remarked: 'I am very pleased with the people here both in the higher and the middle classes' as she returned from a day spent at Tong Castle in the company of the Hartley family.[10] Henry Hartley was a wealthy ironmaster and prominent Methodist, but more significantly mayor of the town. The Macdonalds had made his acquaintance along with his relatives, the Fowlers and Thorneycrofts, all of whom provided mayors for Wolverhampton in the middle years of the century. With friends of such eminence, Agnes and Louisa discovered that access into local society was guaranteed. (There was nothing unusual about Methodists holding public office; indeed Wesley urged his followers to take responsibility in the community, for he argued that those with wealth and talent had an obligation to use them for the good of others. In London, the Macdonalds had seen little evidence of this, but in the industrial towns, where nonconformity flourished, many Methodists held public office. Seeing this at first hand had a profound effect on Louisa and undoubtedly influenced her attitude to the parliamentary aspirations of both husband and son in later years.) Friendship between the Macdonalds and these notable families thrived during the early 1860s, 'rooted in a mutual meeting ground of brains, brilliance and Wesleyan Methodism', one member of the Fowler family wrote.[11] Certainly Mrs Macdonald's diary entries are littered with references to dinners, teas and outings which Agnes and Louisa undertook with these people; reciprocation seems to have been lacking on account of the Reverend Macdonald's invalidity and the poor state of the family finances. The Fowlers and Hartleys were fervent in their pursuit of culture, to which the two Macdonald girls with their knowledge of the London scene added extra spice.

The social aspect of these encounters came as light relief, for as Louisa explained: 'At that time our home life was completely over-shadowed by the long illness of our father, and almost all the sunshine that came to my sister and myself in those days we owed to the affectionate kindness of Mr and Mrs Fowler.'[12] For Louisa, the attraction was in the serious conversation, because unlike Agnes she liked to see herself as a high-minded young woman. The range of subjects included literature, religion and politics, the last being a novelty to her. Despite her father being of the Liberal persuasion, parliamentary affairs did not concern the Macdonald family, whereas amongst the Fowlers it was a matter of great importance and a frequent topic for drawing-room debate. Henry Fowler himself was elected to Parliament a decade later, and his career took him into the Cabinet as Secretary of State for India and won him the title of first Viscount Wolverhampton.

One of Louisa's memories of these years concerned her embarrass-ment at being caught by Mr Fowler with a *risqué* eighteenth-century novel in her hands. She was in the new Wolverhampton Library, an example of Fowler beneficence, when the great man came over to see what she proposed reading. 'He glanced at the title and then told me in the kindest terms and frankest manner that it was not a book suitable for me, and that I had much better leave it unread. It was not a book suitable for a young girl.'[13] Desperate to retain the favour of this family, Louisa hastily replaced the volume on the shelf, mumbling her thanks, never to look at it again. One cannot help speculating that if it had been

Agnes caught red-handed in this way, she would not only have given a pert reply, but probably sneaked back later to see why such reading should be censored.

Agnes derived more pleasure from her visits to London than to the Methodists in Wolverhampton, whom she found rather straightlaced compared with the artists. Agnes's holidays in London were not numerous, but of reasonable duration, enabling her to participate in her sister's way of life. Morris insisted she stay with them at the Red House, and Georgie told her she should feel flattered, for as soon as Morris arrived at the Burne-Joneses' house, he shouted for Agnes to come and amuse him. He told her that no one could tell such entertaining stories and he only wished that such funny things happened to him. Unlike Georgie, who drew and admired whatever the menfolk demanded of her, Agnes retained her own identity: there were no flowing medieval robes in dreary colours for her, but a steadfast adherence to large fashionable crinolines, even though she complained the doors at the Red House were too narrow for these garments. The much admired 'stunner', Janey Morris, Agnes thought too pale and said Janey would do better to wear some bright colours; but with a reputation for being both outspoken and good fun, Agnes's words provoked laughter rather than offence.

In the spring of 1864, when Louisa joined Agnes in London, they paid a joint visit to the Red House, where Edward Burne-Jones recorded their stay in his watercolour painting *Green Summer*. It shows a pastoral scene with Janey, Agnes and Louisa sitting in the garden listening to Georgie reading aloud. 'Our favourite picture' was the girls' verdict, because it captured the mood of those happy days perfectly.

Everyone presumed that Agnes would find her husband in the London art circle rather than amongst the Wolverhampton families, and a letter from Mrs Macdonald to Georgie, written at the time of Alice's wedding, suggested that Georgie was actively canvassing on her sister's behalf, for her mother told her rather tartly to stop trying to marry the girls off. One loss from the family circle was quite enough at a time, and she preferred to take a deep breath and wipe away the tears before more befell. However, it was already too late. Within two weeks of that letter, Mr Edward Poynter appeared in Wolverhampton with what Mrs Macdonald described as 'an enquiry'. Poynter had become a regular visitor at the Burne-Joneses since he had taken over their former rooms in Russell Place. They shared a common interest in art, although

Poynter tended to have a more serious approach to life and stopped short of the puerile antics the others so enjoyed. He was twenty-nine when Agnes made his acquaintance for the first time in March 1865, when she was in London assisting with Alice's wedding preparations. On the night before the nuptials, Poynter joined the family and helped Agnes to clean the large silver tray which was to hold the wedding cake. Agnes's description of the intense young Mr Poynter on his knees with his coat-sleeves pushed back polishing silver for all he was worth is amusing when viewed in the light of the later man. The fastidious artist got himself extremely dirty, Agnes told her sisters, but it was in a good cause. During the course of this romantic little interlude, when Edward Poynter was kneeling before the attractive Miss Macdonald, a proposal of marriage was made and accepted.

Agnes was very impressed by the rising artist, who appeared more mature than the others. His birthplace had been Paris, and he had a very good artistic pedigree, being the son of an architect and on his mother's side descended from a leading eighteenth-century sculptor. His conversation was also impressive, being sprinkled with references to his travels in Madeira, Dresden and Rome and to his acquaintance with Whistler, Du Maurier and Frederic Leighton. Agnes also noted that the post Poynter held at the Department of Science and Art was more prestigious than the one John Kipling filled. Indeed everything about Edward Poynter struck her as professional. The pictures which he had already shown at the Royal Academy demonstrated his proficiency in draughtsmanship and artistic potential. When Agnes met Poynter, he was putting the final touches to his oil painting *Faithful Unto Death*, in which a Roman soldier remained at his post despite the Pompeian lava about to engulf him. It was a painting which was so well received that Poynter's success was assured, both in terms of career and marriage. Agnes favoured the notion of union with a highly-esteemed artist.

The personality of Poynter appeared in *Trilby*, one of Du Maurier's novels, disguised as a character called Lorrimer, who is described as 'a most eager, earnest, and painstaking young enthusiast, of precocious culture, who read improving books, and did not share in the amusements of the *Quartier Latin*, but spent his evenings at home with Handel, Michelangelo, and Dante, on the respectable side of the river. Also, he went into good society sometimes, with a dress coat on, and a white tie, and his hair parted in the middle!'[14]

Apart from art, Edward Poynter's great passion in life was music, something Agnes shared. There were always musical evenings at Georgie's when the sisters were present, and writing home on one occasion, Agnes told Louie that she had played the piano a good deal in the evenings and sung with Georgie. But she could not help noticing that whenever she was playing Poynter was always kind enough to tell her where she had gone wrong. Since she agreed he knew all about music, he was probably correct, and she supposed she ought to be grateful, but sometimes she felt a little sad when she thought it had been good. In fact Poynter's self-assertiveness and complete absence of humour were in later years to prove a great burden to Agnes, making hers the least happy of the four marriages. In Poynter's eyes, the witty and beautiful Agnes Macdonald was a great social asset, likely to attract rich patrons and thus worthy of his proposal of marriage. On 18 April 1865, exactly a month after Alice's wedding, Mrs Macdonald formally noted the engagement of Agnes to Edward Poynter. Although she had anticipated keeping her daughters around her for longer, this was a match which pleased her because Poynter seemed a very mature young man, and one likely to be a success in life.

She had far more reservations about the young man who sought permission to court Louisa, and surprisingly the doubts were shared by her daughter. At the end of August, a month's holiday was arranged with Mr and Mrs Stanley Baldwin in Stourport, near Worcestershire, to revive Louisa, who was dispirited by Agnes's engagement, coming as it did so soon after Frederic's to a member of his flock in Burslem – one Mary Cork, the daughter of another pottery manufacturer. A holiday with old family friends, Mrs Macdonald thought, would help to cheer the girl up. Louisa only wrote home once during her stay in Worcestershire and that letter contained no hint of what was to follow. She returned on 2 October 1865, and the same day there came a letter from Alfred Baldwin, one of Stanley's brothers. So shocked was Mrs Macdonald that she could not reply for four days, and then she penned the following:

My Dear Mr Alfred
You were right in thinking I should be surprised at hearing from you, indeed few things could have surprised me more than the contents of your note. The state of solicitude and perplexity in which my mind has been must be my apology for not replying at an earlier period to your very important communication.

The subject is a very serious one and is engaging our very careful consideration as no hasty conclusion could be arrived at that would be favourable to your request. Mr Macdonald and I think it desirable that we should have some conversation with you before coming to any decision, and therefore we should be glad to see you, if you will call upon us, any time after noon on Wednesday next.

In conclusion allow me to assure you that, while I am deeply concerned for my daughter's happiness, I am by no means indifferent to your own.
I remain
Yours sincerely
Hannah Macdonald[15]

Louisa had known Alfred for just over a month, whereas her mother's acquaintance with him stretched back over many years. Truth to say, Mrs Macdonald disliked the young man. Although some of the Baldwins had visited the Macdonalds in London, Alfred had not been amongst them, for he despised his brothers for wasting time and money in the capital. The Baldwin family was large and had many branches as a result of two marriages which had produced eleven children. Alfred was the youngest in this family, born in 1841 after the death of his father George Pearce Baldwin. At twenty-four, Alfred was already a partner in the family's iron-foundry business and was thus a rich young man. It was not this which Mrs Macdonald objected to, so much as Alfred's arrogance.

He was the grandson of a Methodist minister, but had made great show of rebelling against the faith six years previously. Initially he had been attracted by Catholicism, but then settled on being what he proudly described as 'an extreme High Churchman'. With all the zeal of a convert, he continually proclaimed his faith to everyone and was bigoted towards those who were not co-believers. Even of his sister he remarked that she was a very good woman, albeit a Methodist. This did not augur well for a union with Louisa, who had never doubted Methodist doctrine. The Macdonald parents had demonstrated their religious tolerance in the past, and thus it is unlikely they would have objected to the match purely on grounds of belief. Indeed both Fulford and Jones had boasted just such High Church leanings and had been accepted.

After Alfred's visit to Wolverhampton to discuss his suit with Louisa's parents, it was decided that the final word must lie with the person in question, and for the next three weeks Louisa wrestled to make up her mind. Although she could envisage the problems of marriage to such an autocrat, she was also flattered to have received his proposal, since it was her first. With Agnes flaunting her new status, Louisa felt under pressure to match her sister, and an alliance with the rich Alfred Baldwin would definitely be a coup. Set against that, Louisa had doubts about their compatibility because of their different upbringing and his 'worldliness'. By that she meant his involvement in the worlds of industry and commerce, but the High Church man was horrified and argued for pages against such a definition, taking pains also to justify his freemasonry. He expressed his affection for Louisa in the lofty, religious terms which he thought might be most persuasive to a preacher's daughter, but underlying Louisa's dilemma was the knowledge that Alfred and her parents did not get on. This problem he too tried to see in biblical terms, 'thy people shall be my people' was his cry, but the Old Testament allusion was weakened when he spoke of Louisa's parents as the main bugbears in the situation.

Mrs Macdonald foresaw that someone of Alfred's disposition would not permit a wife to have views or pursuits such as Louisa had developed. Arising from friendship with Rebecca Solomon, sister of the artist Simeon Solomon, and a painter in her own right, Louisa had begun a serious study of art which led to her enrolling at the Wolverhampton School of Art. She had also tried her hand at writing. Short stories were passed on to Georgie in the hope of finding a publisher in London. Alfred Baldwin, with no understanding of the arts, was not considered likely to sympathize with such activities, and neither could Mrs Macdonald imagine this pompous young man fitting into their art-orientated family.

Heart-searching letters passed to and fro, until on 28 October Louisa decided to heed Agnes's philosophy that it was best to marry quickly if the right thing offered itself. Louisa accepted, since she might never again get such an attractive proposal. Alfred was delighted to have secured the hand of the devout little Miss Macdonald and proceeded to bombard her with letters designed to mould her religious thinking along more suitable lines. Religious volumes arrived through the post: the writings of Keble, *Ecce Homo*, and Professor Maurice's *Conflict of Good and Evil*, to name but a few. There were also suggestions as to prayers Louisa could use and sermons she might profitably study. In return Alfred agreed to read some of the books Louisa enjoyed, so she sent him a copy of *Sidonia*, the novel so beloved of the Pre-Raphaelites.

Alfred's impression was not favourable, nor unfortunately was his dog's who ripped it up whilst his master was at mass, although according to Alfred the dog could have chosen *The Ecclesiologist*.

A joint wedding for Agnes and Louisa was planned for 9 August 1866, to be followed two days later by Frederic's marriage in Burslem. The remaining ten months were passed with visits by Poynter and Baldwin. The latter always came bearing gifts, such as a box of cigars, a brace of pheasants or a case of wine, in a vain effort to find favour with the family. He never really succeeded, for in a very frank letter written a month after the wedding, Mrs Macdonald told Agnes to pass on her good wishes to her husband, emphasizing she both admired and appreciated the estimation in which he held Agnes's happiness, relative to that of Alfred and Louisa. She added that though it was hardly a thing to quarrel about, she was inclined to think Alfred pleased himself with the belief that he was a very superior being. Her perception of Edward Poynter might have been a little inaccurate, but she was certainly right about Louisa's husband.

Chapter Six

A Courtly Love?
(1860–70)

Young and inexperienced though she was, Georgie never cherished any illusions that marriage to an artist would be easy, but she had anticipated that it would give her a greater freedom than she had been used to at the manse. In some ways she was to be disappointed, because Edward based both his art and his life on the attitudes expressed by Malory in the *Morte D'Arthur*. This book had been much prized by the Oxford set, for it demonstrated a world governed by the principles of chivalry and courtly love, which the young men who had lost their faith in the Church found curiously inspiring. The ideal of manhood is epitomized by Arthur, a knight of the highest moral calibre, pledged to acquit himself honourably and to serve his lady. It was the view of the lady which fascinated Edward and provided him with a model for his relationships with women. In Malory the lady was traditionally fair-haired, of noble birth and chosen purely for her virtue; in many ways she could be called the original dumb blonde, because the knight placed her on a pedestal and worshipped her as an aloof and untouchable idol who would reward his daring exploits with words of praise. Edward liked to see Georgie in this passive role, inspiring both his art and his adoration, as some sketches on a letter during their engagement show. Georgie is portrayed as a medieval queen with glittering crown, enthroned on a raised dais, whilst Edward the humble suppliant kneels at her feet. Later in the same letter, in a cartoon based to some degree on Rossetti's *Girlhood of Mary Virgin*, Edward drew Georgie sitting at the table sketching, a halo around her head and her long hair luxuriantly curling down her back. On the floor Edward is lying gazing up at his vision of loveliness. Rossetti said of his original picture that it 'was a symbol of female excellence, the Virgin being taken as its highest type'.[1]

Georgie's doll-like figure, neatness of feature, high-minded principles and natural reserve made her a good candidate for the role, but it was not one she wanted to act out all the time. 'I have an inclination to upset all the ideas suggested by the above by using language other than befitting a queen,' she added mischievously under Edward's sketches.[2] For the duration of their engagement, Georgie felt flattered by Edward's view of her and was content to accept her lot because it gave her a place amongst the artists she so wanted to join. As time went on, however, it was a mould she struggled to break. A major problem which arose from Edward's image of Georgie was his inability to visualize something so spiritual transformed by the carnality of marriage, and thus he was tardy about taking steps which might hasten their wedding. As Georgie herself observed: 'Our marriage seemed no nearer at the end of three years and a half than it had ever done,' and it was only through the intervention of a third person in the form of Emma Madox Brown that the event ever took place.[3] Even Edward was deeply troubled by the idea: 'Lust does frighten me, I must say,' he confided to his studio assistant many years later. 'It looks like such despair – despair of any happiness and search for it in new degradation.'[4]

Edward suffered first-night nerves, and the morning after their wedding found him ill. This response to a situation which taxed his emotional reserves became commonplace throughout their married life. In contrast to Georgie, whose emotions were kept strictly under control, Edward was easily moved to laughter or tears and in extreme cases would exhibit all the symptoms of a psychosomatic illness – something Georgie was already familiar with in her mother. On the first day of their married life, in a strange hotel room in Chester, Georgie had to take charge of things, cancel their plans to rendezvous with the Rossettis in Paris and head for home instead. She wisely judged that it would be easier for Edward to come to terms with his newly-wedded state in the security of his own rooms.

The running of the household at 27 Russell Place, Fitzroy Square came easily to Georgie, not because she had learned well at home (indeed she seems to have married with little idea of running a home, for her mother or elder sister had always taken charge), but because the Burne-Joneses had very few rooms, precious little furniture, and since labour was cheap, they employed a young girl as maid. Georgie recalled:

A five or six months' housekeeping in Russell Place did not teach me much, though a couple of small drawings by Edward on the back of my first account-book shew his impression that I practised housewifery as well as music. Lighthearted indifference, however, to many things generally regarded as essential lent boldness to domestic arrangements, and I remember thinking it quite natural that in the middle of the morning I should ask our only maid – a pretty one – to stand for me that I might try to draw her.[5]

Initially such freedom encouraged Georgie to consider developing her artistic inclinations.

During the first year of her marriage she made the acquaintance of Rebecca Solomon, eight years her senior, who had made a reasonably successful start as a woman artist, having exhibited her work annually at the Royal Academy since 1852. This was quite exceptional in Victorian England, where the art profession was regarded as an exclusively male preserve. Even thirty years later, when asked about women artists, Burne-Jones replied, 'They don't exist', and when pressed to comment on those who professed to be such, he retorted, 'They don't count.'[6] Lizzie Rossetti, whom Georgie also came to know well in the first two years of her marriage, was keen to produce her own art work and had received lessons from her husband. She had achieved a degree of competence which enabled her to exhibit her work in 1857 alongside that of Millais, Madox Brown, Rossetti and Holman Hunt, and Ruskin had been sufficiently impressed with her talent to offer her patronage. Since Georgie had shown some competence as an engraver, Lizzie suggested they might work together and write and illustrate a book of fairy stories, a favourite beginning to many an artistic career. The two young women, however, never completed more than two or three pieces of work, which Georgie put down to their own ineptitude: 'It is pathetic to think how we women longed to keep pace with the men and how gladly they kept us by them until their pace quickened and we had to fall behind,' she concluded, but this was an over-simplification of the case.[7]

Lizzie's own painting and ill-health occupied her time, but Georgie could have devoted virtually all her time to the project; the crux of the problem lay in Edward's attitude to his wife developing any sort of independent life. He had been content to help her and her sisters to learn drawing in earlier days because he whimsically viewed them as a medieval queen surrounded by her ladies, passing their time in the bower whilst they awaited the return of their champions. Painting, writing and singing were all acceptable drawing-room accomplishments, but in his opinion it should end there. 'Women have suddenly woken up to the fact that they can do something and they can't,' he complained peevishly, in an effort to retain the passive image he so cherished. 'I like women when they are good and kind and agreeable objects in the landscape of existence – give life to it and pleasant to look at and think about.'[8] It was a far narrower view than the Reverend George Macdonald supported and one which Georgie herself found hard to accept. Surprisingly, the artist's views were more in accord with contemporary opinion than the Methodist minister's, even though they had been arrived at through the study of medieval literature. Biblical and scientific arguments for male superiority made little impact on Edward: to him it was simply 'to educate women only spoils them and takes away their charms'.[9]

Georgie's art work, though continuing after her marriage, gradually declined and within five years had virtually ceased. The fact that she should have to content herself with sketching a serving girl in the dining-room, whilst her husband drew from a professional model in his adjoining studio, goes a long way to demonstrating the sort of encouragement Georgie received. She did get to spend time in Edward's studio either acting as a model or as something of a studio assistant: preparing his materials, clearing away or, if none of this was necessary, reading aloud whilst he painted. She had the satisfaction of aiding her husband's career as well as seeing herself immortalized in his paintings. Everything in the first year of marriage was such a novelty that Georgie was not troubled by his attitude because she believed her work to be inferior anyway.

Evenings were spent amongst an incongruous collection of aspiring writers and painters, whom Georgie found so entertaining that she totally forgot her own family. The characters she met were in complete contrast to the people she had encountered at the manse, but, awestruck, she judged them all to be brilliant and good. Perhaps one of the most bizarre creatures of her acquaintance was the red-haired poet Swinburne, who lived near them and used to appear two or three times during the day as well if he had written something which needed an immediate audience. Georgie thought him 'courteous and affectionate and unsuspicious and faithful beyond most people to those he really loved', but others formed less favourable impressions.[10] The artist Du Maurier, who was later to achieve fame as an illustrator for the magazine *Punch*, wrote home to his mother: 'As for Swinburne he is without exception the most extraordinary man not that I ever met only, but that I ever read or heard of; for three hours he spouted poetry to us, and it was of a power, beauty and originality unequalled. Everything after seems tame, but the little beast will never I think be acknowledged for he has an utterly perverted moral sense, and ranks Lucrezia Borgia with Jesus Christ; indeed says she's far greater, and very little of his poetry is fit for publication.'[11] Nonetheless this homosexual poet with a taste for flagellation and excessive wine ranked amongst Georgie's friends.

Her approach to the Bohemian world was mingled with naïvety and sincere admiration. When things surfaced which she did not approve of, Georgie tried to apply the doctrine of John Wesley, namely 'hate the sin and love the sinner'. Thus she was very fond of Morris, whose violent swearing she found offensive, and also Swinburne, who on occasion appeared so drunk that he had to be sent home in a cab with his name and address fastened to his coat. Underlying everything was Georgie's belief that she was privileged to sit at the feet of genius.

Weekend visits to the Morrises at the Red House, Upton, out in the Kent countryside, were a great pleasure to Georgie. Since the Morrises kept open house for their friends, this was a favourite gathering place for people like Rossetti, Philip Webb (who had designed the Red House), Madox Brown, Charlie Faulkner and his two sisters, Swinburne and many others. Although the bedrooms were not numerous, mattresses could always be found to accommodate the men on the drawing-room floor and an exhilarating undergraduate atmosphere prevailed, where art blended with horseplay and music. Guests cheerfully took part in decorating the house, walls, ceilings and furnishings. Georgie loved it, painting tiles, glass, cabinets, indeed anything which was asked of her. Along with Janey Morris, she learned to embroider under the direction of Morris, and the women produced wall-hangings and 'tapestries' to complete the medieval scene.

These attempts to decorate and furnish the Morris residence led to the establishment of a firm to manufacture handcrafted objects, and in 1861 Georgie found herself part of the workforce of Morris, Marshall, Faulkner and Company. She was delighted by this opportunity to use her skills, but her role, along with the other women in the group, was confined to decorating the men's designs. Never again was Georgie to create work of her own: 'I stopped, as so many women do, well on this side of tolerable skill, daunted by the path which has to be followed absolutely alone if the end is to be reached,' she wrote, but it might be truer to say that she was never given the opportunity to discover if she possessed the necessary talent.[12] What work Georgie did produce has largely vanished or, since it was unsigned, has become attributed to others. She certainly did execute pieces of embroidery for the firm, but those which have survived tend to be labelled as the work of Janey Morris and her sister; similarly the tiles and glass she painted for the firm are mixed in with the work of Kate Faulkner, who, because she did not marry, continued painting tiles for the firm for many years. Those engravings which are credited to Georgie are the ones which bear a marked similarity to the work of Edward Burne-Jones, but are poorly executed. Such accrediting may be inaccurate since Georgie spent more time practising engraving than Edward.

The birth of her son Philip in October 1861 also contributed greatly to the cessation of her creative work. 'It was a sign of change, and the thought of any change made me sigh', she wrote.[13] The baby's appearance caused Edward an emotional upheaval also. When Mrs Macdonald arrived in London to look after her daughter and grandson, she found them both well but the new father in such a state of collapse that the doctor had to be fetched. Edward was disturbed lest the baby might deprive him of Georgie's affection and so change his life. Change their lives it certainly did, but naturally it was Georgie who noticed the effect most. 'I had been used to be much with Edward – reading aloud to him while he worked, and in many ways sharing the life of the studio – and I remember the feeling of exile with which I now heard through its closed door the well-known voices of friends together with Edward's familiar laugh, while I sat with my little son on my knee and dropped selfish tears upon him as "the separator of companions and terminator of delights".'[14] If evening company at Russell Place had to adjust to the baby, so did their weekends: 'We paid other visits to the Morrises after this but none quite like it – how could they be?' Georgie looked mournfully back.[15] Janey Morris had also given birth a few months before Georgie, so that decorous outings in the pony and trap or embroidery for the young mothers took the place of paint-splashing.

Although Edward feared the baby would usurp his place in Georgie's affections, he had no cause to, because Georgie no more relished the idea of motherhood than her own mother had done and was quite determined to pursue her own activities as far as possible. When a visit to Italy with Ruskin was mooted, she saw no objection even though her baby was barely six months old. Shortly before their departure in May 1862, Philip was dangerously ill according to Mrs Macdonald, and Georgie herself agreed he was 'at death's door', but he recovered and within a month was deposited with his Macdonald grandparents and aunts in Manchester, whilst his parents sailed for Italy. It was Georgie's first experience abroad and she delighted in the scenery and architecture, although after some time Ruskin noted that she 'seemed to see everything through a mist of baby'.[16] The purpose of the journey had been a commission for Edward to record some of the treasures of Italy before they vanished, a task which was expected to be lengthy, but after ten weeks Georgie, who had never before been away from England, was very homesick. Despite the breathtaking scenery, 'nothing would serve her but her husband must draw the baby for her on the sand', and they returned early, much to Edward's relief as well.[17]

The baby was the symbol of Georgie's homesickness, though not the root, because she was to leave him behind on other occasions when she accompanied Edward on artistic missions. An opportunity arose for her to work with Edward on a project using her skill at embroidery, after Ruskin secured a commission for Burne-Jones to design and execute wall-hangings for Winnington Hall School near Chester. So early in 1864 Georgie left the young child behind in order to go and teach twelve girls to embroider Edward's designs using the stitches Morris favoured. Although the chosen subject was Chaucer's *Legend of Good Women*, Edward could not resist beginning with some practice pieces based on characters from *Morte D'Arthur*, and ultimately these were the only pieces completed. Twelve girls working simultaneously on a piece of work proved impractical, and Georgie's one and only opportunity to work in partnership with her husband foundered.

The appearance of Philip focused Georgie's attention on the problems of running a home. She was already aware that money flowed erratically when Edward was involved, although at first she felt it was not the wife's place to comment on it. At a time when money was tight, she discovered an uncashed cheque stuffed away in the pocket of an old garment because Edward had no bank account and was too embarrassed to tell the person who had bought his picture. On another occasion Edward impulsively spent their last £8 on a pretty watch he had seen in a shop and wanted to give Georgie. The cost of furniture and other household items which were ordered through the firm of Morris, Marshall, Faulkner and Company began to mount up and sometimes exceeded the income Edward was paid for his designs by the firm, which was a situation Georgie, brought up to have a horror of debt, could not allow to continue. For all his notions of women on pedestals, Edward gratefully relinquished control of the family's finances. 'I know now,' Georgie admitted in her old age, 'that Edward had more anxiety about money in those early days than I then realised; for it was not a subject he talked much about, and it never occurred to me that we should not have our wants supplied.'[18]

It was a natural progression for Georgie to take responsibility for all the business aspects of Edward's art. She was admirably suited to such work by temperament and upbringing, being efficient and inheriting her father's meticulous attention to detail. Although Edward liked to regard art as his province, the monetary aspect embarrassed him and he would far rather let a debt lapse than have to press for payment, whereas Georgie regarded it simply as a case of paying for what you had received. She was prompt in rendering the artist's bill, but equally as quick in reimbursing any money she regarded as overpayment. In a fatalistic way she applied a similar philosophy to her life, believing that happiness had to be paid for by suffering: the greater the happiness, the deeper the despair. It was a melancholic view of life undoubtedly derived from her mother: 'It is a device of mine never to grudge trouble in the pursuit of what seems to me really good and never to grudge payment for it afterwards,' Georgie wrote when an old lady, but in her mid-twenties it formed a bitter lesson.[19]

The payment for her early married happiness began in October 1864 when she gave birth prematurely to Christopher Alvin whilst she was in the throes of scarlet fever. The baby fared well despite his mother's illness and his father being 'in a distressing state', according to Mrs Macdonald, who came to help the family. So ill was Georgie that her life was despaired of for a while, and Edward was beside himself with anxiety; however, the improvement after a few weeks was such that Mrs Macdonald was able to leave them to resume the nursing of her sick husband. Within four days of her departure the baby caught scarlet fever and died. Georgie was numb with grief. In the period immediately following, she wanted only to get away from home, so, taking the two-year-old Philip, she went alone to Hastings to gather her thoughts. This was the beginning of many holidays spent apart, if holiday it could be called; indeed as time went on it became increasingly rare for Edward and Georgie to be away from home together. The next two Christmases also saw them go their separate ways, as Georgie returned to Wolverhampton, looking for strength in Macdonald family unity, and Edward chose to remain amongst his bachelor friends in London. For some unknown reason Edward hated Christmas, and the feeling never left him even when he could celebrate it with his children around him. 'A dull day, I knew it would be,' he wrote, and another year, 'Xmas Day itself a monumental day for dreariness, so as to make me vow never

nnah Macdonald aged fifty-four. Her strong belief in the value of female education
d a profound influence on her daughters.

Reverend George Browne Macdonald, the girls' father, in his late forties, dressed as a Wesleyan Methodist minister.

Carrie Macdonald, the only surviving picture of this sister who died aged sixte
The painting, on porcelain, was done by Mr Chesters in the same week that her T
was confirmed.

Reverend Frederic Macdonald soon after his ordination as a Methodist minister which his mother, understanding the rigours of that life, greeted with the comment, 'God help the poor boy!'.

Harry Macdonald in his mid-twenties in
New York where he was engaged as first
proof reader on the *New York Times*.
There were high hopes for his future bu
he was never able to live up to them.

ilfred Heeley who introduced the
acdonald girls to the sort of
ucation they longed for. He
nained friendly with them all his
e, living at the Grange with the
rne-Joneses for a short time
fore returning to India.

nes Macdonald, described as
rannously beautiful', an
spiration to artists and collector of
rriage proposals.

uisa Macdonald photographed to
rk her sixteenth birthday, but her
sight was so poor that she stood
le chance of being able to read the
ok in front of her and generally
nt round in a misty blur.

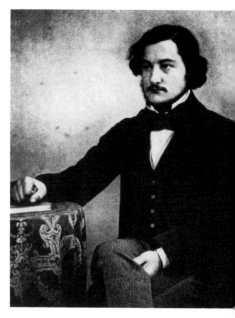

Cormell Price, a school friend of Harry's and lifelong friend of the Macdonald sisters who called him 'our dear brother Crom'. Alice chose the school where he was headmaster for her son Rudyard.

William Morris about the time he enter the Macdonalds' life. 'Altogether the m remarkable man I ever saw,' was Georg judgement.

Kings' Daughters was drawn by Burne-Jones during his visits to the Macdonalds in 1858. All the faces belong to the Macdonald sisters but exact identification is diffic Georgie is probably the centre figure, Alice to her left with buttons down her dress Agnes leaning over the balcony, Louisa with the rabbit and Edith, the child.

most, for I suggested it. At me

Mr Edward engaged

Mr Jones's friend —

It only makes me the sorrier. I am

'r Jones's friend', Morris, sketched in 1856 on a joint letter from Edward and Georgie
the young Fred Macdonald, showing Morris in a typical rage at Red Lion Square.
e other sketch of 'Mr Edward engaged' shows Edward kneeling in adoration whilst
orgie sketches.

ment — then faint in rosemary

*is profane jester possesses a won-
l power of exaggeration, but I'm*

e beardless Edward Burne-Jones is again seen gazing at his fiancée who is drawing a
ll life. The cartoon was obviously influenced by Rossetti's *Girlhood of Mary Virgin*
ich Burne-Jones had seen.

Georgie Macdonald at the age of sixteen after her engagement to the would-be artist Edward Burne-Jones.

e of the few early photographs of Burne-Jones, taken when he was thirty-one.
cording to his wife, he had an immoveable conviction that he looked hopelessly plain.

One of the few portraits of Alice Kipling, who never enjoyed having her photograph taken after Agnes said that photographers always made a hash of her face.

Georgie painted by Poynter in 1869 at the most difficult period in her life. The painting was commissioned by her greatest friend Rosalind Howard, who also gave her the lock of brown hair and pearls which is visible. 'No one will know what it means when we are dead and gone,' Georgie told her friend.

Agnes painted by Poynter at Louisa's request. Louisa commissioned a portrait of herself (*right*) at the same time and the paintings hung in the drawing room of Wilden House.

again to get up on that day.'[20] The only way he found to pass the time on that occasion was to sit reading Burton's *Anatomy of Melancholy*, a favourite book of his mother-in-law's.

The baby's death was a turning-point in Georgie's life, though neither she nor Edward realized it at the time. Grief served only to separate rather than unite them. Edward, who had been carried through the period of Georgie's illness by the strength of his friends, looked to Georgie for love and comfort after Christopher's death, but weak from her ordeal she could offer him nothing; instead she withdrew deeper into herself as a defence against further hurt. Edward felt rejected, as he had always dreaded, and was forced to depend increasingly on his friends, whilst Georgie was left to look to her sisters for support. Her spirits and her health never fully recovered from her sad experiences: 'When we turned to look around us something was gone, something had been left behind – and it was our first youth . . . our Bohemian days were over.'[21]

The plans that had been drawn up for the Burne-Joneses to live at Upton in a new wing to be built on to the Red House were cancelled. Edward suggested that Georgie's health and the family finances would not stand it, but equally important, though not mentioned by him, was his own obsessive desire to stay in London. 'I should dearly like a quiet country time every year if Edward could come too,' Georgie confided in a friend, 'but as he says he cannot work out of his studio, I cannot hope for that.' Even the prospect of a few days away caused trouble: 'Edward remains immoveable on the subject of leaving Town, and makes it a matter of difficulty even to go from next Saturday till Monday to fetch Phil from Bewdley. The small man has been there for more than a month.'[22] The prospect of sharing the Red House had offered Georgie hopes of a closer friendship with Janey Morris and the chance to participate more fully in the working of the firm, but it was not to be. Looking back over her life, Georgie lamented the cancellation of the scheme.

Once the Burne-Joneses decided to remain in London, Morris put the Red House up for sale and moved back to the capital. Through the long difficult years ahead, Georgie came to value the proximity of Morris far more than she thought likely. Edward increasingly attended social gatherings alone, which led him to develop a separate group of friends, in which Georgie had no place. The Little Holland House set, though inviting her occasionally in the past, were really only interested in the artists themselves and did not encourage the appearance of wives and sycophants at their soirées. At one such gathering Edward was introduced to some of the Greek community by Edward Poynter, who had studied with one of their number in Paris. The Ionides have been called the Victorian Onassises, for they were extremely rich and had only settled in London because it was the centre of world trade and finance. They had a genuine interest in the arts, were willing to spend plenty on patronage and were very hospitable. Consequently their Sunday afternoon 'at homes' quickly became popular with hopeful artists.

Edward was spellbound by these Greeks: they were striking in looks, utterly charming and unconventional. Du Maurier noted: 'The women will sometimes take one's hand in talking to one, or put their arm round the back of one's chair at dinner, and with all this ease and *tutoiement*, or perhaps on account of it, they are I do believe the most thoroughly well bred and perfect gentlefolks in all England.'[23] Such behaviour was quite alien in Victorian society, and Edward, who in any case never had any defence against attractive women, was quite at a loss how to take them. 'Two things had tremendous power over him,' Georgie wrote perceptively, 'beauty and misfortune – and far would he go to serve either, indeed his impulse to comfort those in trouble was so strong that while the trouble lasted the sufferer took precedence over everyone else.'[24]

Amongst the Greek Community in that year of 1866 was Maria Zambaco, an auburn-haired woman of twenty-three and the owner of a personal fortune of £80,000 which gave her complete independence. Intriguing stories circulated about her behaviour on the occasion she had been in London several years previously: unmarried and with only a young girl as chaperone, she had amorously pursued Du Maurier round Kensington Gardens. Quite abruptly she had departed for Paris and married a penniless doctor, returning in 1866 with two young children but no husband. She decided to become an artist and took a studio in London. In Edward's eyes she was alluringly beautiful and helpless, though hardly to be described as destitute. He saw her as a damsel in distress and, as the knight, was only too willing to give succour, the only difficulty being that this lively young woman had no intention of playing the game according to the rules of courtly love. Edward met her at a time when he was emotionally vulnerable, for in June of that year Georgie was fully occupied with the birth of her daughter Margaret, and although Edward adored the little girl from the start, childbirth terrified him. Furthermore, two months later, his favourite sisters-in-law Agnes and Louisa were married. He wrote jokingly to Louisa about the desertion of his two wenches, but the idea of two young virgins, similar to those who filled his paintings, being despoiled by husbands horrified and tormented him. So agitated did he become as the event drew near that Georgie had to arrange a distraction. Fortunately, William Allingham had returned to England and urged Edward and Georgie to accompany him to the Isle of Wight where he promised to introduce them to Edward's hero Tennyson. Since this was one of the few alternatives guaranteed to absorb Edward's attention, Georgie agreed to go, even though she would be prevented from attending her sisters' wedding. Silently she accepted this as a further example of the price of past happiness; to Agnes and Louisa their sister's absence was baffling.

After the Burne-Joneses' return from Hampshire events moved rapidly, giving Georgie little time to dwell on the deteriorating relations between herself and Edward. In March 1867 the family were obliged to move house because their lease could not be extended. It was the third move in seven years and thus particularly unsettling. After a life of itinerancy Georgie longed for somewhere permanent, and Edward agreed that this change of house must be their last for a long time. Since the Grange in North End Road, Fulham, was too large and commanded a higher rent than they could comfortably afford, it was agreed to share the accommodation with Wilfred Heeley, who had recently arrived on leave from India with a new wife. His first wife, well-known to both Edward and Georgie, had died tragically of cholera in Calcutta five years previously, and Wilfred was determined that his second wife should benefit from the comparative safety of England for the birth of their child. Babies and young children seemed to dominate Georgie's life not by design, but because others knew they could turn to her for both sympathy and practical assistance. Georgie was only too willing to aid her young sister, Agnes Poynter, during the birth of her child in October 1867, when their mother was fully occupied nursing the other young mother, Louisa Baldwin. Following hard on this came the birth of the Heeley baby and then Alice Kipling's second child, also born at the Grange, so that, Georgie groaned, the house seemed more like Queen Charlotte's than their home.

Alice's return after a two-year sojourn in India promised to be the highlight of Georgie's year, but was in reality a profound disappointment to them both, because it served only to emphasize how far their paths had diverged in the meantime. The ructions caused by the plain-speaking Alice, her ill-behaved son Rudyard and a fractious baby rumbled on in the Macdonald family for much longer than the eight months Alice was in England. Georgie was upset by what she saw as a further example of the transience of former happiness, first in her marriage and now with her sisters. Edward, though fond of Alice, retreated from a house where howling babies and boisterous children made painting impossible, to the more inspiring charms of Mrs Zambaco. Georgie was so caught up in the hubbub that she barely noticed his absence. No sooner had Alice departed for Bombay in October 1868 than the Reverend George Macdonald died, and Georgie's presence with her mother was once more requested.

Thus the beginning of 1869 found Georgie in the lowest of spirits: she was mourning the loss of her father, whom she loved dearly, the sisterly affection of former days seemed broken by Alice, and relations between herself and Edward were deteriorating rapidly. Such misery caused Georgie to withdraw deeper into herself, unable to share her problems with anyone, and faced with a choice between this miserable companion and the scintillating company of Maria Zambaco, Edward naturally chose the latter. A letter Georgie wrote to her sister Louie in January makes it obvious that she no longer had the strength to put on a brave face: 'Margaret's fiendish irritability during her affliction relieves my mind on her account while it depresses my spirits, but Phil has been so meek that it has been almost a relief for him to be a little peevish as he has been today. Edward is out and they are both in bed so instead of having the howl that I feel inclined for, I come to my Louie.' Further on in the same letter she noted with some feeling the 'desperate uncertainty of life', in the face of which she felt helpless, and she ended sadly: 'I leave you my child for a lonely peck at my supper.'[25]

Matters came to a head very rapidly after that letter: Edward disappeared with Maria Zambaco to Dover, apparently intent on going somewhere on the Mediterranean. Georgie was stunned. Although the Burne-Jones/Zambaco affair had become common gossip, she had been too preoccupied, too trusting and too naïve to foresee the outcome. Years later she wrote:

> Never think you have fathomed the depths of the nature of the dearest companion but believe in it always. Remember that of many things it is impossible to speak so that at last one can say, 'I would tell you if I *could*'. That is as near as one can get with all one's striving. And it is enough for this life. To everyone this thing comes differently, but there is a freemasonry between those who have entered on it, which gives me a tender feeling for all I know, it seems to me the best.[26]

Georgie had no idea what to do, being only concerned that her newly-widowed mother should be spared any knowledge or pain. Her sisters, inexperienced in the ways of the world and nursing their babies and their health, she also wished to leave in ignorance. Salvation appeared promptly from outside the family in the guise of Rosalind Howard, the wife of one of Edward's friends. Although four years Georgie's junior at twenty-four, this lady had already developed a dominating personality, which in later years found an outlet in such militant causes as politics, feminism and temperance. Georgie had met the Honourable Mrs George Howard some eighteen months previously, and the friendship which grew up arose as much as anything from the differences in their characters. Georgie was always drawn to the extrovert, and this young woman combined outspokenness, intellectualism and eccentricity with an aristocrat pedigree, being the daughter of Lady Stanley of Alderley (later a founder of Girton College, Cambridge).

Rosalind Howard was the answer to Georgie's prayers: in January 1869 she breezed into the Grange, raised Georgie from the depths of despair, set the household working and without any fuss left enough money to ensure her friend would not be in financial difficulties, as Georgie's attempt to express her thanks in writing show:

> I am more touched by your kindness and thought for me than I can tell you – I do not know how to thank you. Forgive my reserve the other day when you came, but I am obliged to shew it in time of trouble or I should break down.
>
> One day I hope I may be able to explain things better to you – meanwhile believe me I love you and trust you.
>
> Your tender thoughtfulness in sending the picture went to my heart and I gratefully accept your trust – your other thoughtful and sisterly kindness moves me very much too, and if there were need of it I would shew you that I trusted you enough to take it, but happily there is not, and I send it back to you not from pride, believe me, but from simple justice. I have better news of Edward – I will write you more in a few days when I know more. Meanwhile it is not a sign that I do not love you that I do not ask you to come and see me. Trust me and believe me ever.
>
> Your loving friend
>
> G B J

The postscript to that letter revealed Edward's progress, his panic and predictable response to the emotional challenge of running away with a woman:

Thus far I wrote this morning, but Edward is so much better that I may now tell you that he is at home again having been too weak to face the journey when he reached Dover.

For two or three days he was so ill we kept his being at home a secret, that the house might be quite quiet. The irritation of the brain however has decreased very much that he is up and in his studio, but must still be kept very quiet. Forgive the little deceit, it was meant only for good and I did not like it even then. I will tell you as soon as he may see you, and meanwhile it will be a comfort to me to see your face, for my heart is filled with anxiety still.[27]

Georgie dealt with the situation in the only way life had taught her – through Christian belief. She accepted that Edward's folly had arisen from his attempts to comfort someone alone and friendless in London, and she forgave him. She was convinced that this was the right course of action to take and prayed to God for strength to see it through. That did not make it any easier to follow her chosen path, but Georgie was fortified by the Methodist doctrine of her childhood, trusting that God was working his purpose out, though understanding might be hidden from mortal eyes. When Edward demanded complete peace and solitude to sort out his confused mind, Georgie obediently took the children and left the security of her own home for lodgings. They went to Oxford, the city which represented the happy days that were past, and for two months Georgie struggled to understand what had happened. 'We often know the right when we don't do it and sometimes discover it too late,' she wrote.[28] Her tragically brave attempts to come to terms with her predicament found expression in a letter to Rosalind Howard, written soon after her arrival at the rooms in Museum Terrace:

How can I answer your letter, except by thanks for the love it contains, and which I gratefully accept? If words could do it I would answer you at length now, or wait till we meet, and then do so – but no words can explain any difficult relation of any human beings to each other, and none but God can sum up a care and see it clearly. I know that you are generous enough to take me on my own terms, and to forgive me where you think them mistaken – reserving your judgement as to my mistake – and I am very thankful to you for this because I love you, but I hope you will be able further to bear with me if I appear tiresomely reserved as ever on some subjects. I have made up my mind to this, long ago, and mean to keep to it. At the same time, please never be afraid of saying anything *to* me you wish to do, for I know your straightforward nature ought to do that, or anything you think might help me, directly or indirectly, for I need help. Indeed, my dear, I am no heroine at all – and I know when I come short almost as well as any one else does – I have simply acted all along from very simple little reasons, which God and my husband know better than anyone – I don't know what God thinks of them.

Dearest Rosalind, be hard on no one in this matter, and exalt no one – may we all come well through it at last. I know one thing, and that is that there is love enough between Edward and me to last out a long life if it is given us – and I tell you that because it will give pleasure to your kind heart. Also, I must beg you to believe that I have never said an untrue thing to you, and this though you cannot understand it.

I *should* like to see you before you go – I am not far off – could you not run down for a day? Do think of it. All that you say I seriously consider, because you never speak thoughtlessly – and I should like to have another talk with you. I fear you think much too well of me in many ways, and I don't want that – it makes me feel worse than I really am. If I did not know you loved me I should ask you to excuse this egotistic letter, as it is I don't.

With love to you both, and in hopes of seeing you here soon.
Ever, my dearest Rosalind
Your loving friend Georgie.[29]

There was no easy, tidy solution to the problem, and Georgie remained in Oxford until Edward summoned up the courage to visit her. Even then he made it clear that he was unable to stop associating with Maria Zambaco, for according to his chivalric principles it would be wrong to abandon a person he felt was so alone in the world and dependent on him – an Arthurian knight would never desert a lady in need. Equally, Edward was adamant that his love for Georgie remained as strong as ever.

Deeply hurt, Georgie remained in Oxford, but time hung heavily on her hands. She wrote to Rosalind:

I am sick of *me* and wish there was not such a thing. We lead such a quiet life here, and there are a great many hours in every day, I assure you – more than usual. But they pass really not unpleasantly, and I cannot tell you how good rest and quiet are. It feels funny sometimes when Phil is gone to bed and I sit down to read, as if I were the undergraduate to whom these rooms really belong, but it is snug and what I have longed for of late. Edward will come down if he can and so I shan't have been alone long.[30]

Georgie turned to Louie Baldwin as well, for this quiet religious sister was one relative she felt able to talk to and be comforted by; a carefully worded letter brought Louisa down to Oxford for two weeks at the beginning of March, but without alerting the family to Georgie's plight. Her advice, along with Alfred Baldwin's, who arrived at the end of the period to accompany his wife home, decided Georgie on what course to take. Now that she was both physically and mentally stronger for her rest, it was agreed she should return home with the children and attempt to carry on life as normal. Alfred was of the opinion that this positive action, supported by prayer, would make Edward see the error of his ways. Georgie returned to the Grange at the end of March 1869. 'God grant we may have a quiet summer before us,' she wrote to Rosalind on her departure from Oxford.[31] But a depressing scene met her on her return. Edward was in a precarious state of health because of his emotional dilemma, his painting was at a standstill and his relations with his wife were strained. Georgie only survived the rest of the year by taking frequent holidays, some alone, others in Worcestershire with Louie or at one of the Howards' ancestral homes: Naworth Castle near Carlisle, in the wilds of Cumberland. Edward remained in London and continued to see Mrs Zambaco.

By their tenth wedding anniversary in June 1870, the image of the lady on the pedestal had been smashed. The courtly love ideals had gone the same way as Methodism and the worship of 'art for art's sake', all of which Georgie felt had failed her. Edward's behaviour had demonstrated to her that, nearing thirty years of age, she had to look outside the two of them and make a life of her own. Influenced by some quite exceptional people like Rosalind Howard, the novelist George Eliot and William Morris, a strong independent Georgie Burne-Jones emerged with a passionate concern for causes such as socialism, feminism and education.

Chapter Seven

The Memsahib
(1865–80)

Alice was delighted at the prospect of going to India because John Kipling's appointment as architectural sculptor at the Jeejeebhoy School of Art in Bombay sounded prestigious, and there was an opportunity to exchange the tedium of family life for the excitement of the unknown. She regarded the vast distance from England as a distinct advantage since unfavourable comparisons between the artistic merits of John Kipling and Burne-Jones could not be drawn. Although such thoughts might be far from Georgie's mind, Alice was less confident about her other sisters, and indeed following a visit to an exhibition of Indian sculpture in London some years later, Agnes was wont to remark that she was very ashamed of John's mission to that country. A clean break with her family seemed the best solution to Alice, for the special Macdonald family closeness which she had once cherished had begun to be onerous. She felt a subtle pressure on her to become the daughter to bear responsibility for her parents, and inextricably bound up with this was chapel life. As a minister's daughter, Alice felt trapped in an eternal round of Bible classes, missionary meetings and sewing circles, whilst her mother paid lip-service to the notion of voluntary attendance. Alice might be outspoken, but she was not so hard-hearted as to refuse, knowing her father lay ill in bed, for her mother urged her to attend public worship for Papa's sake, because he attached so much importance to it and would be greatly upset if he thought any of his children paid no attention to it. In India, however, Alice and John were free to do exactly as they pleased and both, as children of Methodist preachers, agreed they had received enough instruction to last them a lifetime and proceeded to abandon all formal religious observance.

Another benefit Alice saw in going so far from home was that she would be able to hide her age, about which she was very sensitive, believing twenty-eight to be old for a bride. Furthermore she considered there was some stigma in marriage to a younger man. Alice took such great pains to hide her age that in later years her own daughter was surprised that the difference in her parents' ages should cause her mother so much distress. 'I can't understand why she was so sensitive about age – long before her death she stipulated her age was not to be mentioned in obituary notices or on tombstones.'[1] In India Alice felt sure people would presume the Kiplings had been married for years so that dates and ages would be unimportant.

Once the three-year contract with the School of Art was signed, she wanted the wedding dispatched as quickly and as simply as possible. With the Reverend George Macdonald in poor health, a quiet London wedding from Georgie's home suited the purpose admirably. Everything was conducted in a strictly business-like manner with no undue displays of affection. Staying with Georgie to help with the wedding preparations, Agnes was impressed, reporting to Louie that John and Alice had earned her praise for not being spooney in public; indeed, she concluded they had been models of good behaviour and the bride herself seemed quite unmoved by events. An equally unemotional attitude was applied to the wedding presents, so that anything not liked or believed to be unsuitable for India was promptly disposed of, such as an electroplated palm tree containing a flower vase, which they all thought ugly and tasteless. To Agnes's amusement, Alice announced there was no more space in the trunks for glassware and the grotesque object could be given to her mother-in-law, whom she had already dismissed as a mere knitter of socks.

The wedding took place on 18 March 1865 on a raw, cold morning at the church of St Mary Abbots in Kensington with as few people present as possible. None of John's family came down from Yorkshire and his only supporter was Mr Longden, a fellow artist at South Kensington, who acted as his best man. The Macdonald family was represented by Georgie, Fred and Agnes, who along with Edward Burne-Jones, Aunt Pullein and one or two friends made up the entire congregation. Agnes thought it quite the dreariest place and wedding service she had ever experienced. The small party returned to Georgie's to eat a wedding breakfast which they had prepared themselves and augmented with a hamper sent by Mrs Macdonald; then the bride and groom departed for a round of family farewells.

For all her jibes Agnes was genuinely upset at the prospect of losing her sister to a strange country, believing Alice would never return alive. The grim reality of her elder sister's imminent departure to the other side of the world kept striking Agnes and leave her feeling very sick. Part way through a meal she would suddenly stop eating and consider the possibility of never seeing her sister again. Georgie too was upset by Alice's going, and all agreed that those who were left must stick together at all costs. However, Agnes's new resolution was forgotten a few weeks later when she became engaged to Edward Poynter.

In contrast to the family's distress, Alice maintained her mask of indifference to everything and everyone throughout her wedding and the tear-jerking family scenes that followed. Agnes could not understand her eldest sister's behaviour, remarking that none of them knew whether Alice had enjoyed the day or not. She went through it all like one in a dream and paid no attention to anyone except herself, so in Agnes's opinion she ought to have enjoyed it. Although the odd piece of sisterly spite appeared, for the most part there was genuine grief at the loss of one of their number, and Agnes wished heartily that Providence had allowed them all to remain in England. Yet she noticed John and Alice expressed no regrets at all and wanted to leave as soon as possible.

Mrs Macdonald tried hard to dissuade her daughter from what seemed like a death wish, for in addition to the reports of young Mrs Heeley's demise in Calcutta, horrific pictures of Indian life had filtered through to the manse from missionaries and newspaper reports of the Indian Mutiny which had been suppressed only seven years earlier. Mrs Macdonald's arguments might have carried weight with Harry in the past, but Alice was made of sterner stuff. Despite the pressure of tears and biblical texts, she appeared unmoved and bid her parents and sisters a controlled goodbye, returning to London with John to finish their packing. Agnes noticed that far more attention was given to the choice of tropical kit than had ever been paid to the wedding finery, when Alice went to a warehouse in London which specialized in 'active service kits for all climates'. Under her Uncle Pullein's guidance, she purchased the necessary topee and, as Agnes noted in disgust, a desert hat of the foulest appearance, which so resembled a beehive as to make people recoil in horror. When it was in place, it was impossible to see Alice's face and her voice sounded miles away. A green veil about a yard square and a linen umbrella completed the hideous costume.

On Wednesday 12 April 1865, Mr and Mrs John Kipling left London for Southampton and India. Alice's determination, which had carried her through the emotional family scenes without flinching, nearly failed her when she came to board the ship, for she loathed the sensation of floating on water. Nevertheless, she overcame her misgivings and marched up the gangplank of the P & O steamship *Ripon* with John. Agnes did sincerely hope that Alice would find the journey less dismal than she expected, but her wish was not fulfilled: the voyage turned out far worse than Alice had anticipated. Not only was the Bay of Biscay stormy, but she was in the first nauseous month of pregnancy, and when the ship called at such exotic ports as Gibraltar and Malta, she was in no state to care. At Alexandria they were thankful to step on to dry land. Work had begun on the Suez Canal, but was not completed until 1869, so passengers for Bombay had to travel across Egypt to the Port of Suez by train. The railway journey turned out to be little improvement on the sea passage, being two hundred miles in cramped, stifling conditions. When they boarded the next ship at the head of the Red Sea, temperatures had risen so much that everyone donned their topees as a matter of course and slept on the deck – men on one side and women on the other. The whole experience was like a nightmare, but Alice could only trust that once in Bombay everything would improve.

Sadly, she was mistaken. The timing of their journey had been unfortunate, bringing them to Bombay at the end of May when the hot season had begun and the women and children left the city for the hill station at Nassick to escape the crippling heat. The Kiplings, new to such customs, had made no arrangements, so Alice's first experience of India was of a scorching Bombay summer. Temperatures of over 100°F in the shade, combined with an advancing pregnancy, came close to killing her. It was all so much worse than she had ever imagined, and she hated India. 'I am homesick worse than ever I was in my life – I *cannot* care for this country – or never seem to do,' she wrote.[2] In fact that statement appeared in a letter written fifteen years after her arrival in Bombay but Alice detested India from the moment she landed until her final departure almost thirty years later.

The first months in Bombay were the worst, because John was fully occupied at the School of Art and Alice found herself having to cope virtually alone in a foreign country. The packing cases which had been sent on ahead from England failed to arrive, so they were without such essential items as crockery and were forced to use their limited funds to purchase the basics at extortionate prices. Added to that the Anglo-Indian way of life was alien to everything Alice had experienced or read about. Although provided with an absolute army of servants compared with what she had been used to at the manse, ignorance of their caste restrictions and their language meant that nothing ever met her exacting standards. John Kipling told Edith Macdonald:

> Things are so funnily like and unlike what they should be. A Hindoo makes a shot at the right thing and he hits or misses by chances so that no one thing is quite right – no masonry is square, no railings are straight, no roads are level, no dishes taste quite like what they should, but a strange and curious imperfection and falling short attends everything, so that one lives as in a dream where things are just coming about but never *quite* happen. I don't suppose if I were to talk for a week, I could make you quite realise how far the brains of the native take him and where the inevitable clog of his indolence and that'll-do-ishness stop him short. But it is very odd and strange.[3]

Alice, brought up to strive for perfection, found the whole way of life exasperating.

To her despair, cherished pieces of fine linen and lace which she had brought with her from England became torn and misshapen after being laundered by the *dhobie*, the Indian washerman. From then on she was obliged to wash the best garments herself, but since this was not expected of a memsahib, there were no facilities in their bungalow and she had to press her clothes under a heavy book. Similarly, she longed to take over the preparation of food for John and herself because strong Indian spices were particularly upsetting to a pregnant English stomach; however, her wishes were to no avail. Food was always prepared by an Indian cook in the servants' quarters, then brought over for the family, so no kitchen was provided in the European part of the accommodation. Cravings for cocoa and English biscuits also had to go unsatisfied because such delicacies could only be obtained at great expense. Although the servants could be exceptionally infuriating, they were more than ready to be of service, and John found to his amazement that his bearer took it as a matter of course that he would not only run the sahib's bath, but undress him and pour the warm water over his back. It was a way of life which took a great deal of readjustment.

Situated in the School of Art compound, their whitewashed bungalow was large and airy with the provision of a verandah. Although some of its facilities were rather primitive by English standards, Alice found it far cleaner and in a better state of repair than most of the housing the Methodist Society had found for her family in England. The area surrounding their bungalow appeared to be a flamboyant jungle when they arrived at the end of May, because the gold Mohur trees were in full bloom, but as the summer progressed the area became a heap of swirling dust and was transformed into a mud bath by the autumn monsoon. Nevertheless, it was an image of beauty which remained with Alice's daughter Trix all her life. 'My very earliest memory is of my father walking up and down our verandah in Bombay brushing his beard, my three-year-old mind was more impressed by the emerald aisle of vast length, as it seemed to me, hung with wreaths and sprays of purple flowers and orange trumpets, and dappled by morning sunshine, than by the beloved figure that walked there,' she reminisced.[4]

Alice found it hard to come to terms with the extreme contrasts of India. On the one hand there was the growing prosperity of Bombay, as shown by the massive public buildings being erected under the auspices of the governor Sir Bartle Frere, and on the other the hovels behind these great façades, where the Indians lived. Disease and poverty existed on a scale she had never imagined; beggars, their heads crawling with flies, were a common sight. Near the Kiplings' home on the Bombay Esplanade lay the harbour and the Indian market, both noisy with jostling crowds and rich in smells, whilst not far away was a shady palm grove where coconuts blown down by the wind could be collected from the path. Cool and refreshing though it seemed, there was menace in the shadows and an aura of death hung around the place. Yet a far more tangible monument to mortality dominated the area: by the Esplanade loomed the Towers of Silence, where dead bodies were put out to be taken by the vultures patiently shrouding the turrets. A procession along the road below would provoke a gruesome fluttering of wings as the huge birds prepared for their feast. Painful reminders of this were also liable to be found closer to home, as Rudyard recalled: 'I did not understand my Mother's distress when she found 'a child's hand' in our garden and said I was not to ask questions about it. I wanted to see that child's hand.'[5] It was equally disturbing to discover that the rains might well wash human bones out of a mud wall or a horse's hoof break through some long forgotten grave under the path.

The birth of Joseph Rudyard Kipling on 30 December 1865 was a prolonged and painful affair, coming as it did at the end of a debilitating summer in the city and a miserable Christmas dominated by homesickness and the early stages of labour. Instead of the comfort of mother and sisters when she needed them most, Alice found herself surrounded by alien tongues and faces. Her labour dragged on for six days, 'as long as it took for the creation of the world', she said with feeling.[6] Things were not eased by the horrible revelation that the Indian servants had sacrificed a goat to Kali, the goddess of life and death, in order to speed the Memsahib's recovery. She came out of her ordeal resolved that any future babies would be born in England, for surely she would not survive another such delivery.

Fortunately the baby thrived with his Indian ayah, though his mother took longer to recover her health and spirits. 'I often wonder if this dull depressed woman can be the same she was in England,' Alice wrote to a friend, but she took good care to keep such thoughts from the Macdonald family.[7] Alice did not want to worry her mother, but more important than that she had no intention of giving her sisters the opportunity to gloat over her misery. Family letters were carefully composed and concentrated on giving information about John Kipling's successes at the School of Art along with the sending of copies of the *Times of India*, an English newspaper for the Anglo-Indians. In return she received copies of *The Times* which the family in Wolverhampton had finished with, and these she read avidly in an attempt to maintain contact with what she regarded as the real world. In one letter Alice copied out some curry recipes and enclosed the relevant spices, so that Mrs Macdonald was able to treat her family to the main dish of curried rabbit. Unfortunately their reaction to Indian-style cooking was not recorded; suffice it to say, no other mention is made in Mrs Macdonald's diary of curries being cooked again at the manse. On another occasion Alice enclosed a *carte de visite* photograph showing her son with his ayah, and this provoked great merriment and numerous jokes at Alice's expense. The picture showed Rudyard asleep on his ayah's lap, but the Indian ayah bore a striking resemblance to Alice, and the Macdonald family thought the Indian climate had had a dramatic effect on Alice's skin colouring and were accordingly most alarmed.

Once her health recovered, Alice began to take more of an interest in the Anglo-Indian community in Bombay, whose social life revolved round the governor's family. Invitations were secured to some musical evenings which Lady Frere 'and various swells' attended. Although Alice enjoyed moving in company and making music again, she was disgusted by the people. Few of them had any knowledge or interest in art and music, preferring to gather in cliques and gossip about minor scandals. The most galling thing for Alice was that in this local hierarchy, where Army and Civil Service rank counted for everything, a teacher at the School of Art on a meagre salary and working directly with the natives was treated as the lowest grade. In Bombay and throughout Anglo-India, protocol was observed far more strictly than it ever was in England, and so the Kiplings were destined always to be the last to enter at social events. Methodist doctrines about everyone being equal in the sight of God carried no weight, and Alice was furious, though powerless to effect any change. She consoled herself that the members of the English community were not worth bothering about. 'Indeed take the women all round, they have not brains enough to make such a cutlet as I ate at breakfast this morning!' she said.[8] Remarks like this did nothing to aid the Kiplings.

With the baby looked after and domestic chores performed entirely by the servants, Alice was bored. She took up her former interest of writing poetry and added short stories to her repertoire. Reading, which she adored, proved difficult because the books invariably had to be sent from England, and that was a lengthy and expensive business. It was often only John's good humour which made life bearable for Alice; he drew cartoons and left them around to amuse her, such as this one:

Memo to Mrs J. Lockwood Kipling, School of Art-lessness
Who borrowed her books from holes and corners of the earth?
Who laid them out in pomshus order?
Who drove away and forgot them?
                    Yah!

which was accompanied by a caricature of the situation.[9]

Another interest which Alice resurrected to pass her days was embroidery, not Berlin wool work, about which John was very disparaging ('a terrible achievement', he called it, 'that blazes with the brightest colours and seizes your eyes as a bull-dog jumps at the throat of a thief'[10]), but the style of embroidery she had been taught by William Morris. The quality of local materials she found inferior, and so fine linens had to be sent to her by her mother.

In many ways it came as a relief to Alice to find herself pregnant again in the autumn of 1867, for John had agreed she should return to England for the birth, even though it would stretch their finances to the limit. There was not enough money for all three Kiplings to return, so John remained in Bombay. Alice had been perpetually homesick for the three years she had been in India, so that even the arrival of the weekly mail boat had provoked tears. The prospect of going home made her ecstatic, but in reality turned out to be the greatest disappointment of her life. The intervening years had wrought changes in both herself and her family, and all bar the youngest, Edith, were married, so she had relatives she barely knew. Harry had abandoned the long-suffering Peggy Talboys and married Caroline Gold in New York, and Fred had married Mary Cork, the Methodist daughter of a pottery manufacturer. Alice had met Agnes's husband, Edward Poynter, at Georgie's, but disliked him, believing him to be too full of his own importance. Louisa's husband was another of whom she had a poor opinion, despite having met him but once whilst visiting friends in Worcestershire. Based on letters received from Louisa, Alice thought Alfred Baldwin a sanctimonious philistine, who was fast making his wife as boring as himself. Agnes and Louisa both had babies of similar age and vied with each other in a 'who's got the best baby' competition, which did not interest Alice in the slightest.

On arrival in England in March 1868, she went directly to her parents, who were then living in Bewdley, Worcestershire, following the Reverend Macdonald's enforced retirement, so that they could be near Louisa. Two-year-old Rudyard was to stay there with his cousin, Philip Burne-Jones, then aged five and a half, whilst Alice went to Georgie's for the birth. On 11 June Alice gave birth to a daughter who was christened Alice Macdonald Kipling like her mother, but always nicknamed 'Trix', arising from a chance remark that she was a 'tricksy baby'. This delivery was marginally easier than the first one, but with a baby weighing eleven pounds, Alice did not have a very comfortable time. Trix fared far worse, being born with a broken arm and a black eye and looking so poorly that neither Georgie nor Alice thought she would survive.

When Alice was fit enough to rejoin her son at Bewdley, she found a distinctly hostile atmosphere, for Rudyard had been storming around demanding the same total obedience from his grandparents as he received from his ayah and native bearer. In a matter of a few weeks he had caused havoc with his tantrums and kicked his Aunt Edith. Fred, who called to inspect this phenomenon, declared him to be a powerful problem capable of upsetting any household. The Baldwins were appalled at such behaviour, and Louisa reported to Agnes that Alice's children had turned the house into a bear garden with their behaviour and Ruddy's temper had made Papa so ill that they were thankful to see the back of the family. The presence of such disgracefully behaved children had taught her a lesson she would not forget, and little Stan would most certainly feel the benefit.

It was an upsetting visit for everyone, and confirmed the Macdonald prejudices against India. Harsh words were exchanged which could not be forgotten, and relationships strained to the limit. Mrs Macdonald was also more than grateful to see the Kiplings on their way, for even the new baby, she noticed, was a cross little thing. Ruddy left them in fitting style: after being amiable and well-behaved for a while, he let out ear-piercing screams which had the effect of drying everyone's tears. Mrs Macdonald did, however, spare a thought for her daughter, and wondered how on earth Alice would manage on the voyage back to Bombay with a fractious infant and a self-willed little rebel. All she could hope was that John would be able to handle Ruddy better than Alice, for she said the two-year-old boy could twist his mother round his little finger. The Reverend George Macdonald, already ill when Rudyard arrived, took a turn for the worse and within two weeks of the Kiplings' departure was dead – a coincidence which was not lost on the family.

Alice was bitterly upset by all the comments and criticisms that she had received, believing her family to be bigoted and narrow-minded. 'What do they know of England who only England know,' she said bitterly.[11] Even Georgie, to whom Alice had always felt closest, had been an unsympathetic companion, seeming miserable and detached, and Edward, once so much fun, had hardly been present. Alice attempted to think through her problems on the voyage back to the hated continent. There was no prospect of escaping from India now, because John had accepted a renewal of his contract at the School of Art, and she had learned that she no longer fitted in with the Macdonalds in England. Summoning up her old spirit, Alice determined to make the best of her uncongenial situation. She set herself the task of advancing John's art career, for therein lay the prospect of a rosier future. Architectural sculptor at the Jeejeebhoy School of Art had sounded grand, but the reality was somewhat different. An art school for the Indian population had been set up a few years earlier at the house of Sir Jamsetji Jeejeebhoy with classes in drawing and wood-engraving. Sufficient interest was generated to enlarge its scope with three new appointments in 1865 – Mr Higgins to teach art metalwork, John Griffiths decorative painting and John Kipling architectural sculpture.

Temporary buildings were obtained on the Esplanade and the three artists from England found themselves pioneers in the field. Although employed by the government, pay was poor and they were told they would be permitted to take private work to supplement their income. On her return from England, therefore, Alice decided to canvass for pupils amongst the English community on behalf of her husband. With little in India to occupy wives and daughters, Alice found it easy to generate interest in sketching and painting lessons as a pastime. Success here encouraged her in assiduous cultivation of government officials encountered socially, in an attempt to further John's cause. Whether Alice's efforts were the reason is hard to say, but John did receive commissions to embellish some public buildings in Bombay and to report on cotton production in the province during his two months' annual holiday. The latter was hardly the sort of work Kipling had been trained to do, but in the early days of photography it was more practical to employ an artist to record scenes in pictures as well as words. Kipling's report was obviously well-received, for it led to another commission to tour the North Western Provinces and the Punjab to catalogue the achievements of the artworkers in Upper India.

As a result of their combined efforts, John and Alice found their finances improved, and they began to create a niche for themselves in Anglo-Indian society. The musical, witty Alice of former years reappeared and helped to increase their popularity. Not all were impressed by the couple: 'The sourest and vainest lady this side of Suez', one local newspaper called Mrs Kipling, and the verdict on John was hardly flattering: 'The laziest and most conceited bore', he was pronounced.[12] But they were in general untroubled by such comments: Alice could be relied upon to supply a sharp retort.

Adversity, it seems, played an important role in moulding the characters of two of the Macdonald sisters, for unbeknown to Alice her sister Georgie was simultaneously struggling to emerge from the cocoon Edward had spun around her. Both in time developed formidable personalities, as Trix's opinion of her mother showed: 'Mother had a *very* strong will – but there were curious streaks of sand in her marble.'[13] These weaknesses Alice concealed from all but her closest family. Whereas Georgie used her talents in developing interests outside her family, Alice channelled hers into promoting her family. Loyalty had played a significant part in Macdonald childhood, and Alice simply transferred her allegiance to John and her children. She used her time in India to further first her husband's career and then her children's, for not only did she believe them to be worthwhile causes, but they provided her with distractions not available elsewhere in the accursed country. Her new purpose provided her with a challenge, but did nothing to change her opinion of India, as her husband well knew. 'Mrs Kipling is not at all bright and at times I think I was a brute to bring her out. If I could have a deputy wife it might be arranged somehow, but the state of Society is not yet sufficiently advanced,' he told a friend.[14]

When Alice found herself pregnant in 1870 for the third time, she decided to remain in India for the birth, not wanting a recurrence of previous Macdonald histrionics. The little boy was born in April, hastily christened John and then died a few weeks later. His short life acted as a catalyst for Rudyard and Trix's removal from India, and the following year all four Kiplings were on their way back to England. The six-year-old Rudyard and three-year-old Trix understood this to be a family holiday. In December, however, the children were taken to visit some total strangers, Mr and Mrs Holloway in Southsea, and suddenly found their parents had vanished. It was a traumatic experience in their young lives and left a lasting impression. Trix wrote:

> Looking back, I think the real tragedy of our early days, apart from Aunty's bad temper and unkindness to my brother, sprang from our inability to understand why our parents had deserted us. We had had no preparation or explanation, it was like a double death, or rather like an avalanche that had swept away everything happy and familiar.
>
> Yes, everything had gone at once: Papa, Mamma, home, garden, sunshine, dear Ayah who was never cross, Meeta, bearer, who could make wonderful toys out of oranges, Dunnoo, syce [groom] who took care of Dapple Grey, the fat pony with the saddle ring, the Chokra (boy), who called the other the servants when they were wanted, and who only grinned and didn't mind if I chose to pelt him with my bricks.
>
> Ruddy remembered our lost kingdom vividly, and used to tell me stories of my red-and-green push-carriage, which grew so funnily small for me, and of the broom gharry (brougham) where we sat opposite pretty Mamma in her bright frocks, and drove to the bandstand or along Back Bay.[15]

Instead, the children had six years in which they never saw either parent, receiving only weekly letters and some presents. Rudyard wrote bitterly of these years in Southsea in his autobiography *Something of Myself*, and his biographers have always severely admonished the

Kipling parents for this separation. What is frequently overlooked is that John and Alice were only acting in accordance with normal Anglo-Indian custom, which regarded India as a tour of duty and not as home; consequently children were 'sent home' to England to be brought up in a healthier climate and given a 'proper' education. Only the lowest classes of Europeans kept their children with them in India, simply because they could not afford to do otherwise. Where possible, children went back to a relative in England prior to going to boarding school, but as Alice told a friend in India, she had never contemplated that course of action because 'it led to complications', so a couple who advertised their services in the newspaper were selected. Members of the Macdonald family were certainly out of the question after the previous encounter, but Trix felt her mother should have allowed them to go to their Kipling grandparents in Yorkshire. 'What a lot of misery Rud and I should have been spared if mother had left us with them.'[16]

Discussion of the children's experiences in Southsea is really outside the scope of this narrative, but let it be said they may not have been quite as dismal as Rudyard painted. Trix admitted later in her life that her brother had exaggerated: 'Dramatic licence added some extra tones of black to intensify our grey days', was her tactful remark.[17] To her cousin, Stanley Baldwin, she privately admitted that an English upbringing probably did Rudyard good. 'You will agree with me that he was no drooping lily then – but distinctly a soaring human boy – spiced with devilry. Very much between ourselves dear Coz, I think that in some ways "Auntie" saved his soul alive – he was about as spoilt as he could be when he came home in 1871. Six and a half years old and he had never been taught to read! I don't know what the parents were thinking of or how he escaped learning.'[18]

Alice and John in fact hated the enforced separation from children whom they adored. 'I long to hear from you when you've seen Trix,' Alice wrote to a friend in England. 'I feel the loss of that sweet bright creature even worse than I thought I should.'[19] Furthermore it was an arrangement they could ill afford, but as a result of their Methodist upbringing, both Kiplings had the highest regard for education and were prepared to make the necessary sacrifices. In an effort to ignore the heartache caused by the removal of their children, Alice became more devoted to John and his career. Irrespective of her efforts, John was recognized as a good teacher, sympathetic to Indians and their culture, and a person who genuinely wanted to encourage their art, rather than smother it as inferior to European achievements. In 1875, Kipling's efforts were rewarded when he was offered the post of principal of a new art school to be set up in Lahore, some thousand miles away in the Punjab. The post carried with it responsibility for a museum as well, and the two together meant a substantial increase in salary and prestige for the Kiplings.

Lahore was a much smaller town than Bombay, and its British population numbered only seventy civilians, though the infantry battalion stationed there did increase the numbers significantly. Whilst being pleased that her husband had obtained recognition for his abilities, Alice did not welcome a move in 1875 any more than she had as a child. The household had to be packed up and transported by rail to the Punjab, a journey which lasted four days. Any enthusiasm she might have had was also dampened by Louisa's letter from England telling her of the death of their mother; for all their differences of opinion, Alice retained a deep love for the mother who had brought her safely through a peripatetic childhood. Mrs Macdonald's death was felt all the more keenly by Alice because thousands of miles separated her from the grief of her family, and because her mother's death now left her bereft of parents. She could only take comfort from the knowledge that their last meeting, at the time when the children were taken to Southsea, had been a happy one. Her mother, too, had been reassured by this, for on that occasion she noted that they met in peace and parted in peace without a single misunderstanding or sharp word, for which she heartily thanked God.

After the Kiplings' arrival in Lahore, John became very ill with typhoid. It was not the first illness either of them had had in India; sickness was an occupational hazard of day-to-day living, but the severity of the attack on this occasion threatened to take John's life, and Alice was frantic with worry. She trusted no one else to nurse him and for three weeks dispensed morphia and applied leeches in an effort to save his life. Looking back she said, 'I felt that if only someone belonging to me had been near, it would have given me the only comfort I could take,' but that was not to be, and she struggled on and fortunately John recovered, but the fever left its mark.[20] Although only thirty-nine, he had prematurely aged, with his remaining hair turning completely white and his face looking haggard and drawn. For the first time, Alice had no fears that people would think her older than her husband. After the illness she became almost paranoid in her efforts to cleanse their bungalow and thus prevent a return of the disease. The trees and shrubs which were always to be found round a dwelling in India as a necessary defence against the sun were uprooted, in her belief that they harboured insects and disease. The Europeans in Lahore stared in astonishment and decided that these Kiplings were certainly eccentric. The cleansing operation was so extensive that their bungalow acquired the nickname of Bikaner Lodge, after the desert state.

Alice found it very hard to settle in Lahore. She wrote:

I feel as if I had been here months instead of days. I am perfectly sure the days are twice as long here as in any other part of the world – yet I don't feel settled. Our house is very large for two people, and built on such an inconvenient plan that when we want to go into any of the fourteen rooms we have to run through the other thirteen to get to it. It is ugly too in spite of a wooden floor to the Drawing Room and papered walls – the rooms being the shape of boxes and the walls cut up with big doors which take up all the corners. Its only merit is that being new it is clean – but the situation is bad and all the dust of the Mozung Road passes through the house several times a day.[21]

This did not prevent her from sending to Morris, Marshall, Faulkner and Company for furnishings.

During John's convalescence following the typhoid attack, both he and Alice spent many hours writing and reading each other's work. Following the success of the government reports produced in Bombay, John had begun freelance journalism for an eastern Indian newspaper, the *Pioneer*, published in Allahabad. What began as odd articles in April 1870 developed into a regular weekly column on wide-ranging subjects. Art did feature in the form of advice on interior design for Anglo-Indian houses, which had the effect of making the Kiplings into the arbiters of artistic taste. Other subjects John wrote on were cruelty to animals, aspects of English life and feminism. In such a reactionary country as India, Kipling rather boldly declared: 'The case for the extension of the franchise to those women who possess property and pay rates is logically very strong.'[22] With equal forthrightness he used his sardonic humour against ostentatious displays of religion by 'stray clergymen "anxious to help the movement, you know" and grim English ladies whose appearance would command respect in the wildest scene and who certainly do not need to be kept out of temptation'.[23] Amusingly all John's articles were signed 'Nick'. The origin of this pseudonym is revealed in a pencil heading in one of John's scrapbooks of press-cuttings as Nicotine – for John was a heavy smoker and rarely seen without his pipe.

In addition to journalism, John, like Alice, wrote short stories which were sent back for publication in England in both *Temple Bar* and *Cornhill* magazines. John's stories were gentle romances, whilst Alice had progressed from her morbid poetry to stories which were said to be a cross between Edgar Allan Poe and the grislier parts of the Arabian Nights. It was this short story and poetry writing which was to be so crucial to Rudyard when he returned to India.

Although the move to Lahore started off inauspiciously, it proved the turning-point in the Kipling fortunes. During the summer of 1876, they spent the two months of John's holiday at Mussoorie, a hill station on the edge of the Himalayas, visited by those who could not afford the splendours of the season at Simla. They were, however, summoned from there to Simla by the new Viceroy, who requested John to design and execute seventy banners by the end of the year. These were to be presented to various princes as part of the celebrations at the Imperial Assemblage, or Delhi Durbar as it was then called, when Victoria was to be proclaimed Empress of India. This promised to be a herculean task, to which Alice could contribute, for she had gained some knowledge of textile design from William Morris many years before and had become reasonably accomplished as an embroideress after long practice. The work for the Durbar had little in common with the medieval wall-hangings produced by Morris, Marshall, Faulkner and Company, for they were to be made from Indian silks, satins and chintzes with appliquéd devices. Drawing on information told her by her mother, Trix said that her father designed and cut out the banners, whilst her mother taught and supervised the Indian tailors who carried out the embroidery, but Alice 'worked the most difficult bits herself. With a very slight knowledge of Hindi, she could teach an Oriental to do anything – no bribes, no threats – only helpful understanding.'[24]

The Kiplings were invited to attend the Delhi Durbar and see the results of their handiwork being presented by the Viceroy. Despite it being the beginning of January, the Kiplings were accommodated in a three-roomed tent complete with fireplace for the duration of the celebrations. At their conclusion, the Viceroy sought them out to express his thanks, and chivalrously remarked to Alice 'I hear you yourself worked the angel banner. Angels created by an angel.' He went on to add to her great delight: 'Who would have thought of meeting Mrs

Burne-Jones's sister in India?' To this Alice, who had also done her homework, countered: 'And who would have thought of meeting Owen Meredith as Viceroy?'[25] In London Lord Lytton had made a name for himself in literary circles as the poet Meredith, and as such was acquainted with the Burne-Joneses. Alice's reply was masterly, and from then on the Kiplings found themselves the personal friends of the Viceroy and Vicereine, because they were amongst the few in India who had any connections or interest in the London cultural scene. The new Viceroy was unconventional in his behaviour and Bohemian in his taste, like John Kipling, and the Vicereine and Alice shared a mutual hatred of India. With such eminent friends, the Kiplings were the overnight recipients of everyone's visiting cards, and although plenty of people thought them upstarts with neither rank nor riches to support their position, any protégés of the Viceroy had to be cultivated. Problems of etiquette, however, could not be overcome so easily, and the Kiplings continued to enter dinner-parties last, but when the Viceroy sought them out across a crowded room to discuss the fortunes of their famous relatives the Burne-Joneses and the Poynters, such inconveniences could be overlooked.

Alice stood no chance of competing with the splendid regalia of the wives of well-salaried officials, so she adopted a clever ploy. As the wife of an artist, Alice affected a strikingly plain dress made by herself, which she proclaimed to be in the style advocated by William Morris. She also made a show of wearing no jewellery except her wedding ring, which less charitable tongues said owed more to Mr Kipling's empty pockets than to Mr Morris. Whatever the reason, amongst the glittering company that swarmed around the Viceroy, a clever, witty lady in an austere costume could not be ignored.

By 1880, Alice had spent fifteen miserable years in India, but she could console herself that they had not been wasted. With John now well on the road to success, Alice began to make plans for the return of her children, whose futures she now intended to mould as well.

101

Chapter Eight

The Rivals
(1866–80)

The four Macdonald girls entered marriage, as most people do, with plenty of optimism and only the vaguest notion of the ultimate outcome, but the older girls did set out with clear aims: Georgie intended to develop her art work and Alice wanted to find independence and adventure. More content to let life take its course, Agnes and Louisa seem to have had no real aspirations, were more easy-going in nature and gradually became pale imitations of the two others.

Agnes possessed a similar wit and spirit to Alice, but she lacked her sister's determination and persistence, so marriage to the dominant Edward Poynter, who needed a wife mainly as a drawing-room ornament, eventually dulled Agnes's sparkle and turned her into a rather bored woman. A similar fate awaited Louisa, for though she shared the same high-minded principles as Georgie, she was never put to the test. Consequently she did not develop the same strength of character. It was John Kipling's view that 'Louie has led what they call in Staffordshire a "caded" (sheltered, screened, protected) life and was not originally a weak nature', and that Alfred Baldwin had cast his wife in the role of the little creature at home.[1] Louie played the part admirably, by becoming infused with the same morbid introspection that had dogged her mother, and was given better opportunity to indulge herself.

The struggles and adversities Georgie and Alice encountered in their early married lives helped to define their adult personalities. These women married men who were starting out in their careers and thus in need of practical assistance as well as sympathy from a wife, whereas Agnes and Louisa were expected to slot into the lives of already successful men and be little more than decorations – not easy for girls educated to think for themselves and afforded some glimpses of Bohemian freedom.

During childhood there had been the usual sisterly battles for superiority, but with eleven years separating the youngest from the oldest in the family, such conflicts usually favoured the more senior. Georgie rarely participated, believing these activities purposeless, even hurtful, and preferred to follow her own quiet course of action. Her marriage five years ahead of her sisters forestalled any comparisons of husbands or status, so she kept her own counsel and steadfastly refused to be drawn into arguments, as when Poynter threw out provocative comments about her friends and even her husband.

Alice, on the other hand, found the conflicts irresistible and was regularly at odds with Agnes, but marriage and India put a new perspective on life. Initially she viewed her whole family in a sentimental way, but after the traumatic Macdonald reunion at the time of Trix's birth, she felt antagonism towards them all. Interestingly, her attitude passed to both husband and son, who in their turn were more than willing to score a point for the Kipling side when the opportunity arose. During John Kipling's leave in England in 1879, he stayed a while with the Baldwins. His comments were: ' 'Tis very odd how piety, wealth and a loudly asserted trust in a personal deity seem to make some people apprehensive and gloomy.'[2] What gave Alice the most amusement was a series of articles John devised for the *Pioneer* newspaper. Whilst on holiday in England, he continued to send a regular report back to India under the heading 'English Etchings' which purported to give Anglo-Indians an insight into life in the homeland. Some of these reports concerned the mythical market town of Snoozely in Worcestershire, which in his scrapbook of press-cuttings John's handwritten notes reveal to be based on Bewdley, and the 'friend' in question, Alfred Baldwin. The articles drew attention to the Baldwins' public and private lives, highlighting those aspects Kipling regarded as snobbish and hypocritical:

I asked him how it was, that while, when he came up to town he went to the opera and the theatres, he never encouraged the local theatre. He not only thought that he should lose caste among his co-religionists, but that he should lose influence among the people whom he was trying to influence for good. The local theatre, he said, is low; but at that moment a company from London, whose performance he had there seen, was down on a visit . . . my friend dodged from one argument to another, the real truth being that he was in fear of the Brahmans of his caste. The clergy and the mighty hosts of dissenting ministers are fiercely opposed to the stage, in the pulpit and to the poor; but they cheerfully excuse the backslidings of their wealthy supporters who go to such entertainments in London or Paris. There is a dreadful amount of customary cant and unconscious hypocrisy among the respectable middle classes of England.[3]

These inflammatory remarks achieved a rather hollow victory because the articles were published in India, thus ensuring the Baldwins were kept in ignorance.

Rudyard continued the Kipling/Baldwin feud, allowing it to trickle on at a personal level for much of his life. Aware of the very bad impression he had created in the Baldwin household as a little boy, Rudyard was keen to retaliate by suggesting Stanley was a weak specimen tied to his mother's apron strings, and whenever the opportunity arose, would involve him in violent, messy activities which he knew would cause friction with Aunt Louie. Much stemmed from Ruddy's jealous opinion that the Baldwin cousin was in receipt of everything money could buy, whereas of himself he wrote to Margaret Burne-Jones: 'Pater mourns he has nothing for me to come into save his name.'[4]

The strongest competitors amongst the Macdonald sisters were naturally the two closest in age, who had been bosom companions in their youth, were married on the same day and managed to produce sons almost simultaneously the following year. Louisa knew Agnes peered down her nose at the Baldwins for their involvement in industry and for having to live in the provinces, because the letters which arrived from London stressed Poynter's latest artistic successes and his wife's conquests in society drawing-rooms. There seems a curious irony in the play which Agnes selected for her country sister when she came to stay at Gower Street, Bloomsbury; for the two young women, along with their husbands, attended the Charing Cross theatre to watch Sheridan's *The Rivals*. Although as children both had been brought up to regard theatre-going as sinful, they experienced no difficulty in adopting this custom of fashionable society. Louisa was keen to participate in the life of the capital whenever the chance arose, and since marriage to Alfred had converted her to High Anglicanism, she felt herself permitted to indulge in a pleasure she knew had been Georgie's delight for years. Agnes also had no qualms, for she had given up Methodism on her marriage, and even went so far as to persuade that loyal chapel-goer Edith Macdonald to attend a performance of *The Barber of Seville* at Covent Garden.

Marriage gave Agnes an entrée into a milieu she had always admired but never expected to participate in. Edward Poynter was recognized as a rising star in the art world and courted by hostesses for dinners or country house parties. His attractive new wife, whose repartee was as entertaining as her music, was also welcomed, and the invitations arrived so thick and fast that Agnes complained to Louisa she had been forced to send some refusals. Popularity could be transient, as Agnes was aware, so she determined to enjoy it whilst she could; at the same time her husband assiduously cultivated all the useful contacts possible. Whilst working at the South Kensington Museum with his friend Frederic Leighton (later Lord Leighton), he contributed illustrations to a periodical with Millais. So prodigious was his capacity for work that he continued painting for exhibition. The picture *Faithful Unto Death* had been highly acclaimed at the time of his engagement to Agnes, and the gigantic painting *Israel in Egypt*, which he exhibited at the Royal Academy in 1868, drew much attention, not just for its size, but also for the unusual subject matter and the almost photographic realism with which Poynter had depicted it. Its prompt sale for £850 further enhanced the painter's reputation, as did his election as an Associate of the Royal Academy the following year. With that kind of success coming his way so early, the boast went back to Worcestershire how everyone in London was making a great fuss of the Poynters.

Not wishing to be outdone by such reports, Louisa promptly supplied details of life in Bewdley, for although Agnes made disparaging remarks about Louisa's marriage to an ironmaster, she failed to appreciate that her younger sister had married into a substantial empire. The Baldwin family had many branches and owned not just the forge at Wilden, which was Alfred's principal concern, but also an iron-foundry, a tin-plate works, a worsted spinning mill, a carpet factory and sundry smaller concerns. Alfred was the youngest in the family, but marriage to him conferred on Louisa a status akin to that of lady of the manor, even if it was one founded on 'brass' rather than land. When they returned to Bewdley from their honeymoon, there was a reception appropriate to their station, as Louisa lost no time in telling Agnes. The date and time of the newly-weds' return was supposed to have been kept a secret, but sufficient information was leaked to ensure that the church bells were rung in their honour, and Louisa declared that she dared not show her face at church the following day or they would have had endless visitors. The official appearance of the bride was scheduled for the following Sunday, and then she thought the flood-gates really would open, for she discovered to her delight that life as Mrs Alfred Baldwin commanded a great deal of touching of the forelock.

It is doubtful in fact whether Louisa herself knew the extent of her husband's wealth, for although he settled £4,000 on her during their engagement to ensure she had some money of her own (which figure, set against a Methodist minister's salary of under £200 per annum, must have seemed a vast sum), she regarded money as the preserve of her husband and, provided her basic needs were met, did not concern herself with it, being less avaricious than Agnes. Under Alfred's direction, the Baldwin companies prospered, and in 1870 he bought his brothers out to become sole owner, so that, by the time of his death in 1905, the companies were worth over a million pounds. Despite this, Louisa was well aware that in her sisters' eyes industry was inferior, even sordid when compared with art, so her suggestion that Alfred commission some paintings for their home was a clever one. The ironmaster also found the idea of being an art patron rather to his taste, with the result that Poynter in particular was able to sell several pictures to Baldwin. Obviously the solid realism of Poynter's work appealed more to the businessman than the ethereal images of Burne-Jones, and Alfred had not been too impressed by the latter's efficiency, because the painting *Barbara*, the long-expected and delayed wedding present, arrived four years and four months after the nuptials, whereas Poynter's schedules were invariably met.

The most inexplicable art purchase Alfred Baldwin ever made was a painting titled *Phyllis and Demophoön*, which Alfred and Louisa had viewed in Burne-Jones's studio in 1870. The picture was commissioned by another industrialist, Frederick Leyland, and on completion exhibited at the Old Watercolour Society, but it provoked such an outcry that it was swiftly removed. Some thought that the intertwined couple, one of whom was clearly modelled on Maria Zambaco, was a reference to the artist's *affaire de coeur*, whilst others simply found the male nudity shocking. Alfred Baldwin, who certainly had no sympathy for the Burne-Jones/Zambaco entanglement, nevertheless bought a copy of this picture in July 1871 and hung it in his dining-room.

Rivalry between town and country continued, but Louisa was confident that she had pulled off a major coup when she persuaded her parents to settle in Bewdley virtually next door to her. As one of the youngest in the family she felt she held a special place in their affections and was unwilling to relinquish it even after the wedding. Some of her letters to Alfred before their marriage had attempted to persuade him that Wolverhampton was the ideal place to live, but he responded firmly that if God showed them it was their duty to live near Stourport, then it would be cowardly for them to shirk it. Conveniently it was concluded that God did intend them to live at Bewdley near Stourport, as originally planned. Once her honeymoon was over, Louisa searched there for suitable accommodation for her parents and the eighteen-year-old Edith, already committed to caring for them; within four months, all were close neighbours. Louisa hoped to make herself the focal point for the whole Macdonald family, now married and spread around the globe. Yet despite the presence at Bewdley of her parents, members of the family instinctively turned to Georgie. Whenever Alice returned to England she deposited herself at Georgie's, and Harry, coming back from New York for the first time in ten years with his wife Caroline, chose to test the climate of opinion with the calm, dependable Georgie before approaching the others. However, in 1869 she did not find his presence welcome at the end of a year in which she had almost lost her husband to another woman.

Harry received a prodigal's welcome from his mother, overjoyed at the sight of her favourite child, and fortunately she also adored her 'daughter Harry' from their first meeting. Louisa was equally impressed by this new sister-in-law because she could stand up to Harry without fainting or being upset by his rebukes, and it was quite evident that Caroline had devised a tactful way of persuading Harry to follow her line of action. Indeed Louisa, who had never cherished any great affection for this elder brother, believed that the family were seeing Harry at his best for the first time, though she felt there was still room for improvement and the removal of Harry's entire liver under chloroform might lead to better humour. By this time Harry was a proof-reader for the *New York Times*, but still cherished the dream of a permanent return to England. This visit was therefore taken up with the search for work. There are indications that Harry's health was bad, with two accidents in the space of a few weeks – one where he fell and nearly drowned and another at his mother's house when he alarmed her by cutting himself badly from a fall whilst dressing. At the end of 1870 he and Caroline returned to America. The pinnacle of his achievement in that country was to become financial editor of the *World* newspaper, despite Caroline's reports of his worsening health. To their disappointment they never had any children, and Harry never returned to England again. He continued to believe that one day he would rejoin his family, but his father was dead, and his mother died five years after his visit. Fred alone maintained contact with Harry, from a sense of Christian duty rather than through any affection. The two met in New York during one of the Reverend Frederic Macdonald's Methodist missions, and Rudyard also sought out his uncle when he visited America, but his sisters put Harry out of their minds after his departure in 1870.

Accounts of Harry's illness suggest there might indeed have been a physical problem, but it is less easy to discover one in the cases of Agnes and Louisa. Both girls enjoyed excellent health before their marriages, but within two years a deterioration into varying stages of invalidity and delicacy occurred. The severity of Agnes's condition fluctuated, but the 'touchy nerves' that she believed the whole family were blessed with could be relied upon to render her indisposed if a tedious social function threatened. Louisa's malady, by comparison, became an established way of life as she sought to gain the attention and sympathy of her workaholic husband. The needs of Baldwin and Company occupied most of the owner's waking hours, and nothing, apart from religion, which was worn like a hair shirt, was ever permitted to intrude. The idea of a great love between Louisa and Alfred was promulgated by Louisa in an effort to satisfy her craving for affection, and her journal records the hours spent lying down, longing for the moment when Alfred would walk through the door. She said that she felt the heartache of a child waiting for its mother to arrive and restore it to happiness. Other remarks of Louisa's to the effect that she and Alfred were so deeply in love that they had to make a special effort not to exclude the young Stanley resembled romantic fiction, because Alfred was so busy working he never noticed the child, and Louisa so preoccupied with her hypochondria that her son was often forgotten.

Louisa evolved the role of the patient martyr as the most successful way of engaging Alfred's sympathy. She could console herself that in one small area she was indispensable to her husband, because the great man did have an Achilles heel. He was terrified of thunderstorms, and if one threatened he retreated to the cellar of the house, to be cradled in his wife's arms until the danger passed (how he coped at the works is not recorded). But since thunderstorms were a comparatively rare occurrence, Louisa settled down to almost sixty years of ill-health, moving between periods of great distress and minor recoveries, whilst those around her danced attendance. Her illness began after Stanley was born on 3 August 1867, even though her mother described it as an easy birth and was pleased with the way Louisa recovered. Six weeks later she had a relapse. It is hard from this distance in time to determine whether childbirth was responsible for the mysterious ailment, but a letter from Georgie to Louisa six months afterwards hinted at a gynaecological cause: 'The organ you mention is very well understood and one hears constantly of women who suffer from the very source you mention and yet live afterwards to be the smiling mothers of thousands.'[5] That was not a fate Louisa had in mind, for she had already moved into her own bedroom, which was never again to be shared with the beloved Baldwin, only with her sisters when they came visiting. Her joyful accounts of sitting up in bed talking with Georgie suggest a very real attempt by both of them to recapture their former girlish happiness.

Louisa's new absorbing interest in her health provided her with the excuse to visit London regularly. The Baldwin family doctor who attended her at first favoured humble remedies like limewater and milk, followed by therapeutic hot seawater baths at Hastings, but when no lasting cure was effected, Louisa decided she needed the advice of a more eminent London doctor. Alfred accompanied his sick wife to consult Dr Charles Radcliffe, the leading Methodist physician who had always attended the Macdonalds during their London days and was still called to the Burne-Joneses. From Dr Radcliffe, Louisa progressed to the highly-acclaimed Sir James Paget. Predictably, the more prestigious the physician, the more expensive the cure: limewater and milk were abandoned in favour of stronger remedies and some amusingly naïve letters of Louisa's record her inexplicable collapse following consumption of a complete bottle of champagne along with a little sherry and beer, all recommended on account of her health. The day after this concoction, Louisa resorted to cramming down as many beaten eggs in wine as she could manage. She was sure something was wrong, and it was all most discouraging.

The diagnoses were as bizarre as the cures. One idea involved an irritation of the spinal cord, which though painful and tedious she believed to be curable, and it was the physician's suggestion that a German bath would be efficacious. Later, another idea gained credence, and Louisa announced that though her heart was not diseased, it had far too rapid an action and needed to be put right.

Fortunately a Continental cure was recommended – at Cannes this time. Sir James Paget obviously understood the needs of his patient very well, for Louisa was acutely aware that she alone amongst her brothers and sisters had never travelled abroad. Married to a patriotic Englishman like Alfred Baldwin she was hardly likely to do so. He never took a holiday, though occasionally was persuaded to accompany Louie to the coast, returning to his business as soon as one of her sisters was able to join her. By contrast Agnes Poynter and her husband were frequent visitors to Europe; Georgie had been to Italy with Edward and Ruskin, and of course Alice's travels were unparalleled. Even young Edith had been taken to Switzerland by Fred and his wife, and with Harry in New York, that left Louisa as the only untravelled member of the family. With the weight of medical opinion on his wife's side, Alfred was not in a position to refuse, but though Louisa's journeys to 'take the waters' continued for years, Alfred only found time to join in the first one; her subsequent expeditions had to be undertaken in the company of Agnes or a friend.

Louisa's strength noticeably returned when she stayed with her London sisters, and she was able to view art exhibitions, call on old friends like Webb, Morris, Faulkner and the Solomons, attend concerts with the Poynters and even go to such plebeian entertainment as Mascali the conjurer at the Egyptian Hall. There was certainly an element of magic in his performance, but it was so wrapped in vulgarity that Louisa found it purgatory to endure. Nevertheless, she decided that Mascali understood the needs of his public perfectly, since they apparently enjoyed what she could not bear. Back in Worcestershire, her sensitive spirit languished once more on the *chaise-longue*, re-enacting her mother's philosophy that the more refined the lady, the greater the delicacy. Louisa felt obliged to spend a great deal of her time on her back: taking her meals supine, being pushed out into the garden in a bathchair or taken for a drive in the specially converted carriage her husband had to buy for her. The young Stanley Baldwin was taken care of by a nurse and grew up knowing his Mama was an invalid, who often had to be shut away in a darkened room. It was only his Aunt Edie, then in her early twenties, who enlivened his childhood. She was a regular caller at the Baldwins because Louie sent for her to run errands or just sit and read aloud. After Mrs Macdonald's death, Edith moved in permanently with the Baldwins to take over the running of the household and bring up her nephew, since it was recognized that

Louisa's illness prevented her from carrying out such chores. Stanley was grateful for the company of this light-hearted aunt, who devised exciting games for him, listened to his lessons and took him for walks.

Agnes's condition was never as drastic as Louisa's. If rivalry extended to the sphere of health, then the accolade surely went to Louisa, because Agnes was perfectly capable of travelling abroad with her husband and did not need to be carried in a litter like Louisa. Edward Poynter's attitude to work was similar to Alfred Baldwin's, and when the two men met socially, they discovered much in common, despite coming from quite different walks of life, and respected each other's profession. Life with Poynter was not easy for Agnes: she discovered that the dedication which she had so admired was in fact single-minded, even ruthless, ambition, which was not relieved by the slightest indulgence towards either wife or children. Few regarded themselves as his friends, and most referred to him by his surname, believing him to be hardly the type of person to welcome familiarity. Those friends of his student days who lived in London learned to their cost how Poynter could turn into a harsh critic. In a public speech he attacked Whistler, saying 'during the two or three years when I was associated with him he devoted hardly as many weeks to study', and Du Maurier was similarly dismissed as having a 'dangerous tendency towards laziness' as Poynter sought to give the impression that none worked harder than he.[6] Mrs Macdonald agreed, but was unable to sympathize with behaviour which had prematurely deprived her of her own husband. As she remarked to Louie, man was not wound up to go for more than six days, so if people like Poynter insisted on going against the face of nature, which she interpreted also as the law of God, then they had to take the consequences.

Poynter's incivility towards those he considered inferior was common gossip amongst the artistic fraternity and varied from criticism of colleagues to downright rudeness towards his models. One story which circulated about him concerned a dinner-party given by the artist Alma-Tadema, where the meal had been poor. In disgust, Poynter stormed across the dining-room, picked up the speaking tube which communicated with the kitchen and shouted: 'Cook, you are a damned fool!'[7] Some of the man's intolerance is echoed in the reminiscences of W. Graham Robertson, who was friendly with Poynter's son Ambrose. 'Poynter himself I always found difficult of access though he was kind to me in his remote way; putting up occasionally with us boys in his studio

111

and suffering us in his house, though I think not gladly. Many of his old friends have assured me that his heart was in the right place, but I feel the same could not be said of his liver, and chronic dyspepsia is not improving to the temper.' But Robertson was sweetened by Ambrose's 'lovely witty mother, who fascinated me as she did everybody'.[8]

Such a prickly character as Poynter did not fit easily into the Macdonald world, and beyond the contact necessary to appease his wife he remained aloof and avoided being enmeshed by her relations. Agnes in turn raised objections to visiting his father and step-mother in Dover, announcing petulantly that if she was not happy she became ill. The idea of going to stay with her mother-in-law was abhorrent, but when Poynter insisted, she declared that she would prefer to endure the inconvenience of staying near by and visiting daily to spending one night under the same roof. Edward ignored Agnes's protestations and for at least one Christmas left her behind in London whilst he departed for Dover as he had arranged.

Marriage to Poynter alienated Agnes from her family, not just on account of her husband's arrogance, but also because of her own initial rejection of them in favour of the glitter of society. Despite living close to Agnes, Georgie only saw her sister when their paths crossed socially. She had rendered assistance when Agnes was involved in childbirth and their mother was taken up nursing Louie, but once back on her feet Agnes had disappeared off to Italy with Poynter, and Georgie had resumed her own life. Since both moved in the art world it was natural to share acquaintances. Burne-Jones was equally as keen as Poynter to find patrons from amongst the rich and famous, but Agnes's opinions of people were sometimes at odds with Georgie's. Rosalind Howard, regarded by Georgie as intelligent and vivacious, was considered very tiresome and argumentative by Agnes. Most of the time Agnes and Georgie went their separate ways, but when Georgie did invite the Poynters to a dinner-party, Agnes opined that Georgie only invited them as bait for others, a comment which infuriated her sister.

Relations with Alice also remained cool. Such pretensions as the Poynters had were hardly likely to find favour with the down-to-earth natures of Alice and John Kipling. Agnes was left with only her childhood companion Louie, for the younger unmarried Edith tended to be ignored by them all. The rivalry which dogged relations between Agnes and Louie at the start of their marriages mellowed as their sons became inseparable companions. Agnes felt that the close fellowship which had existed between her and Louisa had now passed on to their sons, and both sisters welcomed this unexpected turn in events. The two children were frequently in each other's company when their parents were abroad or, in the Poynters' case, at Wortley Hall, for the artist had secured a lengthy commission to decorate Lord Wharncliffe's billiard-room, entailing four huge classical paintings and the Earl's portrait. The work was spread over several years and necessitated periods in Yorkshire at the stately home, with the happy participation of Agnes.

The social scene ceased to have the same magnetism as it had in former days, but Agnes was careful not to refuse the more prestigious invitations which came her way as her husband rose in public esteem and office. The Wharncliffes particularly had brought Agnes into contact with nobility and even royalty, for the Prince of Wales and his good friend Mrs Langtry were also on the Earl's guest list. It was through the good offices of Lady Wharncliffe that Agnes was presented at court, just ahead of 'The Jersey Lily' herself. Although Agnes's social standing relied entirely on her husband's status, she did her best to establish a niche for herself as an accomplished pianist. Music had been one of the few things she had been prepared to work at in her childhood, and after her marriage she found it a useful pastime. She took lessons in both singing and piano and spent several hours a day practising. At soirées, she was often requested to entertain the party and would accompany others, including her husband, who also enjoyed singing. Music and involvement in society were only distractions from boredom and an underlying knowledge that marriage to Edward Poynter was a disappointment. Agnes's letters refer to him being busy and often away from home. On the occasions he was there she found him too preoccupied to indulge in light conversation, with the result that life was rather miserable for both.

Louisa had more of a conscience about being idle than Agnes. Though illness had been one of the few things the Reverend George Macdonald had been prepared to accept as a reason for inactivity, Louisa still felt the need to do something. Since she found herself with abundant leisure, she resorted to the constructive pastimes of the manse that she had once been so keen to abandon. Making clothes for the poor and needy was begun, but Louisa always made sure there was someone else to do the distribution. Wood-engraving, which had been her favourite occupation in girlhood, was never taken up again, but her writing did make a reappearance. Lying down, she was able to work on various pieces of fiction which she always referred to as her 'tales'. Georgie, who became a regular visitor to Wilden House, where the Baldwins had moved when Alfred became head of the company, encouraged her younger sister in this pursuit. Louisa records in her journal that they often spent mornings working together on their manuscript books, later reading work out to each other. Even when Georgie had returned to London, chapters of writing were exchanged through the post, but none of Georgie's work has survived. It seems likely that she destroyed it herself, for she never held a very high opinion of any of her efforts, whether artistic or literary. Louisa was different: heartened by the praise which Alfred lavished on his wife's attempts, she parcelled her manuscript up and sent it on to William Morris for criticism after Georgie had read it. Morris was slightly embarrassed by its arrival: 'I will try to be sincere, but you know it is not very easy to say what one thinks if a friend's work is *not* to one's mind: you after all are the best person to say whether the book ought to be printed. I know you are clever and thoughtful, and are not likely to be wrong about it.'[9] Burne-Jones also squirmed when confronted with a copy of *The Story of a Marriage*, which Louisa had written, attempted to praise the parts which he felt could never have been better expressed and tactfully suggested there were a few parts, but very few, where if he had been listening to her reading it out, he might have ventured to suggest an alternative phrase, but so seldom, because it was a masterly effort. In later years she took to sending her work to Rudyard for approval and advice on publishing, and he was reasonably restrained in his remarks, though he did say that her collection of short ghost stories, *The Shadow on the Blind*, was too wordy and cliché-ridden: 'What you want is heap plenty blue pencil,' he told her, adding more gently: 'The tales are good and more than good but you give the impression of wanting forty pages to turn in.'[10] John Kipling said privately that he thought it 'the oddest thing that she should want to write poetry at all seeing she has many dainty ideas but little notion of how to put them and absolutely no ear for rhythm and cadence'.[11]

Other things which occupied her time were regular lessons in German, French and Italian, learning enormous chunks of Shakespeare by heart, and religious studies. At least an hour was set aside every day for Bible reading and devotions, in addition to daily worship with Alfred. The consignment of books which Alfred ordered regularly from the London Library always contained a preponderance of theological texts, such as *The Bishop of Worcester's Charges to the Clergy* and what Louisa considered were Barrow's wonderful sermons about slander and evil speaking, as well as a little poetry and some George Eliot novels, once Georgie had introduced her to the famous novelist.

Religious observances did not help to bridge the gap between the sisters, but their children did. With Alice in India, Rudyard and Trix were virtually orphaned in England, and all the sisters undertook some responsibility for their welfare, although Rudyard's memories of these years have led his biographers to cast the Macdonald sisters in the role of wicked aunts, who ignored him totally. This is not true. The Kipling children received visits from at least one member of their mother's family every year and were kept in constant contact by letter. In August 1872, the summer following their arrival at Southsea, it was Macdonald family policy to spend their holidays there. Grandmother Macdonald, Aunt Agnes and Ambrose arrived unexpectedly at Lorne Lodge where the Kiplings were being looked after, and old Mrs Macdonald thought the children seemed well and happy. During the following weeks the cousins played on the beach and picnicked together, whilst the adults, including Mrs Holloway, watched. When the two Poynters departed, their place was taken by Aunt Louie, Stanley, Aunt Georgie and the two Burne-Jones cousins, all of whom went to see the little Kiplings, who were found to be well and happy, and in Louisa's opinion, vastly improved. Mrs Holloway, they decided, was a very nice woman indeed. The daily contact between the families continued, and was so successful that when the holiday ended in the middle of September, Louisa arranged with Mrs Holloway for Rudyard to return to Wilden with Stanley. For the next six weeks, Rudyard stayed with his Aunt Louie, who took her duties as godmother very seriously, teaching Ruddy to recite his catechism and making sure he attended church regularly with Alfred and Stanley. Although Rudyard returned to Southsea at the end of October, he was in London again for Christmas, staying with 'the beloved Aunt Georgie [who] is several kinds of angel from heaven' and his Uncle Ned.[12] Trix was less fortunate, finding herself left behind with the Holloways most of the time, possibly because she was barely three years old and the continual shifting about was thought to be too disturbing. What was far worse from her point of view was the separation from Ruddy, the only link with her real family.

At the Grange, Rudyard was made much of: 'I had love and affection as much as the greediest', he remembered even in old age.[13] They were exhilarating days when Uncle Ned fooled around pretending to make voices issue forth from draped chairs in the hall, or engaged the children in burying something he maintained was part of an old pharaoh, who required all the rites of Mizraim and Mephisis. There were visitors like Morris, Price and Rossetti to the house, and in addition to Philip and Margaret Burne-Jones, the two Morris girls called and all became involved in amateur dramatics to entertain the grown-ups. It is interesting that Burne-Jones found it far easier to play with the boisterous Rudyard than with his own son, thus making Philip into an outsider. He seemed to inherit all the most melancholic characteristics of both parents, which did nothing to endear him to any of his cousins. Even his grandmother had noticed he was a strange boy, remarking that after a month in his company, she was convinced Philip possessed sufficient powers of worry to wear his mother out, which was perhaps borne out by Georgie's continual concern about her son's unhappiness and inability to make friends. Rudyard, meanwhile, found a very good friend in Margaret Burne-Jones, and she was the only one of his cousins he felt comfortable with. W. Graham Robertson, a theatre costume designer, well known as an æsthete and dilettante, detected similar traits in the girl as in her brother when he wrote that she was difficult to get to know because she 'has the Macdonald reticence and reserve developed to an abnormal degree', but Ruddy apparently found in her the same warmth as in Aunt Georgie.[14]

It would have been hard to find two more different personalities than Rudyard and Stanley Baldwin, for the latter had been brought up very strictly and sombrely. Not surprisingly he was the only member of the family who got on well with the humourless Edward Poynter, and Stanley was proud to own to a friendship with this uncle, which lasted from his earliest memories until the artist's death. Rudyard could not resist trying to lead the well-behaved Baldwin cousin astray whenever the opportunity arose, as it did in the summer of 1879. Alice had returned to England and collected her two children to take on holiday. The twelve-year-old Stanley was invited to join them. Trix recalled: 'We had a lovely holiday at a farm in Epping Forest. I don't know how mother survived it, we were so absolutely lawless and unchecked. Our cousin Stanley Baldwin came for a six week visit and we infected him with our lawlessness too – even to donkey riding. He brought a bat and tried to teach us cricket, but we had no time for it – it entailed too much

116

law and order.'[15] Instead Rudyard taught his cousin to raid the dairy, get himself plastered in mud by wading into ponds and steal the baking which the farmer's niece had put to cool. The farmer warned Mrs Kipling that the two boys were doing each other no good, but it was not until Ruddy and Stan attempted to sit down to a meal covered in manure and blood, having spent the day assisting in pig slaughter, then playing in the muck heap, that Alice objected. After the long separation from her children, she was indulgent and reluctant to discipline them at all.

For Stanley Baldwin, such a way of life must have been a revelation, compared with his lack of freedom at home. His father brought him up to be very aware of his position in the neighbourhood. Even his fifth birthday was celebrated with all the pomp and ceremony befitting a crown prince. The village of Wilden was draped with yards of evergreen over the road and hung about with banners and posies for the occasion. At half-past three the temperance band led the two hundred Baldwin employees and their families to the meadow where the games were organized – climbing the slippery pole to win a sixpence or bobbing in the water for a penny, as well as the traditional three-legged and sack races – followed by as much tea and cake as could be downed. The workers' wives, obviously knowing which side their bread was buttered on, presented the young master with a two-handled cider cup, an engraved glass, a cup and jug, sugared cakes and a basket of apples, all of which Louisa found very touching.

Marriage had originally pulled the Macdonald sisters apart, but nostalgia and loneliness gradually brought them together again, as they sought in sisterhood the affection they had failed to find as married women. The death of their mother in February 1875, which upset all the sisters deeply, began a melancholic addiction to anniversaries and events connected with their childhood. Agnes was inconsolable because for her it seemed to symbolize a far greater loss. Her reaction to the event was reminiscent of Georgie, for Agnes retreated into a shell, ignoring both husband and son and only wanting to be with Louie so that they could talk over former times and visit the grave. It brought both women closer than they had been since marriage. The melancholy which had been very much a part of Hannah Macdonald's nature surfaced again in her daughters as they looked back with longing on their lost childhood. Agnes wrote and told Louie how she would regularly fetch out the letters they wrote to each other in 1865 and reflect tearfully on how intimate they were in those far-off halcyon days, but even the letters could not compensate completely for their lost youth. Louisa similarly cast her eyes backwards, not just in obsessive celebrations on anniversaries, but also by hoarding letters and relics of their past. Even the letters which had passed between the young Carrie and Wilfred Heeley were fetched out, read and grieved over. By 1880 much of the former rivalry had gone, to be replaced by a melancholic closeness dependent upon the past. Even Alice, separated by thousands of miles, felt a little of it now that both parents had died and her former aggression towards her sisters melted away, but experience had taught her to be more self- reliant. She found more affection with her husband, and later her children when they were restored to her, and remained distanced from her other three sisters by a fundamental difference in attitude.

Chapter Nine

Dear Little Epigram
(1870–80)

In 1870, Georgie hoped that the worst of her matrimonial problems were over and in one sense they were, because Edward had abandoned Maria Zambaco at Dover and returned to Georgie. Despite protestations of love for his wife, however, he maintained a liaison with the Greek lady for several years. Details of its progress are vague, but Georgie's son-in-law Jack Mackail, who was commissioned by the Burne-Joneses to write a biography of Morris that met their approval, was surprised at the duration. In a note to a member of the Ionides family he wrote: 'I see the letter is dated Nov 1872: I had thought MZ was all over by that time, but my chronology is very confused about that very confusing and complicated business.' He added rather tantalizingly: 'How extraordinarily interesting one could make the story, if one were going to die the day before it was published.'[1] He certainly did not die before publication, and Georgie made no effort to enlighten him further: indeed she continued destroying much of the material once he had used it. In this as in several other relationships where she was involved, it was her main concern that no one's work or character should suffer misinterpretation by later generations. All these men were great in her eyes, no matter what follies they committed.

'I think I need spend no more time in this looking back,' she told her friend George Eliot, but that was not so easy when figures from the unhappy past had a habit of reappearing.[2] A portrait of Maria arrived at the Grange painted by Rossetti at Edward's request and framed in a most unusual way, with a locking door so that Edward could drool in private, yet 'return an evasive answer to an inquisitive world'.[3] Soon after, he began work on his own picture of Maria as a commission for her mother, and so absorbed was he by the project that he dismissed the pleas of his children to accompany them and their mother to Whitby for a holiday with George Eliot. The picture confronting Georgie on her return was a blatant declaration of love for Mrs Zambaco, because without the restraints imposed by public exhibition, Edward felt free to employ every device possible to symbolize his devotion. Maria was shown with Cupid, whose arrow was wrapped in a piece of paper bearing the names of both artist and model. In Maria's hand was a miniature of Burne-Jones's *Le Chant d'Amour*, and the flowers surrounding her were irises and white dittany, representing flame and passion in Edward's favourite language of flowers. There could be no mistaking the meaning; moreover he had never painted such a love picture of Georgie.

She was in an impossible position because it was obvious this *femme fatale* provided the much-needed inspiration for Edward's art, and any attempt to remove her would destroy his work. Georgie unwillingly condoned a situation she knew to be wrong, but she was heard to say, 'If I thought things never would be any better than that I would throw up the sponge all round. I wouldn't care so long as there was hope even after a million years.'[4] Finding truth in one of their favourite Macdonald family maxims, 'bare is the back without brother behind', Georgie turned in bewilderment to her friends. Although one of the first to admit she found it difficult to form close relationships, she knew four people who helped her through these years and set her on a course she would follow for the rest of her life.

Perhaps because she always held a low opinion of her own abilities, Georgie was irresistibly drawn to strong characters, three of whom history has judged to be 'great': William Morris, George Eliot and John Ruskin. The fourth, Rosalind Howard, also played a part in public life, but her very forceful personality led her along increasingly eccentric paths, and she has largely been forgotten. There was an element of hero-worship in Georgie's attitude towards her, yet Georgie was anything but a sycophant. Georgie's advice and criticism were valued for their honesty and common sense: 'Of what offended the moral sense she could be scathing in condemnation, and few if any were more harmoniously alive than she to follies and absurdities; but to no one and of no one did she ever say an unkind word.'[5] She was indeed a fiercely loyal friend. In return, Georgie gained affection and new causes in life. All four people campaigned on national issues, which led her to look outside herself and get personal worries in perspective. These people possessed the confidence to write or speak out publicly, and though

Georgie would have shrunk from such a challenge once, by 1890 she too was prepared to declare her convictions in public, even when she knew them to lack general backing.

In time of trouble it seemed natural Georgie should turn to her oldest friend, William Morris. His marriage also reached crisis point when Janey Morris made it clear she preferred the Mediterranean warmth of Rossetti to the Icelandic chill of her husband. Once the Red House days were over and the Morrises returned to London, Janey took refuge in one of the many undiagnosed ailments so favoured by Victorian women, which released her from matrimonial obligations and allowed her to seek recovery on the south coast with whom she chose. Morris and Georgie, both abandoned, looked to each other for solace in a purely platonic way. Regardless of the level of intimacy between Edward and Maria or Rossetti and Janey, Georgie had such strong views about the sanctity of marriage that she never considered sexual infidelity.

Morris had known Georgie since she was sixteen and the acknowledged property of Edward Burne-Jones. He was fond of her and worked his first piece of illuminated manuscript, his poem 'Guendolen', especially for her in 1856. Once Janey entered Morris's life, she replaced Georgie as the inspiration for his poetry, but it is clear that, by the late 1860s when the Morris marriage was in difficulties, Georgie had regained her former place. The Earthly Paradise poems, which were published from 1856 onwards, are believed to contain references to Georgie, and Mackail's tactful introduction to a later edition suggests that he too guessed this, for he wrote: 'There is an autobiography so delicate and so outspoken that it must needs be left to speak for itself.'[6] Morris's pencilled comment in the margin of the original manuscript, meant only for Georgie's eyes, read: 'We too are in the same box and need conceal nothing, don't cast me out – scold me, but pardon me.'[7] Much of the poetry that came later was not only dedicated to Georgie but also inspired by her. He presented her with a beautiful handbound illuminated copy of The Book of Verses in 1870 and a further volume The Lovers of Gudrun inscribed 'Georgie from W. M. 15th April 1870. This is the first copy of the poem with some alterations inserted: I wrote it in June 1869 William Morris.'[8] His single attempt at novel writing concerned the love of two brothers for the same woman, and when partly written, Morris gave it to Georgie 'to see if she could give me any hope, she gave me none, and I have never looked at it since', he told Louisa Baldwin.[9] Evidently autobiography in the guise of fiction frightened Georgie.

Strangely she regained the status of 'the lady on the pedestal', but for Morris rather than Edward. It was a convention which suited them both. They viewed the great love and respect between them in a spiritual light, of a higher order than anything sexual. Morris, for all his passionate displays of temperament, said sex was a 'mere animal arrangement', and in a letter to Charlie Faulkner he spoke of marriage in terms of legalized prostitution wherein man has 'adorned the act variously as he has done the other grotesque acts of eating and drinking'.[10]

Few letters between Morris and Georgie have survived. Following his death, she asked for hers to be returned, and a large boxful was burned. When Morris's daughter May appealed to Georgie for letters to use in a work about her father, Georgie replied: 'I turn to my archives and find that the letters from your father that I have kept only begin in 1876,' a clear indication of the ambiguous nature of their friendship before that period, for Georgie, like her mother, was a compulsive hoarder.[11]

If Morris supplied the love Georgie would have liked to receive from a husband, then Ruskin sought to be a father figure to her, but this she found the hardest relationship to handle. The first meeting with John Ruskin occurred during her engagement, when she went with Edward to the basement of the National Gallery to meet the famous art critic who had done so much to further the ideals of the Pre-Raphaelite Brotherhood. Georgie was completely overawed by the man and did little more than listen as he explained the finer points of the Turner collection he was cataloguing. Edward was flattered that such a famous personage was prepared to notice him and laud his work. After his marriage Edward readily became Ruskin's protégé, and it pleased him to see how much the forty-two-year-old critic liked young Georgie. She is 'a country violet with blue eyes and long lashes and as good and sweet as can be', Ruskin told an acquaintance, and on learning that Georgie had never travelled abroad, arranged an all-expenses-paid journey to Italy for the Burne-Joneses in 1861.[12] In order that the couple should feel less embarrassed at accepting his generosity, he spoke of himself in fatherly terms: 'Love to all my babies, ever your affectionate Papa' was a favourite ending to his correspondence at this time, and so delighted was Georgie with any recognition of Edward's talent that she welcomed the paternal affection the celebrated man was showering on them both and asked Ruskin to be her son's godfather.[13]

122

Ruskin appeared to encourage her own art.

I am delighted to hear of the perverse woodcutting. It will not I believe interfere with any motherly care or duty, and is far more useful and noble work than any other of which feminine fingers are capable without too much disbalance of feminine thought and nature. I can't imagine anything prettier or more useful than cutting one's husband's drawings on the wood block – there is just the proper quantity of *echo* in it and you may put the spirit and affection and fidelity into it – which no other person could – only then work hard at it – keep your rooms tidy and baby happy – and then after that as much woodwork as you've time and liking for

– advice which only aided the withering of Georgie's creativity.[14]

Within a short time Ruskin's affection became embarrassing to her, because it obviously arose from an older man's infatuation with a young woman. 'You're more my childie than ever, if ever you were one,' he told her. His letters became addressed exclusively to Georgie, and the salutation changed from 'dear children' to 'my dearest little narrow Georgie' (a teasing reference to her admission that she was poorly educated) and eventually to 'my darlingest Georgie'.[15] He told her she was haunting his dreams and preventing him from working, and in an allusion to Keats's 'Eve of St Agnes' he jokingly asked her if, when he next came to dinner at the Grange, she would arrange for him to stay on hidden in a cupboard in her house, from which he could gaze out in silent adoration. There were invitations for her to go and visit him without Edward or accompany him secretly to the opera. Then he suggested they could make it 'even more naughty' if Georgie came to dinner with him alone afterwards. It was an extremely difficult situation for Georgie to handle because she had immense respect for Ruskin's reputation and was well aware of the debt Edward owed the critic. All she could do was to take a careful road and humour her admirer with little in-jokes. It became an accepted convention between them for her to call him 'St C', which one letter reveals was 'Saint Crumpet'. The origins of this nickname have been lost.

Ruskin was beginning to suffer from personality problems which later led to two mental breakdowns, and as time went on also became enamoured of Margaret Burne-Jones, who many said was 'a second-generation Georgie'. On occasions, both Burne-Jones females went to stay at Ruskin's home at Brantwood on Lake Coniston, but Margaret began to escape from these holidays as she felt uncomfortable in the old man's presence. A sprinkling of his letters to Georgie have survived, but those of Ruskin to Margaret were destroyed by Margaret's daughter Angela Thirkell in the 1950s because she thought them 'the kind of letter that Mr Ruskin ought not to have written to a young girl'.[16]

Despite all the problems Georgie had in handling this friendship, it was one she never regretted. The advantages that Ruskin's favour conferred on Edward were obvious, and she was sure she too benefited. 'I sat at the feet of those great ones,' she said in later life.[17] As a wide-eyed young woman, eager for learning, Georgie was determined to make the most of every opportunity. She studied Ruskin's books *The Seven Lamps of Architecture* and *The Stones of Venice* in detail, then discussed the ideas with William Morris and the author. Ultimately Ruskin's view of art in society became absorbed into her own philosophy so that her granddaughter remarked with amusement: 'I think she honestly believed that *The Seven Lamps of Architecture* on every working man's table would go far to ameliorate the world.'[18] Although Ruskin's ideas remained with Georgie all her life, their intimacy conveniently began to wane with the increase in Georgie's commitments and his deterioration in health.

Almost as an antidote to these equivocal male friendships, Georgie formed attachments with two women who became her closest confidantes. The friendship with Rosalind Howard was not surprising in view of their similar age and their marriages to artists, although the Howards belonged to the aristocracy. When measured against Rosalind Howard, Georgie did regard herself as inferior, and likewise when compared with George Eliot. In both cases it was the other's intellect and outspokenness, not their rank, which Georgie admired; indeed in the case of the novelist, intimacy was of dubious social benefit. 'She is not received in general society, and the women who visit her are either so émancipée as not to mind what the world says about them, or they have no social position to maintain', a contemporary wrote.[19] Novel-writing might have brought George Eliot fame, but her personal life ensured her infamy. It was well-known that the self-styled 'Mrs Lewes' was not married to the man with whom she lived, because a quirk in the law prevented divorce from his adulterous wife. For all her affirmation of the sanctity of marriage, Georgie Burne-Jones was extraordinarily tolerant of those whose behaviour was at variance with her own, and quite disregarded public opinion.

Rosalind Howard and George Eliot offered Georgie affection when her need was paramount, and acted as substitute sisters to her. Rosalind was impetuous, had passionate likes and dislikes, and in her daughter's opinion, 'was more wrecked by her own temperament than anyone else'.[20] There was much similarity between the personalities of Rosalind and William Morris: both could be brilliant, stimulating and funny, and exhibited a penchant for challenge and eccentricity. Back home on her country estates Rosalind would ride off wildly on horseback or encourage dangerous games, such as swinging over chasms on ropes or chasing along the unprotected roofs of Naworth or Castle Howard. Over and above this was a propensity for violent change in mood. 'My mother's power of speech when angry was wrecking and shattering,' her daughter wrote, but at best 'her flow of talk was like a flow of lava, and made her an hypnotic speaker on the platform'.[21] It was a personality few found easy to comprehend and fewer still thought attractive, yet it acted on Georgie Burne-Jones like a magnet. 'You are one of the few people of Earth with whom I find it easy as well as pleasant to be quite open, for if you don't always agree with me you are not easily offended,' Georgie told her.[22]

Contrary to appearances their friendship was not one-sided: Rosalind admired the quiet studiousness of Georgie, and the two of them shared a love of music and literature. Following Georgie's stay at Naworth in the summer of 1869, Rosalind commissioned a portrait of her friend from Poynter, and a letter from Georgie in September reported on the picture's progress.

> Such had been my incredible promptness united with my brother-in-law's that the portrait was already begun and the hair arranged in curly wise by the time I got your request about it. However, Mr Poynter had managed to effect a compromise and I hope you will like it. It is very dear of you to care for my likeness and it gives me great pleasure to sit for you. I have stipulated that your little locket shall be distinctly visible in it, and though no one else shall know what that means when we are dead and gone, you and I shall while we live.[23]

The portrait with its secret symbol of affection – a heart-shaped pendant of pearls surrounding a lock of brown hair and inscribed 'Georgie Jones from Rosalind Howard' – hung in the drawing-room of the Howards' London home at Palace Green.

In 1869 Rosalind was a convert to the cause of feminism, having just read John Stuart Mill's *The Subjection of Women* and promptly joining the front ranks in the women's suffrage movement. She regarded her friend Georgie, recently abandoned by Edward, as a likely recruit.

Rosalind's relations with her own husband were tempestuous, and despite providing him with eleven children she was full of inhibitions at the merest hint of sex, becoming frantic at any suspicion of flirtatious behaviour in her presence. By the 1880s this, added to irreconcilable differences in political opinion, persuaded her and George Howard to lead separate lives. Georgie did not fully agree with Rosalind's views and evinced little interest in feminism, only reading reports of meetings and never attending any herself. 'I wonder you care for me, considering my ignorance of politics – I wish I knew more of them as a nice, good abstract subject of conversation! Seriously, I do wish I cared a little more about the female suffrage question – it seems such a piece of indifference to the troubles of my "sister woman", but enthusiasm is not to be got up at a moment's notice,' Georgie told her friend.[24] In fact she never became deeply involved with the 'Votes for Women' campaign, being always more concerned for the provision of equal education for girls, both at school and university level.

She regretted her own lack of formal education: 'How I wish I had a trade to which I could turn and support the household,' Georgie lamented to Rosalind, 'but it is too late. Margaret must have one.'[25] She sought the correct books to teach her daughter the elementary subjects and then arranged for her to attend one of the newly-founded girls' public day schools at Notting Hill, in the hope that Margaret would go on to university. Such ideas were in advance of their time because very few women's colleges even existed. However, when Edward had cause to visit Cambridge, Georgie arranged that Margaret should go as well 'to see the prospect that lies before her of a woman's college – (only she must go to Oxford). Miss Helen Gladstone has kindly promised to take her over Newnham and Girton, both if there's time.'[26] In the end Oxford provided Margaret with a husband, but never the university education Georgie so desired.

It was George Eliot who encouraged Georgie most in her educational aspirations, aiming to distract the younger woman from her marital unhappiness: 'Go on conquering and to conquer a little kingdom for yourself there. When one sees the foolish and the ignorant happy it is possible to doubt the good of a larger vision, but nobody ever envied narrowness of mind in misery.'[27] The novelist was largely self-educated through books and attendance at public lectures on such diverse subjects as chemistry, theology and language. So successfully did she pursue her learning that by the age of twenty-six she had published a translation of a German text and eight years later was editing the *Westminster Review*. She was an inspiration to Mrs Burne-Jones, who had never taken the initiative with her own education. Under George Eliot's guidance, Georgie improved her slight knowledge of French and German, borrowing the novels of Balzac to read and studying passages from Goethe's *Faust*. She worked on passages set by her friend and together they produced literary translations. Encouraged by her success in this, Georgie took private lessons in Latin, which amused Edward: 'Georgie is lexicious deep at this moment – Greek, Sanscrit and Ural-Finnish,' he told a friend jokingly.[28]

The friendship with George Eliot was unusual in that the novelist was twenty-one years Georgie's senior, and despite their similar backgrounds her progress in life had been on a different plane. Notwithstanding the national recognition George Eliot received, she was retiring by nature. Her unconventional 'marriage' left her very vulnerable, and she therefore rarely went out in society; those eager for her company had to meet her on her own ground. As a result the Priory where the Leweses lived near Regent's Park became open house on Sunday afternoons for the more Bohemian elements of society. Georgie recalled:

It was at her own house and from that day (18 February 1868) began our friendship with her and Mr Lewes. She was very like Burton's portrait-drawing of her, but with more keenness of expression; the eyes especially, clear and grey, were piercing: I used to think they looked as if they had been washed by many waters. Her voice was a beautiful one, sometimes full and strong and at others as tender as a dove's. . . . Occasionally we dined there, or they drove over to the Grange on a weekday afternoon – they never dined out – and the general conversation that went on at such times, I am bound to own, was chiefly very funny, with much laughter and many anecdotes.[29]

Not everyone considered George Eliot's looks pleasant: Louisa Baldwin was taken by her sister to worship at the novelist's shrine during a visit to London, and it was her opinion that the great lady was at best plain, whilst her consort was one of the strangest-looking men she had seen. Indeed, many people said they were the ugliest couple in London. For all that their Sunday afternoon salons grew crowded. Georgie Burne-Jones felt ill-at-ease in the noisy bustle, so George Eliot set aside Friday afternoons as a quiet time for their meetings. Only three or four women enjoyed such intimacy; it was the view of George Eliot's biographer Gordon Haight that they worshipped the novelist with almost lesbian devotion. Georgie thought her friend's personality charismatic, combining lofty ideals with deep sincerity and a genuine concern for fellow humanity. Women found it easy to pour out their troubles to her, even those as reticent as Georgie. In the early days of their acquaintance, when the Burne-Jones/Zambaco affair was in full swing, Georgie found herself pouring out her troubles to the sympathetic ear and was promptly embarrassed by her garrulousness: 'I think much of you and of your kindness to me during this past fortnight, and my heart smites me that I have somewhat resembled those friends who talk only of themselves to you. . . . Forgive me if it has been so, and reflect upon what a trap for egotism your unselfishness and tender thought for others is. The only atonement I can make is a resolve that what you have said to me in advice and warning shall not be lost.'[30]

The affection between the two women never revealed itself in a sexual light, but rather resembled that of an older sister comforting her junior in time of trouble. George Eliot, lonely herself, warmed to the intense little artist's wife – 'dear little Epigram' she called her on one occasion[31] – but as their friendship grew, this was replaced by the pet name 'Mignon', referring to Georgie's daintiness. George Eliot's sense of isolation is seen in letters to Mrs Burne-Jones: 'What helps me most is to be told things about others, and your letters are just of the sort I like to have.'[32] 'Your words of affection in the note you sent me are very dear to my remembrance. I like not only to be loved but also to be told that I am loved. I am not sure that you are of the same mind. But the realm of silence is large enough beyond the grave. This is the world of light and speech'.[33] The friendship was not exclusively between the women, because Edward Burne-Jones also admired the novelist. 'There is no one living better to talk to for she speaks carefully, so that nothing has to be taken back or qualified in any way. Her knowledge is really deep, and her heart one of the most sympathetic to me I ever knew,' he wrote.[34] Since both families were fond of music, they often attended concerts together, and when the famous Wagners came to visit George Eliot, she made a special point of taking them to the Grange.

The closeness of the two families enabled George Eliot to participate in a family life her unconventional liaison precluded. The Leweses happily indulged in outings with Philip and Margaret Burne-Jones, attended pantomimes and brought little gifts for them. So natural had this relationship become, that in 1877 it was proposed the two families should spend Christmas together, until George Eliot intervened,

128

fearing that they were imposing too much on their young friends. She wrote:

> Dearest Mignon, I have been made rather unhappy by my husband's impulsive proposals about Christmas. We are dull old persons, and your two sweet young ones ought to find each Christmas a new bright bead to string on their memory, whereas to spend the time with us would be to string on a dark shrivelled berry. They ought to have a group of young creatures to be joyful with. . . . So pray consider the kill-joy proposition as entirely retracted, and give us something of yourselves only on simple black letter days when the Herald Angels have not been raising expectations early in the morning. . . . I am not afraid of your misunderstanding one word. You know that it is not a little love with which I am Yours ever M E Lewes.[35]

Their closeness continued until 1880 when George Eliot suddenly married John Cross. Georgie was aghast, for she had no intimation of the event and received only the briefest of notes from her friend. After all their former confidences, it seemed Georgie was not to be trusted with this most important one, and she was deeply hurt. 'Dear Friend,' she began, 'I love you – let that be all – I love you, and you are *you* to me "in all changes" – from the first hour I knew you until now you have never turned but one face upon me, and I do not expect to lose you now,' but it was a letter she could not bring herself to post for six weeks.[36] At the end of the year the tie was completely severed on George Eliot's death at the age of sixty-one.

In the short term, Georgie received moral support from all four friends and recognition of her own individuality, and in the long term she gained a new political awareness. In her childhood there had been no Macdonald involvement in politics, and neither did Edward have regard for the subject, so it meant little more to Georgie than might a new fashion in clothing. The Franco-Prussian War in 1870 aroused her interest as it did many people's. 'Of course we are much excited about the war and its consequences in Paris – and I expect we should agree with you very much in what we feel about the thing,' she wrote to Rosalind, then holidaying in Italy. 'I never saw so much excitement in the streets for news, everyone is talking of it, or walking along reading newspapers'.[37] But it was the Bulgarian Atrocities six years later which really engaged her sympathies. She discussed the situation endlessly with Morris, who had become treasurer of the Eastern Question Association. Burne-Jones was equally loud in his condemnation of violence, but had no intention of engaging in party politics. 'I know nothing of politics, I very heartily want them swept away if God would send a besom, but the summer has been made really nightmarey to me by thinking over these doleful miseries – and it seems a shame to be comfortable, to be happy,' and since his patrons now numbered Members of Parliament and influential aristocrats, strong political allegiances were ill-advised.[38]

Georgie, however, was fascinated by the political manoeuvrings and attended meetings with Morris, even though Edward disapproved. Her report to Rosalind of the meeting in January 1878 shows just how committed she felt by this time. 'The great meeting at Exeter Hall last Wednesday evening was a most successful and impressive one – the place was crowded with men all eager and serious and almost entirely unanimous – the deep determination of one portion of England not to go to war will really save us. I believe the tactics of the other side are not to laugh at us and say there is no war party, you have frightened yourselves for nothing – I hope we may hold them to this.' The descriptions of Morris's public speaking were equally enthusiastic.

> It is such a blessing to hear him put truth into straightforward words as no one else does at present – for he is free from all the usual forms of public speaking and in fear of no man. How I wish you had heard his song sung at Exeter Hall by a great part of the 3,000 present to the 'Hardy Norseman' – the organ played it and between every verse there was a pause for shouting and clapping which raised the roof. It was such a good thought to have the organ for it was played during the hour before the meeting during the filling of the hall and not only drowned the noise of the entry but gave a kind of solemnity to the whole proceedings. It was poorly played which was a pity,

added the musical Georgie.[39]

Since neither Janey Morris nor Edward Burne-Jones had much sympathy for Morris's political activities, it fell to Georgie to be the natural critic of his speeches, listening and commenting in much the same way as she used to do with his poetry. On one occasion, Edward, who preferred to remain sketching in another room during such orations, heard raised voices, and asked Morris: 'Well were you quarrelling with Georgie?' 'No!' came the reply. 'Georgie argued very well, but I put her down!'[40] Georgie thrived on all this because the burning zeal, the rousing speeches and the organ music had much in common with the Methodist meetings of her youth, but as she herself had chosen socialism as a cause, she embraced it all the more warmly.

The new decade found Georgie entering her fortieth year a more independent and self-assured person. The friendships with George Eliot, Rosalind Howard and John Ruskin were on the wane, though the bond with William Morris was as strong as ever. Edward too had settled down; his affair with Maria Zambaco had been replaced by innocent infatuations with young girls, very often the daughters of patrons, who enjoyed being painted by the celebrated artist. They could conveniently be placed on pedestals and worshipped without hurt to anyone, and it was an arrangement Georgie accepted with amused tolerance.

Philip Burne-Jones was then aged eighteen and causing continual worry to his parents. All his life he had found it difficult to make friends and settle to anything. His school days at Marlborough had been so problematical that he had had to be taken away and coached at home so that he could follow his father to Oxford. His indifference and quite erratic changes of mood made Georgie particularly anxious, so at Oxford it was arranged that Charlie Faulkner would keep a firm eye on him to prevent further problems. Margaret Burne-Jones, then aged fourteen, was a quiet, serious girl, in many ways a younger version of her mother, apart from a lack of aspiration for a brilliant academic career. She preferred instead to sit on the sidelines of the glittering London society her father painted. He was totally enslaved by his daughter and denied her nothing despite Georgie's reservations about such indulgence: she felt she had little power to change the situation.

London life had never been Georgie's real desire, but Edward had always protested he could not work outside his studio at the Grange. By 1880 their income and the legacy which Edward's Aunt Catherwood had bequeathed them ensured sufficient money for Georgie to consider buying the sort of house she had always wanted in the country. Knowing Edward would never agree to that, she suggested the seaside, whose restorative powers might appeal to him. Provided it was Brighton where the Ionides and several other leading families had moved, Edward was prepared to consider the idea, but that was hardly what Georgie had in mind. After announcing there was nothing suitable to be found in Brighton, she compromised by suggesting Prospect House, a small cottage in Rottingdean, close to Brighton. This was purchased, and from then on Georgie divided her time between Rottingdean, which she adored, and London, where her husband spent most of his time. Although not the perfect solution, the purchase presaged for Georgie some of her happiest years, and the Burne-Joneses and all the Macdonald relatives came to feel that she and the Sussex village were the heart of the family. Here too Georgie was able to find expression for all the political philosophies and skills she had learned during the previous decade.

Chapter Ten

The Family Square
(1880–93)

Early in the 1880s Alice began to plan for the return of her children to India: 'John would grow younger with his son and daughter by him – a process he sadly needs for he is getting dreadfully absorbed in things, he is rarely now the conversational companion he used to be,' she told an Anglo-Indian friend, Edith Plowden. 'To me the companionship of these bright young creatures would be new life. I have never been cheerful except by excited spurts ever since I came out last.' Moreover, the cost of keeping two teenage children at separate establishments in England was proving extremely onerous. 'People are beginning to find it impossible to keep their families at home – everything in England is so costly . . . our income which would be good if we were all here under one roof does not bear division and subdivision by exchange – we are really feeling the pinch at present,' she admitted at the end of 1881.[1]

Ultimately it was the financial burden on the family which led to the early reappearance of Rudyard and Trix. It had been intended that Trix, who left India when she was two, should remain in England until her eighteenth birthday, then return and be launched into Anglo-Indian society in search of a suitable husband. At the same time Rudyard would also be ready to come back to India after completion of a university education, but this plan misfired. 'Oxford we cannot afford,' Alice told Edith Plowden.[2] In addition, as the United Services College at Westward Ho did not offer scholarships, there was no chance of Rudyard following in the steps of his cousin Philip Burne-Jones. Although Rudyard enjoyed the company of artists and himself sketched for amusement, he had no intention of copying his father or his uncles. At one stage he contemplated being a doctor, but his headmaster, Crom Price, had also pursued that career for a short while and advised Georgie to let Rudyard attend a post-mortem at the Middlesex hospital so that he could see exactly what was involved. That decided Rudyard: 'I think I threw up my immortal soul', he told Trix, and began to consider other professions.[3]

Since it was not to be medicine or art, literature was the obvious choice because Rudyard found great joy in writing and received every encouragement from his family. During visits to the Grange he had also been fortunate enough to meet some of the leading literary figures of the day. At school he wrote verses in much the same way as his uncle Edward Burne-Jones had sketched, namely to amuse his schoolfellows, but his mother took an altogether more serious interest in his efforts, requesting that she receive copies of all his work. Fearing that this might not happen she even circularized all friends and relations with the request: 'I wish when Ruddy sends you any verses you would let me have a copy. He promised I should have all he did – but he is not sending them – and as time and distance do their fatal work I am sure that his Mother will know less of him than any other woman of his acquaintance.'[4] Some of Rudyard's work was meant purely to entertain the Burne-Jones cousins and the two Morris girls. They had begun a magazine together called 'The Scribbler', 'published' at the Morrises' house in Turnham Green and then laboriously copied out by hand several times over by Jenny Morris. All the children wrote articles for it, although Rudyard, who was away from London at school in Devon, was a less frequent contributor. All offerings were anonymous, but Rudyard's usually took the form of poetry and were often the same verses as he was contributing to the school magazine.

Alice paid great attention to Rudyard's literary efforts and chose twenty-three of the poems she had collected to be privately printed in a book she entitled *Schoolboy Lyrics* (an addendum to the book was what Rudyard later described as 'a scandalous sepia-sketch of Tennyson and Browning in procession and a spectacled schoolboy bringing up rear', drawn by his father).[5] Rudyard was quite unaware of his mother's enterprise until he returned to India later and was then embarrassed by this display of maternal pride. Alice was obviously keen to have her son's talent recognized because she personally distributed copies of the book in the more influential strata of Anglo-Indian society. Rivett-Carnac, then private secretary to the Viceroy, recalled in his memoirs how Mrs Kipling brought him a booklet of about thirty pages in a brown cover for which he was very grateful because in later years, when Rudyard Kipling's fame had spread, he was able to sell the booklet for

£80 'and for a valuable addition to our library purchased with the money, we have to thank the family of Kipling'.[6] Such financial gain on the part of recipients was hardly Alice's aim, but she hoped by putting examples of her son's work in the right hands she would be able to find him employment.

Following her old friend Crom Price's advice that Rudyard ought to make use of his writing ability, Alice looked for a commercial outlet for him. 'His bent seems so strenuously towards literature that I believe that will be his outcome. We therefore propose if all be well to have them, both Trixie and Ruddy, out here in two years' time and get him newspaper work. We should be together – a family *square* for a few years at any rate and I think we should be very happy.'[7] Since John was fully occupied at the art school, she undertook the task of finding an editor willing to take on an inexperienced schoolboy. Cultivating the right entrée was a challenge Alice thrived on.

During the winter of 1881 she found her time taken up helping John with an exhibition of Punjab native arts and manufactures. Although it had been planned some eighteen months previously, most exhibitors left sending their materials until the last moment, and John found himself working from dawn until dusk every day and needed Alice's assistance to get the exhibition ready for the Christmas Eve opening. 'John never rests, or sits down save for 20 minutes at lunch and my hours are nearly as long,' she complained to Edith Plowden. 'I have undertaken the arrangement of textiles – cotton – woollen – silk – embroideries and leather, and as each of these classes is divided into 32 districts and things have come in so irregularly that each day I have to undo about half of the work of the day before, it is not quite a holiday.' Nevertheless, Alice had a talent for efficient organization and enjoyed helping with this and several other exhibitions. Her only real complaint was that, when she returned from work every day, there was always 'a pack of cards on the table but I have no time to return and see very few people'.[8]

After the excitement of the exhibition everything seemed an anticlimax. Alice managed to take three weeks' holiday in Allahabad with some friends ('he is a High court judge', she proudly reported), but she was rather despondent that John had to dismantle the exhibition and could not be with her. She was further annoyed to read about her relatives in the newspaper. Early in March 1882 Agnes Poynter, then aged thirty-nine, surprised everyone, herself included, by giving birth to another son. The first Alice knew of it was in a paragraph in the *World*: 'I learn that she must have been taken ill at a dinner party! And has been herself guilty of taking "an unpardonable liberty in another person's house". I won't pretend that I am not very much amazed by having had no letter from anyone of my sisters. They treat me in this way and are yet surprised when I say that out here I feel cut off from them all,' she wrote in exasperation.[9] Rudyard took a schoolboy's delight in his aunt's social indiscretion: '*Est-ce que mes tantes sont donc folles?* Suppose the other Aunts indulge in second editions. Shan't we become venerable! At first I had a confused idea that I was an Uncle or a grandpapa, but on mature reflection I find that I am only another cousin. Never mind. I ain't cut out of any expectations and I wish her joy. Can you imagine Uncle Edward's face?'[10] These irreverent remarks amused Alice, only to be annoyed to find six weeks later that no one had considered Trix might like to see her new cousin. 'My sisters seem much too occupied to take much notice of her – she had not up to last mail seen Mrs Poynter's baby.'[11]

There were problems with Trix at this time. The girl had been transferred from the Holloways in Southsea to live with three 'very cultured' ladies in London. Although these ladies were reputedly on friendly terms with many leading literary figures, Rudyard was sure his sister was unhappy 'crushed up with the solemn company of spinsters', and urged his mother to move her to younger people.[12] Trix's letters home at this time contain the first indication of the depressions and mental instability which were to dog her adult life. Alice's comments reflected her concern for this fourteen-year-old daughter: 'She seems to have got – who knows how or where – some morbid religious notions and is tormenting herself with fear we shall be disappointed in her in some way.'[13] The same Macdonald fear of failure, which had tormented Harry many years previously, seemed to be working its way into another strand of the family. Trix certainly did not have as much attention and love from her aunts as Rudyard, but once she was living in Warwick Gardens, South Kensington, with the elderly blue-stockings, she saw more of the Burne-Joneses. A letter to Rudyard gives some idea of Trix's activities and those of her cousins:

This has been a specially amusing week, for I went to the Grange for half-term holiday and Phil's new adoration, Oscar Wilde, was there – only at supper luckily, for he is a dish I love not, and I don't think you would either. To look at he is like a bad copy of a bust of a very decadent Roman Emperor, roughly modelled in suet pudding. I sat opposite him and could not make out what his lips reminded me of – they are exactly like the big brown slugs we used to hate so in the garden at Forlorn Lodge. He has a pleasant voice spoiled by a very affected manner – and his black bow-tie – the floppy sort – would have made a very good sash for me. He talked incessantly, and at any pause Phil, who sat next to him, gasped: 'Oscar, tell us so and so,' and set him off again. He hardly seemed to look at Margaret, who was as white and beautiful as a fairy tale, and took very little notice of Aunt Georgie. Uncle Ned was unusually silent, and winced, I think, when Oscar addressed him as 'Master'.[14]

Back in India, Alice struggled to save enough money for the two children's passage from England. This necessitated postponing her own departure for the hill station until John's holiday, and then choosing the cheaper less prestigious summer venue of Dalhousie. Since there were only three or four English women left in Lahore during the summer months, Alice found herself predominantly in masculine company and she made good use of the opportunities presented to secure work for her son. The new parent newspaper of the Allahabad *Pioneer* was the *Civil and Military Gazette* which was published in Lahore. Alice saw this as the obvious target for her attentions because Rudyard would then be able to live at home with them. So persuasive were the Kipling parents that 'Nickson' (the pseudonym Rudyard occasionally used in his journalism, based on his father's) was offered immediate employment. Alice made it clear that her son was to finish his term at school and come to India on a monsoon passage so that he should not have to endure an Indian summer immediately, as she and John had had to seventeen years earlier. Trix at fourteen was far too young, in her mother's opinion, to be able to withstand the rigours of the Indian climate, so she was obliged to remain behind. It was a separation she hated, and only the promise that her mother would collect her the following spring and an arrangement that she could spend part of her school holidays in the Worcestershire countryside with the Baldwins made the situation at all palatable.

Rudyard was apprehensive about returning to a country and parents he barely knew, and not until Trix belatedly joined them in December 1883 did the clouds disappear. Rudyard wrote enthusiastically of that period: 'We delighted more in each other's society than in that of strangers and when my sister came out, a little later, our cup was filled to the brim. Not only were we happy, but we knew it.'[15] Trix's memories of those years also confirmed this: 'Just at the time when most boys cast off home life, Rudyard returned to it like a duck to its pond. I really believe that the happiest time of his life – and mine – was when we all lived together after I came out to Lahore.'[16] Alice was also profoundly happy for the first time since she had arrived in India. They all feared the many years of separation would lead to problems and disappointments, but absence had indeed made their hearts grow fonder, and there was a determination that nothing should destroy the 'family square'.

The room John decorated for his daughter's return almost overwhelmed her, though it was a far cry from the Morris furnishings she had been accustomed to at Aunt Georgie's.

> A beautiful room he had designed for me was waiting me with its lacquered furniture patterned in graffito, its high dado of Indian cotton, and its charming painted fire place where my initials were so twined among Persian flowers and arabesques that they seemed part of the design – I had never had a room of my own, really furnished for me before, and it all seemed part of the magic. My father's pet ravens Jack and Jill, the little grey squirrel on the creeper covered trellis and my brother's bull terrier Buzz, carried on the enchantment.[17]

Now that the family square was complete, all insisted on doing everything together, and reports of their evening entertainments sound very reminiscent of earlier Macdonald ones. Trix recalled that literary activities were the most popular (music could never be considered because she was tone-deaf and unable, she said, to distinguish 'God Save the Queen' from 'Home Sweet Home'). Shakespearian evenings were an especial favourite, when all talk during the evening had to comprise quotations from the bard. As Trix inherited her mother's excellent memory, she fared well, but with his talent for improvisation Rudyard would try and catch the rest of the family out by inventing lines. The Kiplings' familiarity with Shakespeare proved an unexpected social asset in Anglo-Indian society, as one contemporary recalled: 'There was a great run on Shakespeare and after dinner some selected play . . . would be read . . . each person taking the part assigned to him or her.'[18]

There was an even greater emphasis on writing within the Kipling family than there had been in Alice's childhood. Both John and Alice saw their works published, and Rudyard became assistant editor of the *Civil and Military Gazette*, despite the son of one of the proprietors recalling in the *Pioneer*'s anniversary edition: 'As a journalist Rudyard Kipling was far from being a great success. His father had induced my own father and the other proprietors of the two papers to give the young Rudyard a post on the Lahore paper. But in the day-to-day business of journalism Kipling did not by any means shine.'[19] It only left Trix to make her mark on the publishing scene, though it even seems possible that Trix had already seen her work in print. In a letter to Margaret Burne-Jones, Rudyard referred to various stories of his sister's which he had had printed and was proposing to send his cousin. Within the family group there followed a great outpouring of both prose and poetry. The family's first month's holiday together at the hill station at Dalhousie in the summer of 1884 saw the production of *Echoes*. This was a collection of verse parodies written by Rudyard and Trix under the supervision of Alice, printed at the offices of the *Civil and Military Gazette* and sold at the end of that year. The following summer, when all four Kiplings were together at Simla for a month, led to a joint effort called *Quartette*, featuring contributions from them all, and this was once again published and sold from the newspaper offices in Lahore.

Rudyard was delighted with the close attention his mother gave to his writing, as a letter to Margaret Burne-Jones reveals: 'I believe I can honestly say that Polo is the only thing I keep from her and by the same token the only thing outside the office work that she has not the fullest authority in and uses it, bless her.'[20] Rudyard, so long deprived of any sort of helpmate, was only too willing to let his mother have the full rein she wanted. She acted as first reader, editor, censor and critic of his work during these years; she was never one to mince her words, 'with now and then some shrivelling comment that infuriated me', Rudyard wrote later, 'but as she said, "There's no Mother in Poetry, my Dear" '.[21]

His father, though generally a more indulgent person than his mother, seems to have approached Rudyard's work in a surprisingly objective manner. He told Margaret Burne-Jones:

It is of less than no use snarling at Ruddy. The temptations to vulgar smartness, to over emphasis and other vices are tremendous. One test of success here is frequent quotation by other papers. The boy is much quoted but it is not always his best work. I was personally sorry *Quartette* came out but he set himself to it so eagerly I didn't like to baulk him. I hoped someone would rap his knuckles for the unwholesomeness of 'The Phantom Rickshaw' and the coarseness of 'The Tragedy of Teeth' and some other reasons – notably my own share, written years ago to pass time when I was recovering from typhoid, but the Indian press has only given praise, his

139

knuckles await rapping. I'm too near, too little of a judge and too personally interested in his eager vivid life to do much. Anything from you or his aunt would sink deep. No need to fear hurting him, he has the sweetest nature possible so far as criticism is concerned. None of us here hesitate to express opinions and we talk in the plainest frankest way.[22]

This applied most certainly to Alice.

Trix recalled the complaints her mother levelled at Rudyard for his handling of women characters in *Plain Tales from the Hills*. 'No, Ruddy, no! Not That!' 'But it's true,' he protested. 'Never mind; there are lots of things that are true that we never mention,' came the retort.[23] Indeed it seems that many of the comments Rudyard wrote about women in that book caused his mother anxiety: 'It's clever and subtle and all that and *I* see the morality in it but, O my boy, how do *you* know it? Don't tell me about "guessing in the dark". It is an insult to your old Mother's intelligence. If Mrs Hauksbee enlightened you, I'm not sorry that she has gone home,' was the parting comment about a character in the book who was known to be based on a real lady in Simla.[24] Others by contrast praised Rudyard's understanding of the female mind, remarking: 'What a lot you must have taught your son about women.' 'On the contrary,' Alice snapped back, 'what a lot my son has taught me!'[25]

It could not have been easy for Rudyard to accept the strict discipline his mother expected to exert over him, but there were plenty of occasions when his newspaper work took him away from his mother's jurisdiction. What temptations he was prey to then are unknown, although during his first year back in the country one Indian leader tried to bribe him with money and then a Kashmiri girl. 'She was very handsome and beautifully dressed, but I didn't see how she was to be introduced into an English household like ours,' he wrote to his aunt Edith Macdonald with apparent innocence.[26] Alice's reception of such a paramour at Bikaner Lodge defies imagination!

Over the years Kipling scholars have tried to play down the influence that Alice Kipling had on her son's life and work, but this is to misunderstand the nature of the woman. She had grown into a formidable power, absolutely determined to shape her children's careers in the same way as she had her husband's, and none of the family thought of challenging her rights in the matter. Her effect on Rudyard's early writing can only have been for the good because she set the highest standards and would tolerate nothing slovenly or crudely expressed. Interestingly her opinions, like her work, were far less sentimental than her husband's. 'Nasty but powerful,' was her verdict on one story which she recommended for publication, whilst another she demolished totally with the command: 'Never do that again.'[27] Rudyard inherited his mother's sharp eye for the amusing foibles of human nature, which ultimately, under her guidance, brought him overnight fame.

1885 was the first year that summer was spent by all four Kiplings at Simla. Alice had taken the young Trix to Dalhousie (or Dullhouses as her daughter called it) the previous year, but Simla was the only hill station which mattered in Anglo-Indian society. It was situated right on the edge of the Himalayas, some two hundred and forty miles from Lahore, and as Rudyard explained to Aunt Edie Macdonald: 'Simla is built round the sides of a mountain, 8,400 feet high and the roads are just ledges. At first they turned my head a good deal but in a little I was enabled to canter anyhow and anywhere.'[28] It was not an easy place to reach because, being too steep for the railway, the final fifty miles had to be traversed by pony or ox-cart. Alice found neither method congenial: 'The lady Mother is not good at these capers. She tires on rugged paths, steep as a house side,' came the report.[29] However, the rigours of the journey had to be endured by all who wanted to savour the 'delectable mountains'.

The season opened in April, when the weather was cool and log fires were still the order of the day. At this time the Viceroy and the whole Anglo-Indian government moved from Calcutta to the hills to stay until October. Whilst temperatures were lower than in the plains, where cholera regularly arrived with the heat, the rainfall was quite phenomenal at Simla. In the summer between thirty and forty inches a month was normal – 'it is so wet in Simla', Alice complained during her first stay in 1881, 'so suicide inciting these days of drifting mist, driving rain and concentrated misery'.[30] Only in September and October when most had already returned to the plains again did the climate become idyllic. The population at Simla fluctuated wildly with the seasons, for not only did a large contingent of Anglo-Indians arrive for the summer, but they also brought with them servants from the plains, because hill servants had a reputation for being good-for-nothing. Since Simla consisted only of steep hills, it was necessary for a memsahib to take three or four native servants purely to carry her around, pull her rickshaw or, if she chose to ride around the hill station, to run on ahead to the destination and stand there in all weathers holding her pony until she was ready to return. Accommodation in Simla was always extremely expensive and much sought-after. Top-ranking members of the Viceroy's entourage had their own permanent houses in the town, whilst others rented property for the season. Lower down the social scale, people like the Kiplings could only afford rooms in one of the hotels, although sometimes they were fortunate enough to have the use of James Walker's residence (proprietor of the *Civil and Military Gazette*) for a few weeks. Despite the expense, Alice regarded their annual sojourn there as a worthwhile investment in her children's future, because with the Viceroy and the Commander-in-Chief present for most of the season, the potential for advancement was limitless. The financial burden was eased in 1885 by Rudyard's official assignment to Simla by his newspaper and the extra allowance he received to enable him to participate in the social scene, which entailed as 'much riding, waltzing, dining out and concerts in a week as I should get at home in a life time', he reported to his cousin Margaret.[31]

Alice arrived in Simla with her daughter in May, whilst John was obliged to remain in Lahore until his leave in July. She determined to get both her son and daughter launched into viceregal circles by one method or another, for this was vital if they were to make any headway. Lord Lytton, who had been so kind to the Kiplings in former years, had finished his tour of duty and with him went their popularity, because his successor, Lord Ripon, was unimpressed by the Kipling style. The year 1884, however, saw the arrival of the next Viceroy, Lord Dufferin, a cultured Irishman, great-grandson of the dramatist Sheridan, a romantic and a dandy. 'If Lord Dufferin had not come I think poor Anglo-India would have gone crazy with vexation and apprehension,' John said, 'but we have no end of confidence in the new man.'[32] With the stars of Poynter and Burne-Jones very much in the ascendant, Alice Kipling knew she stood an excellent chance of creating the right impression, added to which the Irish blood in her Macdonald veins could conveniently be remembered.

Alice wasted no time making an impact, for the Viceroy was heard to declare: 'Dullness and Mrs Kipling were never in the same room together', and soon the Kipling family found their name added to the Viceroy's open list, which meant they were automatically invited to all social events.[33] Their comparatively low status was of no consequence to Dufferin, who was the most sociable Viceroy Simla had ever known, and his entertainments were larger and on a more splendid scale than his predecessors'. Not everybody agreed that the Kiplings should move in such exalted circles: John was incensed to read regular weekly criticism of his family in letters to the *Times of India* and *Indian Daily News*. Ironically, a Mr Macdonald, a former newspaper editor, was the perpetrator, using his retirement to settle old scores in public. His accusation that the Kiplings were social climbers was perfectly true. They were, however, little different in this respect from others, but it galled many to have to observe their obvious success.

The following season in Simla had the Anglo-Indian community agog at the sheer audacity of the Kipling females. Even their tall attractive daughter Trix had become as haughty as her mother, so that the shy sweet maiden called 'Rose in June' in Dalhousie earned the sobriquet 'The Ice Maiden' in Simla. She cared little now that she had Archie as her regular escort – the Viceroy's eldest son and aide-de-camp, Lord Clandeboye. As John had noticed soon after Trix's arrival in India, she always seemed more at ease amongst older men, probably as a result of a lack of friends her own age in England. Her undoubted beauty, to which both photographs and contemporary reports bore witness, meant she was never short of admirers. Her father enjoyed playing a small part in her success by designing outfits for her to wear at the latest viceregal extravaganza. 'I painted for her for the Calico Ball, a dress; white, light blue and dark blue with ornaments taken from Mooltan pottery, which she was supposed to represent,' he told Edith Plowden, 'and I hear it was a great success though I didn't see it put together.'[34]

Intimacy with such eminent people was not restricted to Trix, for John went on to describe the private drawing lessons he gave to Lady Helen Blackwood, Lord Dufferin's daughter, remarking that it was not at all uncommon for His Excellency to wander in unannounced to pass the time of day. 'Lord Dufferin, who frequently comes into our sketching room, professes to be greatly struck by the uncommon combination of satire with grace and delicacy, and what he calls the boy's [Rudyard's] "infallible ear" for rhythm and cadence.'[35] John had also taken responsibility for the Simla Ladies Sketching Club which met twice a week, the pretentiousness of whose members did not escape the bluff Yorkshire man: 'Have I the courage to say, "Believe me ladies, the greatest part of you are wasting your time and aiming at the impossible?" ' he asked Edith Plowden.[36] This question was naturally rhetorical, for in the honours given out at the beginning of the following year, John Lockwood Kipling became a Companion of the Indian

Empire for services to Indian art, which had of course covered a far wider span than the idle rich of Simla.

Alice was very satisfied with her family's achievements by the mid-1880s and settled down to reap the benefits. In a personal sphere she took an active part in the Simla Amateur Dramatic Society which put on fortnightly performances in the Gaiety Theatre located in the town hall building along with the library. Those Monday matinées were recognized social functions, receiving the Viceroy's invariable support and detailed coverage in the newspapers. One surviving photograph of these dramatic occasions shows Alice costumed in a Quaker hat in a performance of what was termed a *tableau vivant* – 'Auld Robin Grey' – and the other performers listed as several army officers and the daughter of the Commander-in-Chief. There are some photographs showing Trix acting alongside her mother; Rudyard also took part. Alice was also a regular participant in the Vicereine's philanthropic activities, one of which was a needlework class at the Simla Work Society, where the Simla correspondent for the *Civil and Military Gazette* noted that eighty ladies 'who have their social duties to attend to' stitched clothes for the poor, the orphans and the inhabitants of asylums. The correspondent concluded it was but 'a very small ripple in the ceaseless stream of charity at Simla'.[37]

The Kipling family provoked much gossip during the 1886 season, when the Viceroy's son proposed marriage to Miss Kipling. John and Alice were flattered, whilst the rest of Simla gleefully anticipated this presumptuous family's imminent come-uppance, for no matter how cultured these Kiplings considered themselves, marriage into the aristocracy was beyond the realms of possibility. Alice too was aware of that but did not lose her nerve when the Viceroy called to discuss his son's indiscretions. 'Don't you think, Mrs Kipling, your daughter should be taken to another hill station?' he began tactfully. 'Don't you think, Your Excellency, that your son should be sent home?' was her reply, and society watched in awed silence as Lord Clandeboye boarded the next boat to England.[38] Would nothing stop these Kiplings?

Amazingly, relations between the Dufferins and Kiplings were unaffected by this interlude, and those watching took good care not to upset the artist's wife who had the ear of the Viceroy, and whose lightning darts provided great amusement to all bar the victims. One young girl newly arrived on the social scene was described by Alice as 'nearly as big as her mother and crouching and stooping in such a ridiculous manner that presently I imagine she will go on all fours'. Another young hopeful was 'very plain till her cousin Mrs Lambert's daughter came – and by her transcending ugliness made Miss Black seem almost beautiful'. Those already established as married women did not escape: 'Mrs Young is evidently spared for more illnesses, as she is now recovering,' Alice told Edith Plowden. 'You will be shocked to hear that she is going to perpetuate her kind – these delicate women are wonderful and often accomplish feats of childbearing we strong ones shrink from. I daresay she will have quite a large family of incurables.'[39] It is a great pity Alice's letters to Louisa Baldwin are not extant!

The attention which Trix drew in society was perhaps a little too great for her mother's liking, for as Trix later told some relations, she was sure her mother was jealous of her success. Alice needed to be the centre of attention and was reminded of those former days when her attractive sister Agnes put her in the shade. Rudyard well understood his mother's feelings and scribbled a little poem in 1884 making it appear to come from Trix, in a well-meaning attempt to heal his mother's pride.

> The young men come, the young men go,
> Each pink and white and neat,
> She's older than their mothers, but
> They grovel at Her feet.
> They walk beside Her rickshaw-wheels –
> None ever walk by mine;
> And that's because I'm seventeen
> And she is forty-nine.[40]

In view of Alice's acute sensitivity to the merest hint about her age, this was a Rudyard effort *not* swiftly published around Simla!

There was no encouragement from Rudyard for Trix's amorous conquests, because he wanted his sister to make her name with her poetry rather than her beauty, which he saw as a threat to his own happiness. When Lord Clandeboye's successor, a young journalist, appeared on the scene, Rudyard vented the full force of his anger: 'You can't realize how savage one feels at a thing of this kind – an attempt to smash the Family Square and the child barely eighteen too.'[41] His own matrimonial prospects seem to have been heavily influenced by his adoration of his mother. 'When I marry it must be a lady well versed in domestic knowledge, not less than twelve years my senior, and by preference some other man's wife. Thus only can I hope to pass

145

gracefully from the comforts of the four square hearth to the comforts of "my own",' and though much of this was written with tongue in cheek, there was a fundamental truth in it. Another letter also spoke of 'the pearl' which he expected to find for a wife, who would be 'as sweet and as perfect and almost as old as my Mother'. The overwhelming affection Rudyard felt for this parent, which is evident from his correspondence, is summed up best by his remark: 'Love is a scarce commodity and I hold the best is a Mother's.'[42]

During 1887, it was apparent the family square was breaking down. Rudyard's journalistic talent had been recognized by the proprietors of the *Civil and Military Gazette* with the offer of a post on the more prestigious *Pioneer*. His delight was tempered by the knowledge that he would have to move eight hundred miles away from the family to Allahabad. This was opportune because, although he had enjoyed five happy years spent in the bosom of the family, he was rising twenty-two, and his mother still expected to maintain a strict control over almost every aspect of his life. In addition there was the likelihood that Trix too would leave, for that summer at Simla she became engaged to a Lieutenant John Fleming, although by the time she was ready to depart for Lahore in the autumn, the engagement was over. This was a relief to Rudyard because he disliked Fleming intensely. 'I believe in Trix immensely, but that wretched worm on the hook, Jack Fleming, is still allowed to write to the girl, whereby methinks he will enjoy in full those torments which were my share when I received a similar poem from Flo Garrard four years since,' he told Margaret Burne-Jones, referring to a girl for whom he had cherished an affection since Southsea days. 'Trix seems to have made a choice which has not endured three months since he *jawâbed* (jilted). Let's hope the next lover will be better. For my little maiden I have nothing but sympathy because she's very sorry and upset in her poor little mind.'[43]

With Alice's encouragement, the Fleming attachment trickled on, and the following summer the engagement was renewed. Alice thought that marriage would dispel some of the dark worries which beset her daughter. For all her beauty, Trix was the definitive introspective personality, with few female friends and a heavy dependence on her mother. Problems arose when she joined in the vogue for spiritualism at Simla. Unlike Alice, who had been able to enjoy a little table-turning in her youth without ill-effect, Trix was more highly-strung and tended towards unhealthy self-analysis.

146

Several years before, Simla society had flirted with the celebrated Madame Blavatsky and her theosophy; messages were said at the time to float down from the ceiling on palm leaves and teacups materialize under bushes. John had attended one of her séances and declared Madame 'one of the most interesting and unscrupulous imposters' he had ever met.[44] In the Simla drawing-rooms such psychic phenomena were regarded merely as a novel way of passing a dreary wet afternoon. Alice was more tolerant of this hocus-pocus than one might suppose because its practitioners cleverly appealed to her pride, telling her what great supernatural powers she had inherited from her Highland ancestors. Flattery always worked with Alice, and though she knew both husband and son strongly disapproved, she continued to dabble and encouraged her daughter to do likewise. It is said that Trix became extremely competent at reading a crystal ball she acquired – a singular heirloom which has passed down the family to the present day. Sadly the crystal ball was unable to warn Trix of the problems which lay ahead of her, and continual practice with it led in Rudyard's judgement to her mental breakdowns: 'This soul-destroying business of spiritualism has affected her mind profoundly,' he was to write as late as 1927, but a proneness to emotional instability was recognized by her mother before Trix ever returned to India.[45]

Spiritualism and Fleming were a lethal combination actively encouraged by Alice in the face of opposition from husband and son. It worried Alice that Trix never chose male friends her own age, for her dancing partners were usually older married men and thus unavailable as potential husbands. Perhaps remembering her own youth wasted on broken love affairs, Alice took up the cause of Lieutenant John Mureluson Fleming, one of the few eligible suitors who had appeared. He was a soldier seconded to the Survey Department in Mussoorie, and at thirty, only ten years Trix's senior, but John was uneasy about this alliance. He told a friend:

> Trix has renewed her engagement to John Fleming and I don't like it. She has knitted up the ravelled sleeve at Simla and they sprang it on me suddenly, the week before I was leaving Lahore [for England]. Came the young man eager for an answer, powdering down from Simla to Lahore for half an hour's talk with their [Trix and Alice's] sanction. What could I say or do? I only hope with all my heart the child is right and that she will not one day when it is too late find her Fleming but a thin pasture and sigh for other fields.[46]

John's brief encounters with Fleming had shown him sufficient to realize that the couple's interests diverged widely. John thought him a dour Scot with no interest in art or literature, but Alice was swayed by his Highland pedigree.

The marriage of Trix Kipling to John Fleming followed on 11 June 1889 at Simla, but Rudyard's absence was conspicuous. In a manner reminiscent of his uncle Edward Burne-Jones, Ruddy could not bring himself to watch whilst one of his favourites was given to another man. Moreover the time had come for him to spread his own wings. The period spent at Allahabad had eased Rudyard away from his family, although he still regarded his mother with deep affection: 'I go to Lahore next Monday and by Wednesday will be with Mother again,' he told his friends in Allahabad. 'She, the Mother, is very anxious to see me again and I confess that I should like to feel her arms round me once more before I go.'[47] But Alice found difficulty in accepting Rudyard's new-found independence. 'Living alone has made you so old and uninterested,' she told him, adding: 'You'll have to be civil, Ruddy.'[48] As the fault-finding persisted, Rudyard said, 'I knew in verity that I had come back to the old life and the way thereof. But not wholly for it is owned that I am no longer ownable, and only a visitor in the land. The Mother says it is so and the Sister too and their eyes see far – "You belong to yourself" says the Mother and the Maiden says: – "You don't belong to us at any rate" '.[49] Such remarks hurt from people he cared deeply about, and since submission was no longer possible, a clean break from the claustrophobia of the family square was the sensible solution. In March 1889, just three months before Trix's wedding, Rudyard embarked for America, with friends from Allahabad.

In the October of that year, Rudyard paid a visit to the long-forgotten Harry Macdonald, the uncle he had never met. Harry was then aged fifty-four and destined only to live another two years. 'My uncle reminds me pathetically from time to time that I am the only one of his blood-kin who has come to him for thirty years; speaks of me as "my boy" and yarns away about literature. The Aunt, who does not care for books, is different, but I am making good headway there.'[50]

It was to his other uncles and aunts that Rudyard repaired later that year, when he moved from America to England, and although he enjoyed being taken into society by the Poynters, it was with Aunt Georgie he felt most at ease. Despite the many years he had spent in England, everything seemed alien to Rudyard, and he too suffered an awkward emotional adjustment to this new life. Only the arrival of his mother in London helped him through his problems. John and Alice came to England in 1890 to put in hand Her Majesty's commission for an Indian room at Osborne House. This was to be their last holiday in England before John's tour of duty ended in 1893, and so thoughts were already turning to resettling in England. Pleas on John's part to allow Stanley Baldwin to go back out to India with them to widen his experience fell on deaf ears at Wilden, but to everyone's surprise Edith Macdonald announced that she would accompany her sister and brother-in-law for twelve months in 'the gilded orient', as Rudyard described it to her. Alice, who felt lost without her son and daughter to look after, was delighted at the prospect of her youngest sister's company.

The reality of India proved nearly fatal to Edith at the modest age of forty-two, because she promptly fell prey to one of the familiar fevers and expected the same medical attention that Louisa received at home. John, normally the most patient of men, became exasperated by his sister-in-law's insistence that she was dying and by the regular visits of the Bishop of Simla to administer the last rites. 'Alice and Trix are a good deal worn and knocked up by incessant watching and nursing, for not half an hour passes but she asks for something. Both Doctor and Nurse say they have never seen a case like it, for fever so bad and so long continued generally leaves the patient with very little will even tho' the head be clear,' he told a friend, 'But with Edie her constant cry is – "Now give me something, I am sinking." And she has been able to take nourishment and stimulant enough for a man at work.'[51] It was with thankfulness on all sides that Edith finally recovered enough to sail back to England.

Alice and John had celebrated their fifty-sixth birthdays by the time they packed up their belongings to return to England. Alice felt little regret at leaving the country she had consistently hated since her arrival, but she could not help but be proud of her family's achievements. John was the recognized expert on Indian art, and Rudyard the star of the London literary scene. The England which she and John had left so eagerly twenty-eight years before was still very much home in Alice's mind, and moreover now housed Rudyard and Trix, when Fleming's duties permitted. There also awaited her the other Macdonald sisters, whose love and faithfulness Alice hoped to regain after such a long interval.

Chapter Eleven

Middle Age
(1880–1900)

The four husbands of the Macdonald sisters were able to point to considerable achievements in their respective fields by their middle years, receiving public recognition and enjoying general acclaim. Their wives were thus freed from financial and family constraints and given the opportunity to develop their own interests.

First to be honoured was John Lockwood Kipling when in 1887 he became a Companion of the Indian Empire. Alice was elated: John undoubtedly deserved the decoration, but more importantly she felt sure her sisters could no longer dismiss Kipling as a second-rate artist. The honour, only one step from a knighthood, was proof of his ability and the esteem in which he was held. It also encouraged her to set her sights higher. No firm plans had yet been made for their retirement to England, so she believed it still within the realms of possibility that greater rewards might yet fall to John, especially since the Duke and Duchess of Connaught were now residing in India. One immediate result of the royal presence was a commission for John to decorate the Duke's billiard-room at Bagshot House in Surrey. The carved panels were admired by the Duke's mother, Queen Victoria, and led to a far more important appointment to design and execute an Indian dining-room for Her Majesty at Osborne House, which Kipling's quotation shows cost £2,250. During the Kiplings' sojourn in England early in the 1890s, John was presented to the Queen as a friend from India of Prince Arthur, Duke of Connaught. This was to be the summit of the Kipling pater's social achievements, whilst in the literary field English publication in 1891 of his book *Man and Beast in India* was noteworthy. Alice revelled in her husband's success, knowing none of her sisters' husbands had yet been able to equal it.

Burne-Jones took the step of hyphenating his name in 1885 purely for the purpose of identification, as he tried to explain to his old friend F.G. Stephens: '. . . not from pride dear Steev, but solely from dread of annihilation'.[1] Alice had her own opinions about that, but was hardly in a position to say anything, since she had persuaded John to adopt his mother's more distinctive family name of Lockwood in preference to the common John by which he was known within the family. Irrespective of his prestigious-sounding surname, Burne-Jones's work enjoyed great popularity during the 1880s, so that both commissions and money flowed more freely. From a personal point of view, he always felt in calmer waters and able to control the emotional attraction he always felt towards his models. Under these more auspicious circumstances his painting flourished, and public recognition of his talent came in 1894 when the outgoing prime minister Gladstone was instrumental in bringing about a baronetcy for him. As a result of personal friendship with Gladstone's daughter Mrs Mary Drew, Burne-Jones liked and respected him as he did few other politicians, yet still had grave reservations about accepting such an honour. To be known henceforth as 'Sir Edward' went against everything he professed. Even when he had finally made up his mind, he told a friend that it was not without a pang that he left the working class. In answer to de Morgan's enquiry Burne-Jones mischievously replied 'why did I accept the baronetcy? To please Morris!' and went on to say that his friend's continual invectives against the bourgeoisie irritated him and he would be delighted if in the future the title the Right Reverend Mr Morris was given to him.[2] As Edward guessed, Morris was disgusted that his friend should have gone over to the other side, but, Burne-Jones pleaded: 'How am I to remain a Liberal? All my friends are Tories: the Tories are such dear chaps.'[3] Edward's dilemma about the baronetcy was intensified by Georgie, whose views concurred with Morris's. Although it pleased her to see Edward's work given the status she always knew it warranted, Georgie was wholeheartedly committed to socialism and believed such honours were wrong. If it had not been for the strong argument which Philip Burne-Jones put forward in favour of accepting the distinction for the sake of future generations – and himself in particular – the title would never have been taken. Nevertheless it remained something of an embarrassment, and on first hearing himself addressed by his full title, the baronet retorted bitterly: 'I wonder it doesn't stick in your throat.'[4] Georgie could generate no enthusiasm for something so contrary to her principles, and even Edward's designs for the new crest and motto were ignored: 'I scarcely dare tell Georgie, so profound is her scorn,' he told a friend.[5]

Poynter, who unlike Burne-Jones had all the demeanour of a titled man, was not thus honoured for a further two years, yet his reputation as an establishment man grew steadily. He painted and exhibited with robotic regularity, collecting public offices as he went. He moved up the Royal Academy ladder to be its President in 1896, with other appointments such as Slade Professor of Art at University College, London, and Director of Art at South Kensington on the way. Georgie Burne-Jones became his unexpected champion in 1894 when his name was put forward for the directorship of the National Gallery. A letter from her ladyship to the Earl of Carlisle, George Howard (the husband of Georgie's dear friend Rosalind) contained the following request: 'Mary Drew tells Edward that *now* is the time when a letter from you to her father [Gladstone] about Poynter would she believes have great weight.'[6] Carlisle's letter was obviously forthcoming because within six weeks the post was offered and had been accepted. Support for this unendearing brother-in-law arose not through the family connection but because Georgie believed him the best man for the job. Poynter received his accolade, a knighthood, in 1896, the same year as his presidency of the Royal Academy, but Alice was quick to observe that it was only a knighthood and he had thus not yet reached the level of Burne-Jones; however in 1902 the honour was upgraded into a baronetcy. Agnes had always longed to be addressed as 'Your Ladyship', believing this to be a distinct advantage, but by the time it came to pass, her interest in the social scene had waned. She was haunted by health problems which led to an early death, and her time was now spent more in the spa towns of England and Europe than in London drawing-rooms.

Louisa was only too aware that she stood little chance of receiving a title, since ironmastery, though lucrative, was never more than a 'respectable' trade. But such things had ceased to concern her, as both she and Alfred had set their sights on spiritual rather than earthly rewards. In any case Alfred Baldwin was held in great respect in Worcestershire and was the recipient of various minor public offices, culminating in his adoption as Conservative candidate for the Bewdley division, whence he was returned unopposed to Parliament in 1892. As a wealthy man and very much the 'lord of the manor' in Wilden, he took his responsibilities seriously and had a genuine regard for the welfare of his workpeople. Their spiritual needs were regarded as paramount, and so in 1882 he was moved to build a church in the village at an initial cost of £3,000, then to endow it and the parsonage from his own pocket. Two years later he arranged the building of a village school adjacent, and both institutions were entirely supported financially by the Baldwin family until recent times. Such enterprises offered scope for Louisa's talents, but she was so taken up with her own infirmity that she had no interest outside herself. Georgie in fact had a far better idea of what was happening at Wilden Church than Louie, because Alfred took advice from Burne-Jones and William Morris on ecclesiastical decoration. Wilden Church remains one of the best examples of Morris and Co.'s* church work because every window was designed and manufactured by them; the gold altar frontal now displayed in a case on the wall was designed by Morris especially for Edith Macdonald to embroider, and the angel drapes which adorn the altar at Easter bear testimony, like the windows, to the skill of Burne-Jones. It is most fitting that Wilden Church contains the only memorials to all of the Macdonald sisters together.

Although Louisa's horizons were usually limited to her sick bed, in literary matters she did look further afield, especially when a few of her short stories and poems appeared in magazines. These were followed by four longer works published as books, some paid for privately and others assisted by Rudyard: 'I've written to Methuen telling them to look out for a collection of stories from you and advising them to read them,' he told her as yet another parcel of manuscripts arrived for his appraisal.[7] To the modern reader, the works of Mrs Alfred Baldwin are uninspiring. They join the clutter of consciously literary and patronizing moral writings which now gather dust in second-hand book-shops. Although Louisa tried her hand at children's stories, adult short stories, novels and poetry, she never displayed any of the talent of her famous nephew. Her collection of ghost stories *The Shadow on the Blind* probably represents the pinnacle of her achievements, for the sinister and supernatural intrigued Louisa as much as Alice.

Some of the shortcomings of Louisa's writing arose from her narrow life where no new experiences fuelled her imagination. She had made herself so housebound in Wilden that Miss Edith Macdonald became the recognized escort of Mr Alfred or Master Stanley, and many people forgot Mrs Alfred's existence. For Edith this meant an opportunity to enjoy a status she never imagined possible when left to care for her

---

* Morris, Marshall, Faulkner and Company became Morris & Co. in 1875.

ageing parents, and it made her all the more determined to live life to the full. She took an active interest in the welfare of the villagers, participated in events at the village school and Sunday school, surprised many by becoming the first female churchwarden, supervised the running of Wilden House, attended to the needs of her nephew whilst at home and school and still succeeded in being at the beck and call of Louisa.

Boredom undoubtedly lay at the root of Louisa's problem. Despite the Baldwins' position of authority in Wilden, which should have enabled Louisa to carve a niche for herself distributing benevolence in the manner of Lady Bountiful, it was not sufficient to satisfy the talents of someone like Louisa. She could not help but yearn for the stimulating London cultural scene which two of her sisters enjoyed. When Alfred's position as Member of Parliament for Bewdley took him away from home for the parliamentary sessions, Louisa urged the leasing of an apartment so that she could stay in the capital. Although too indisposed to be seen around Worcestershire, Louisa roused herself sufficiently to join her husband in London, where she passed the time doing the rounds of eminent physicians, taking bizarre treatments in expensive nursing homes, and having tea with her sisters Agnes and Georgie. When exhaustion overcame her, she returned to the waiting bathchair in Worcestershire.

Georgie showed surprising sympathy and indulgence towards this 'invalid sister', as she called Louisa, although in letters to friends she spoke of the tedium of 'those people who are stronger than they seem',[8] and to Rosalind Howard she urged: '*Don't* let us all become the dreaded invalids about whom you and I once exchanged sentiments!'[9] But, like all those closest to Louisa, she never questioned her sister's illness, and in 1881, Georgie reported to Rosalind that for several days they despaired of Louie's life, but that Louisa had recovered thanks to the well-meaning sympathy of husband and sisters. Georgie was closer to Louie than any of her sisters, remembering that it had been Louie who had come to her aid in Oxford after Edward's infidelity. Georgie said of her feelings for Louie: 'She and I have always been deeply attached to each other, but we have developed along different lines and much that gives me help does not feed her and vice versa – but it is wonderful what chasms love will span.'[10] The chasm that had to be bridged in this case was not illness but religion. Louisa, like her mother, allied her hypochondria to obsessive religious observances which appear to an outsider as an excuse to indulge in futile self-examination. Georgie had given up formal religion on her marriage, but retained strong personal convictions which provided the strength she required from time to time. Louisa, by contrast, was ostentatious in her rituals, receiving regular personal ministry from the new curate at Wilden, reading as many tracts and personal testimonies as her mother and liberally besprinkling her writing with texts. All this was now alien to Georgie.

Agnes might have also fallen prey to the same problems as Louisa had she not discovered a new focus for her affection. The birth of a second son Hugh in January 1882 was not 'the dread event' Agnes anticipated, but rather her salvation. It had been a great embarrassment to find herself pregnant at thirty-nine, some fifteen years after Ambrose's birth, and an even greater one when the child arrived two months prematurely after Aggie felt the onset of labour at the house of one of Edward's important patrons. The whole episode provoked much amusement and gossip at Poynter's expense, leading to speculation as to whose baby it really was; few people could credit that the pompous forty-six-year-old artist was still so amorous. Rumours about Hugh Poynter's illegitimacy have clouded his name down to the present day, although his paternity was quite evident by the 1960s when, like two previous generations of Poynter males, he went completely blind.

As the other Macdonald sisters settled into comfortable middle age, Georgie Burne-Jones, armed with a confidence and energy which had previously eluded her, decided to enter public life. Her early Methodist training had taught her that it was everyone's duty to serve the community in some way, whilst close friendship with people like Morris, Ruskin, and Rosalind Howard channelled Georgie's thinking along socialist rather than Methodist lines. The Social Democratic Federation and Socialist League had her interest and sympathy during Morris's involvement, but she never felt compelled to participate as actively as Morris's daughter May. Much of this stemmed from her own reluctance to be in the limelight, as well as a private belief that for all Morris's rousing speeches and noisy rallies little impact was made on the people whom it was intended to help.

Her own entrée into public life arose from a request made to Edward to lend support to the South London Art Gallery. This enterprise had evolved from an initiative by Ruskin in the 1850s aimed at bringing education to the working classes. Since the working classes were identified as living mainly in South London, it was decided to move the working men's college across the Thames to Blackfriars Road, and there it developed into a free library with a loan collection of pictures decorating the walls. Despite such humble beginnings, the Art Gallery attracted auspicious patronage from Gladstone and Leighton. The help of popular names like Burne-Jones and Watts was sought in 1887 as part of a declared policy for the art gallery

> to grow until it becomes the National Gallery of South London, not dependent on subscriptions collected with difficulty, but supported by the nation as a public art gallery, placed where it is most wanted, where the daily lives of the people most need such refreshment, and where the great artisan class, whose work beautifies the wealthier part of the metropolis, live with so little of beauty either natural or derived from art.[11]

Edward had no hesitation in sponsoring such a noble project through donations, the loan of his pictures for exhibition and service on the gallery's committee. To Georgie this was a real opportunity to put socialism into practice and, along with the wife of George Watts, she volunteered her help.

Her enthusiasm astonished Edward, because his wife was not content with merely attending meetings, but went out and urged Edward's patrons to give money and lend some of their art collections for exhibition. Even the distinctly Tory Sir Edward Poynter found himself under pressure from Georgie to open the gallery's first travelling exhibition of pictures in his capacity as President of the Royal Academy. With meticulous attention to detail, Georgie personally undertook much of the organization, including the mundane but necessary tasks of collecting the works, arranging the insurance cover and getting pictures suitably framed. 'I haven't seen Georgie for days,' Edward moaned to Watts. 'She's under a heap of Rossiter's [Treasurer of the Art Gallery] correspondence for the last seven years. I can see only the top of her head, I believe she is pretty well.'[12] Georgie was then in her fifties and had at last discovered a penchant for committee work which generated abundant vigour in her tiny frame. She 'commands and forbids with increasing energy . . . and looks younger than she has done for many years', Edward complained wearily.[13] So passionately did she believe in the whole concept of a South London art gallery that during 1894 Georgie was perfectly happy to serve as the only woman member on a small committee convened to pass the ownership of the gallery over to the local authority. 'I cannot tell you what trouble it has taken to transfer the whole thing to public control and establish it – but it is done at last,' she wrote proudly to George Howard.[14]

Without question Georgie Burne-Jones thrived when she had a cause to espouse, and the new Local Government Act of 1894 offered a perfect opportunity. Under the terms of the Act, villages with over three hundred inhabitants were permitted to elect a parish council to manage those affairs outside the Church's jurisdiction. At a time when women were not enfranchised, it is surprising to find that not only could they vote in parish elections, but they could also put themselves forward as candidates. For Lady Burne-Jones it was the occasion she had longed for to put into effect those socialist principles she so fervently believed in, and to the astonishment of family and friends, Georgie put herself forward as an Independent candidate for the parish of Rottingdean (it being unusual at that time for candidates to have a specific party allegiance). Edward was dumbfounded by the energy which emanated from his tiny wife: 'She is so busy – she is rousing the village – she is marching about – she is going like a flame through the village,' he reported to a friend.[15] Activities which took the teetotal Georgie into all the Rottingdean public houses canvassing electors did not meet with Edward's approval, but he could not help admire her determination in the face of apathy and even abuse. The 'Open Letter to the Electors of Rottingdean' which she wrote, had printed and distributed around the village he thought most impressive, and insisted in showing it to visitors at the Grange in Fulham, demanding constantly: 'What do you think of our Georgie?'[16] When polling day arrived, he went down to Rottingdean to lend her moral support and was heard to cheer loudly when she was returned, the only woman amongst nine men.

This minority position did not daunt her: 'Women can think and understand in matters that men would pass over. In private life women are often like the mortar between bricks – they hold the house together – men know this and expect it of them: and I hope before long it will seem just as natural to them to consult women at the Parish Council about things they understand as it is now to do so by the fireside,' she wrote in a subsequent letter to the electorate.[17] These feminist ideas, inculcated by George Eliot and Rosalind Howard, might have appeared common sense to Georgie Burne-Jones, but were too advanced for the women of Rottingdean and it was several years before another woman could be persuaded to join her on the council.

Her political allegiance was openly paraded in Rottingdean, as one of her pamphlets declared: 'In this particular village for instance there are more working people than any other class, but as they have not sent one of themselves to the Council this year it is not properly representative of Rottingdean. It will be as it is in Parliament, when working men send rich members to represent them. They may enter the House of Commons with the best intentions in the world always to vote for the good of their Constituents; but when a division comes they cannot help seeing the matter through their own spectacles and that is very seldom in the same way that a working man would see it.'[18] Coming from a titled lady, remarks like these sounded dangerously radical to the Rottingdean gentry and were quite incomprehensible to the ordinary villagers.

Support of a sort for Georgie's political venture was forthcoming from her son Philip, then aged thirty-four and dallying with an art career in London. Whilst his mother was serving on a committee investigating the enclosure of a public footpath, Philip stirred up public opinion against the landowner by a strongly worded letter to the local newspaper, followed up by a moonlight sortie to uproot the offending posts and wire and throw the debris back on to the owner's property. Such overzealousness required careful handling on Georgie's part to prevent legal action and discredit for her work.

Although Lady Burne-Jones's electioneering platform was both socialist and feminist, minutes of parish council meetings indicate that her activities were hardly radical, being concerned with the provision of street lighting, allotments, a fire brigade and similar communal facilities, in perfect harmony with her fellow-councillors. She did, however, initiate the idea of a paid village nurse: 'It was done simply as a thank-offering after the birth of my only daughter's first child, and it was a satisfaction to me that the Nurse was one of our own villagers, for it encouraged me in a belief I have that men and women can be found in Rottingdean and other villages who are capable of learning anything that can be taught them,' she wrote, in a clear echo of the philosophy of William Morris, then in poor health near the end of his life and able to lend no more than moral approval for his friend's actions.[19]

Participation in village life increased Georgie's love of the place, and when Aubrey Cottage adjoining their own Prospect House came up for sale in 1889, she persuaded Edward to buy it and convert the two into a larger home, spacious enough to accommodate the regular visits of family and friends. Their extended home was called North End House, a name derived from the road where they lived in Fulham and their geographical position in the village. To Georgie Rottingdean was home, but to Edward it was never more than an occasional retreat, and he eschewed involvement with the inhabitants and village life in general. Georgie's affection for the little seaside village was transmitted to members of her family, and Rottingdean became a focus for the Macdonalds and their offspring. Louisa and Agnes rented houses around the village green for a few weeks most summers, and all four women were able to revive their delight in sisterly company for the first time in seventeen years in the summer of 1882, when Alice was home on furlough from India to collect her daughter Trix. Even though their views had diverged widely over the years, they made conscious efforts to rediscover common ground. Macdonald family connections with Rottingdean were further strengthened by the next generation, when Margaret Burne-Jones's wedding took place there, as did Stanley Baldwin's to the daughter of Aunt Georgie's wealthy neighbours, the Ridsdales; and Rudyard Kipling, returning to England from America, brought his wife and family to live opposite 'the beloved aunt'.

When Alice and John Kipling returned for the last time from India in 1893, there was speculation in the family whether they too would settle in Rottingdean, but this did not come about. The Kiplings availed themselves of Georgie's hospitality for their first few months in England, whilst they assessed their position, but they decided eventually there was little to interest them in that locality. After living abroad for so long they felt no allegiance to any particular area and wanted to decide the matter to their best advantage. London was considered, but Alice did not relish the idea of being seen merely as the poor relations of the Poynters and Burne-Joneses. After three months' procrastination, John and Alice announced their intention of taking a house in Tisbury, a village some dozen miles from Salisbury in Wiltshire. Without relatives or friends within a hundred miles it seemed a peculiar choice, but one which had been arrived at through careful planning. Close to the Kipling house, The Gables, was the impressive country seat of the Honourable Percy Wyndham. His mansion, called Clouds, was one of the main gathering places for a select group of aristocrats known as 'The Souls', and Alice, with daring presumption, felt sure John and herself would find a place in this group.

It was a bold move which offered little chance of success. 'The Souls', a loosely-knit circle of intellectuals, contained only the élite in society.

159

The Kiplings did not have the necessary breeding, and Alice was depending heavily on other points in their favour. Their son Rudyard had already achieved worldwide recognition as a writer and would thus be of special interest to the set. Moreover, both artist brothers-in-law had painted members of 'The Souls', although Burne-Jones was essentially the painter they admired. Through their generous patronage he became friendly with Percy and Madeline Wyndham and another key figure, Arthur Balfour, the future prime minister. Since the 1870s, Edward, Georgie and their children had been occasional weekend guests at some of the country houses of 'the Souls', although Georgie's attendance had almost ceased as she felt her political views were at odds with those of the group, and Morris was disparaging about association with such high Tories. Nevertheless it was noticeable that he did not refuse to execute their commissions; Clouds was designed by Phillip Webb in line with Morris's ideas and the interior almost totally furnished by Morris & Co.

None of these things affected Georgie's admiration for and friendship with Madeline Wyndham, whose quiet serious-mindedness had enabled her to become a reasonably accomplished artist, a needle-woman in the Morris tradition and, more significantly, a competent art enameller. A common interest in literature had also drawn the two women together, and Georgie was sufficiently encouraged to introduce Mrs Wyndham to her novelist friend, George Eliot, as somebody she greatly admired. Although Georgie's visits to Clouds were now very much in the past, her son and daughter maintained the friendships they had formed with younger members of the group. Margaret and her husband Jack Mackail, undeterred by political views which did not concur with their own, enjoyed the cultured atmosphere of 'Saturday to Mondays', and Philip Burne-Jones cultivated these people as he did all upper-class contacts, in the hope they might further his social ambitions.

There were in fact similar motives behind the appearance of the Kiplings on the fringe of this set, for after years of easy acceptance into viceregal circles, Alice was not prepared to retire into insignificance. In Lahore and Simla they exploited the fact that they were the only people of proven artistic merit in the small community. In London, this was not possible, but out in the provinces Alice felt they might well be able to resume a life similar to that they had left behind in India. Things did not get off to a good start. After the high life of Simla, Tisbury seemed dead. The Kiplings had no wish to become involved in village life and kept themselves aloof throughout the seventeen years they lived there. The Wyndhams spent much of their time at their London house and at first barely noticed the newcomers down the road. Worst of all, John was completely unable to come to terms with his new situation, as Rudyard reported to his cousin Margaret: 'Pater ties himself in knots over his house renting arrangements in Tisbury: he has a house on his hands he doesn't want and is very funny about it.'[20] Added to that, both Alice and John felt the cold terribly and were troubled by chilblains and various minor ailments which depressed them. Without the routine existence of the art school and museum, John was at a loss to fill his time and indulged in 'what I can only call obstinate idleness', as Alice remarked impatiently.[21] It took him several years to rediscover the delights of being a freelance artist. In the meantime he confided in an Anglo-Indian friend: 'I think my main grievance is the want of company and I fear I worry Alice a good deal by complaints of the loneliness and dullness of this sepulchre. It is true we are two – but I have a fidgetty craving for society, for somebody fresh to talk to.'[22] After many years of globetrotting, John found it hard to accept staying in one place, whereas Alice settled down gratefully. Once Rudyard was in America, John needed no further excuse. He hastened out to Vermont to be with his son, and together they explored part of Canada. John had no problem coping with Rudyard's formidable wife, Carrie: 'A good man spoiled,' he described her, but it was less easy for Alice who found herself confronted by a personality similar to her own. Carrie also found difficult the few months spent at Tisbury in the summer of 1894, so when the younger Kiplings returned to England to make a permanent home, it was to Rottingdean and the less abrasive company of Aunt Georgie that they turned.

Advancing years were mellowing Alice. Whilst John indulged his urge to travel, she went to visit her sisters. There was a determination on all sides to heal the differences of the past and 'dear old Alice' was welcomed by them all. Surprisingly Georgie and Alice, who had been closest in their youth, discovered they now differed the most in their opinions. Georgie's new political awareness meant that politics was a subject they had to try to avoid, but with the newspapers full of the colonial struggles in South Africa, it did not prove easy. Even the normally placid Burne-Jones held strong views on events in that area. 'Let's have no more dominant races, we don't want them – they only turn men into insolent brutes,' was one of his comments which Georgie recorded with pleasure, but which was like a red rag to a bull to the Kiplings.[23] Rudyard and his Uncle Edward respected each other's views and avoided confrontation, so they were able to delight in one another's company as of old.

The death of William Morris in October 1896 was a loss which deeply affected all the Macdonald sisters. Apart from Edward, he was their most important link with the days of their girlhood. Even Alice in India had retained some limited contact with him and, through her sisters, felt the bond to be unbroken. Louisa and Agnes's friendship with Morris had been sustained by correspondence and meetings with him at the Burne-Joneses, where his second home was. His declining health had been obvious to them all for some while: Georgie said, 'It is no shock – for we have watched it drawing near for a long time – but we know that the conditions of life are changed for us now.'[24] Summoning up the private religious convictions which had sustained her for so long, Georgie was able to view the future with optimism: 'Now we turn from his grave and find him still living, I believe his power is only just beginning to be recognised and that he will have more influence upon his fellow creatures in some ways than any man this century. I cannot yet realise the idea of loss as applied to him – and we who saw him so weary cannot grudge him his rest.'[25] Though distressed by the death of one whom she had dearly loved, for Edward's sake Georgie tried to maintain a cheerful exterior and set about ensuring Morris would not be forgotten by producing a suitable tribute: the Mackail biography. Dejected in spirit and low in health following Morris's death, but unlike her sister Louie, determined to make light of it all, Georgie made this reply to an invitation she wished to decline: 'Please don't say to *anyone* that it is a matter of health – but only of regretted impossibility – for I know the weary rumour that springs up immediately and exaggerates the simplest ailment. After seeing mortal illness one is shy of that.'[26]

When Margaret's letter arrived unheralded at Tisbury in 1898 with news of her father Edward Burne-Jones's death from a heart attack, there was complete disbelief. Louisa, staying with Alice at that time, passed the sad tidings on to Agnes saying that Georgie's death would have been more probable. As they mingled their tears and lamented their loss, Georgie took a more positive approach, thanking God that Edward had been permitted to die in her arms in the night and adding that perfect love cast out fear. Georgie summoned up astonishing powers of self-control, as Sydney Cockerell, who had been Morris's secretary, noted when he visited her a few days after Edward's death. She had 'that air of determined resignation that I had seen in her after Morris's death', he wrote. 'She was very well she said and very thankful to have known these two men, as she had known them.' Significantly she told him: 'We must pay for the wine that we have drunk,' an echo of her belief that happiness always had to be paid for by suffering.[27]

The interment of Edward's ashes was at Rottingdean, in a corner of the churchyard he had chosen the previous year, and as the ashes were lowered into the grave, Georgie came forward to place a small bunch of heart's-ease on the casket. Her simple gesture of love was made with the flowers Edward had included in her portrait fifteen years previously as the symbol of one who loves until death. In her hour of need Agnes was the only sister who came to her; Alice and Louisa did not feel strong enough. Georgie struggled on with life, attending parish council meetings as before: 'I am almost quite well bodily, and am thankfully accepting every mental and spiritual help that my nature can assimilate but it is such a time as every mortal to whom the like happens must go through by himself, and only God knows how he really fares,' she said bravely.[28] For all the sisters the deaths of William Morris and more especially Edward Burne-Jones were a reminder of their own mortality.

Chapter Twelve

The End of a Generation

Agnes was greatly troubled by the impending old age that all the sisters faced, for the resultant break-up of their sisterhood and the unbearable loneliness for the last to die lay on her mind. In a letter to Louisa she spoke of her worries but tried to make light of them by referring to one of their much-loved childhood fables about a fox trying to transport a gaggle of geese across the water in a small boat. This she said might hold the key to their plight if only she could remember how the story ended. There was a genuine concern for the welfare of all her sisters evident in Agnes's letter and in much of the correspondence which passed between the other sisters towards the end of the century. There emerged a new awareness of the sisterly bonds which united them, and this was further strengthened by the death in New York of Harry Macdonald, whose sad life was ended by cancer of the throat in 1891, at the age of fifty-six.

He had clung to the forlorn hope that he might one day return to England, if only to die, but when he made his plans known on diagnosis of the illness, doctors warned him that burial at sea was more likely than in the land of his birth. 'Come at once, my dear brother and see me for the last time,' he pleaded to Fred.[1] In response to this summons, both Fred and Rudyard set out for America. It proved too late, and they arrived unable to do more than offer condolences to his widow and attend to the formalities following the funeral.

Harry's life had been a tragic waste. He had ability, as the academic results in his youth showed, but was laden with guilt about the past and moved restlessly from one job to another. For a brief moment in 1859, the year after his arrival in New York, there was optimism in the family. He published his own translation of a French novel by Octave Feuillet, demonstrating that though he might not have inherited his grand-

164

father's religious fervour, he did have the same grasp of languages. Then doubts about his achievement seized him and effectively paralysed further effort; the book remains an isolated example of what might have been. The deeply ingrained Methodist creed, which demanded rigorous self-examination, gave him no peace, so that even his marriage to the uncomplicated, practical Caroline brought only limited happiness, because he feared he was unworthy of her.

The belief that he had failed the Macdonald family haunted him constantly and was in his eyes the cross he had to bear for his transgressions; it was made all the more painful by the way his sisters disassociated themselves from him, with no visits and few letters. Apart from contact on his trip to England in 1869, when he made his peace with his mother, he only ever saw Fred and two of his nephews again. The Reverend Frederic Macdonald, bound for a Methodist Conference in Cincinnati in 1880, spent a few days in New York and noted: 'Our brotherly affection had never diminished, but we had seen nothing of one another during a long period in which each of us had changed and developed in many respects.'[2] For Fred it was obviously a visit of duty, but Harry clung pathetically to this straw. Despite a lack of encouragement from his mother, Rudyard also renewed family ties with Harry, and Stanley Baldwin, sent out to America to stimulate transatlantic business for the Baldwin company, called on his unknown uncle. That was all Harry had to appease his guilt, and in a final sad letter to Louie he spoke of the love he had retained for all his sisters, as strong at the end of his life as in their childhood, a love he would take with him into eternity. The manner in which Alice had totally rejected him from the day he sailed for America in 1858 remained a deep wound. It had been his intention to seek her out and ask forgiveness, but with the passage of time the great gulf of silence overawed him. The reconciliation never took place, and Harry died as guilt-stricken and unhappy as he had lived. His sisters found it impossible to mourn a brother who had made their childhood a misery and then become a complete stranger.

The loss of Edward Burne-Jones affected them in an altogether deeper way, because Alice, Agnes, Louisa and Edith had accepted him as their brother from the start, and over the years all had grown far closer to him than to Harry or indeed Fred, who was set apart from the family by his calling in much the same way as their father. Edward's death plunged his sisters-in-law into despair, whereas Georgie showed a quiet determination to pick up the pieces and carry on for the short time she believed was allotted to her. Despite the problems their marriage had traversed twenty years earlier, Georgie's prediction that there was more than enough love between them to last a lifetime was proved true. She never swerved in her loyalty and affection for the person she had loved since childhood, and for all his infatuations Edward was totally dependent on her. He had been terrified she might die before him, for he knew that survival without her would be fraught with anguish. In the event, Georgie was able to draw comfort from the knowledge he was spared that, or the loss of his faculties which he also dreaded.

Another of Edward's great concerns in later life was that after his death someone might try to write a biography of him: 'You can tell the life of those who have fought and won and been beaten, because it is clear and definite – but what is there to say about a poet or an artist?'[3] A man's work must be his monument, Edward believed, though he was aware others would not be content with that. On one occasion only did he speak of his worries to Georgie and then asked her to write his life: 'For you *know*,' he said simply.[4] Once she recovered from the initial shock of her loss, she accepted the obligation. A letter written five months after Edward's death to the artist F. G. Stephens reveals her intentions:

> I have decided to write a memoir of my husband and to involve your help in the work – as I am doing that of other friends for no *one* person can ever pretend to be able to draw a faithful portrait of another, however near or dear. My wish is to be able to raise up and leave in the world some image of his personality apart from his work – though that of course must always remain the background to any record of his life – and to preserve as many of his own words as possible. . . . There are so few left now who can recall those early days when Gabriel was in his glory and Edward and Morris sat at his feet and rejoiced in his light.[5]

Writing aided Georgie's rehabilitation because she substituted work for grief and was able to delight in her memories: 'Some times I fairly lose myself in the past. What good days we have known, haven't we?' she told Stephens.[6] A purpose and a deadline – for Georgie firmly believed that her own life was drawing to a close – spurred her on and prevented her from sinking into mournful inactivity. With the enthusiasm and energy which distinguished her work in local politics, this woman of fifty-eight set herself a rigorous schedule. She admitted to Stephens it was tiring, 'but still a deep source of deep satisfaction'.[7] Her biography of her husband, entitled *Memorials of Edward Burne-*

Jones, was finally published in 1904 and is still regarded as the main source of information about the artist and his work, although of his personal life it has been said the book is as interesting for what it omits as for what it includes. The writing went on alongside routine parish council duties and extensive renovations to North End House at Rottingdean designed to improve living conditions for the servants. Georgie busied herself with local charities and the organization of a handicraft show in Rottingdean which she said had been requested by villagers who had read Mackail's life of Morris and were inspired to produce their own works of art.

Symbolic of the ending of her former life was the decision to give up the Grange in Fulham. Georgie had long felt her home to be Rottingdean, and with the lease of the Grange due for renewal, it seemed sensible to relinquish the large house. In the months immediately after Edward's death, it was not an easy decision, but Georgie was typically realistic: 'The pain of leaving the Grange is great, and these last days of it almost overwhelming, but I do not doubt it is right and best for me to go.'[8] At the time of writing that, she was spending a few days in Wilden with Louie, but returned to Rottingdean for her first Christmas as a widow and found great comfort in the presence of her son Philip. Though notoriously unreliable where his own affairs were concerned, he proved a tower of strength to his mother. Not only did he provide her with emotional comfort, but he was unexpectedly efficient in winding up his father's business affairs and sorting out the studio at the Grange. The bond between him and his mother had always been stronger than that with his father, and despite his wanderings around Europe and America in the succeeding years he always contrived to return to her every Christmas as the firm anchor in his unhappy aimless life.

The presence of Rudyard Kipling at Rottingdean was an immense help to Georgie. For four months in the summer before Edward's death, the Kiplings had shared North End House until the Elms, the house across the Green, became vacant. During this time both families had grown very close. 'I like their children and love themselves, so that it is a gain to have them near,' Georgie told Morris's daughter Jenny.[9] Even the forthright Carrie, who had failed with her mother-in-law, found favour with the beloved aunt: 'She is a very remarkable woman, and you can imagine the difference it makes to my life to have them come in every evening as they do,' Georgie wrote after Edward's death.[10] In return she was able to provide them with solace in 1899:

during a visit to Carrie's American parents in Vermont, Rudyard and his eldest child Josephine were taken ill with pneumonia. As Rudyard's life hovered in the balance, causing international concern, his favourite daughter died. He was devastated, and though he later lost his only son in the First World War, this daughter's death was the single most shattering experience of his life. 'Much of the beloved Cousin Ruddy of our childhood died with Josephine and I feel that I have never seen him a real person since that year,' Angela Thirkell said.[11]

The unexpected death of one so young, for Josephine was only eight years old, united all the family. When the news reached England, Agnes immediately telegraphed her sister Alice and offered to go and stay at Tisbury until John returned from America with the family, 'but Alice says she can fight the dreadful – best alone. And I can understand that,' Georgie reported.[12] She herself returned to Rottingdean from London to prepare the Elms for their return. 'Rud will be changed as I am changed since last year,' she gently warned Carrie. 'Mystery it all is – but we are part of it, and no trouble that happens to us is a new one in the world. God bless you, most dear ones, and keep you by the way known only to himself and yourselves.'[13] However, this tragedy struck at the core of her faith: 'I cannot help thinking that the death of the young is not in the *plan* of our being, and that we are ourselves greatly responsible for it. Indeed I believe we are at the beginning only of the art of living,' she confided in a friend.[14]

The tragedy isolated Rudyard from his mother, whereas Carrie, whom John Kipling described as struck 'stone dumb' by the loss, found her mother-in-law the only person to whom she could unburden herself, doing much in the process to heal their former divisions. It was his cousin, then Sir Philip Burne-Jones, whom Rudyard turned to. The two had been in each other's company in childhood, but at that time Rudyard had had a closer rapport with Margaret. However, after her marriage there was a change in relations between Philip and Rudyard: 'They grow more attached,' John noticed. 'Phil has a great capacity, under half-assumed triviality, for sympathy and affection. He is not the happiest of men these days. The superficial side of society he has mainly cared to cultivate is a somewhat bland and unsatisfactory diet for a continuance and he seems now inclined to turn more to Rud who is helpful comradeship to his own age.'[15] They proved of mutual assistance, and for a while Philip spent his time in the Kiplings' company, painting the well-known portraits of Rudyard and Carrie.

Relations between the Burne-Jones and Kipling families remained close despite opposing political opinions polarized by the Boer War. Knowing that socialist and imperialist views could never be reconciled, each kept their own counsel and thus the peace, but differences were never far from the surface, as John Kipling's letter to an old Anglo-Indian friend illustrates:

> Jack Mackail who, like Aunt Georgie, Phil etc is an . . . anti-Boer war advocate, came down to fetch his daughter back. I find his notions are on so lofty and merely academic a plane that they have but little concern with any of the actualities of life and so don't count. As man, a scholar and a parent he is quite delightful and his notions of highly advanced Socialism etc may be as high as they like, so long as they are out of my way.[16]

Fortunately they generally were, and family unity was preserved. Only once did Georgie Burne-Jones and Rudyard Kipling find themselves publicly on opposing sides.

No comment was passed about the Drill Hall and rifle training which Rudyard brought about in Rottingdean, although it was known that the pacifist Lady Burne-Jones did not approve. In May 1900 news of the relief of Mafeking filtered through, sparking off public celebrations to mark what was regarded in the village as a victory after the two-hundred-and-seventeen-day siege. Georgie saw it in quite a different light, and to Rudyard's dismay a huge blue banner appeared strung across an upstairs window at North End House. The provocative message WE HAVE KILLED AND ALSO TAKEN POSSESSION inflamed the villagers, and an angry crowd gathered shouting abuse at what seemed a blatant lack of patriotism. Attempts were even made to set fire to shrubs next to the house. Georgie's granddaughter recalled that for some time there was considerable danger from a populace infected by the Mafeking mood until Rudyard Kipling came over from the Elms to pacify the people and persuade them to go away. The incident only served to reinforce the villagers' belief that her ladyship was distinctly odd, and when Kipling decided to move some twenty miles or so from Rottingdean to Burwash a couple of years later, the rumour was that it was not just the tourists he sought to escape.

The passive little woman who had sat in awe of the artists was proving embarrassingly unpredictable, as her granddaughter Angela remarked: 'Single-minded people can be a little alarming to live with and we children had a nervous feeling that we never knew where our grandmother might break out next.'[17] The villagers were of similar opinion. The female parish councillor who spoke of improving housing and living conditions was peculiar yet harmless, but someone who displayed banners like that was very suspicious. Stories circulated in the village about her ladyship forcing servants and workpeople to listen to strange readings. Angela Thirkell recalled:

> She would have a worthy carpenter or wheel wright to the house once a week to discuss the socialism in which she so thoroughly and theoretically believed. All the snobbishness latent in children came to the fore in us as we watched the honoured but unhappy workman sitting stiffly on the edge of his chair in his horrible best clothes while my grandmother's lovely earnest voice preached William Morris to him. Then there were times when she believed that a hideous but favoured maid was worth educating. In the evening there would be an embarrassing ritual and the maid would sit in the drawing room, though at a respectful distance, and read aloud to my grandmother from such books as she thought suitable to the domestic intellect on 'The Distribution of Wealth' and 'Early Italian Painters'. How we hated it all and how uncomfortable it was for every one concerned except the kind giver of these mental feasts. There can rarely have been a woman who was so absolutely unconscious of self, though it was carried to such a pitch that even her sense of humour fell into abeyance. Now and then her humour did get the better of her, as when she described a visit she had paid to some poor family who had an invalid child 'surrounded with medals for abstaining from vices of which he was incapable'.[18]

Angela's description of her grandmother being 'absolutely fearless, morally and physically' is borne out by reports of her being driven around the countryside in 1900, at eight miles an hour in a 'victoria hooded' motor car. When Rudyard told her he proposed hiring a vehicle, 'the beloved Aunt who feared nothing created, said "Me Too!" '; and he reported proudly: 'She takes to the motor most valiantly', which since his early driving experiences sound like episodes from 'Wind in the Willows' says much for Georgie's courage.[19] The locals, in awe of the newfangled contraption, were less impressed and wondered about the sanity of a sixty-year-old lady who could engage in such activities.

Alice had no intention of travelling in her son's dangerous machine and indeed from 1898 onwards found her time and energy fully taken up by other matters. After ten years of marriage spent travelling round England and India Trix suddenly appeared at The Gables, suffering

170

from symptoms of great stress. The marked contrast of interests and temperament between the Fleming husband and wife which John Kipling had remarked on caused friction in the marriage and led Trix into a nervous breakdown. Alice insisted on caring for her daughter unaided, but it was the opinion of the London doctor sent down to Wiltshire by Captain Fleming that Mrs Kipling's personality only exacerbated the problem. Despite Alice's protestations, a full-time nurse was installed to look after her daughter, and then plans made to take Trix away to recover elsewhere, but the doctor reported to Captain Fleming: 'Mrs Kipling was on the verge of frenzy at any suggestion of such a thing and Mr Kipling, though ready to be firm when he was with me, yielded before his wife's excitement at once.' The letter went on to describe the difficulties which the nurse had met at The Gables and why it had been necessary for her to leave. 'Your wife will go on well now with her mother, whose nervousness is less when they are quiet together and is too familiar to your wife to have the harmful influence it would seem, to a stranger, to be likely. . . . Your wife is quite as determined not to be separated from her mother as the latter is not to allow her to leave her.'[20] It is quite obvious from the letters which passed between the doctor and Captain Fleming that the medical man believed Alice Kipling to be as neurotic as her daughter. Alice became alarmingly hyperactive (as Rudyard had remarked the previous year: 'The main point is not to flutter the mother'[21]), whereas Trix withdrew deeply into herself so that at times she was little more than a vegetable, unable to communicate or do anything for herself. Fortunately this situation proved temporary, but she became totally dependent on her mother. Alice responded warmly to this: having lost her son to another woman, she was overjoyed to form a close relationship with her daughter. Over the next few years mother and daughter were inseparable; when Trix was capable, they wrote poetry together, the results being published in an anonymous book titled *Hand in Hand: Verses by a mother and daughter*. They experimented in the homely pursuit of cookery, taking a particular interest in foreign recipes, but ironically this daughter and granddaughter of the Reverend George Macdonald took no pleasure in eating: in fact Alice's extreme thinness worried John.

One unfortunate outcome of the two women's new-found intimacy was an enhanced interest in psychic phenomena, which did nothing to improve their grasp of the real world. Alice had never taken the same interest in it as Trix, but after several months in her company, watching her daughter transcribe poetry received from Macdonald Highland ancestors through automatic writing, she was easily persuaded that their Celtic blood bestowed special powers on all members of the clan. The patient John Kipling suffered: 'The brunt of the worst of it fell on me, and for a long time I did nothing but attend to my burden. Things have cleared up at last,' he wrote at the end of 1899, 'and we may fairly hope for peace. Meanwhile I have lost a good deal of my respect for the medical profession and especially for those who profess to know about the nerves and brain. Also I have acquired some highly heretical notions about husbands and their relatives.'[22] He was himself caught between the demands of Captain Fleming, who wanted Trix returned, and Alice, who was equally determined to hold on to her daughter. For the odd week, John was able to go to Rottingdean or to his old friends the Pinders in the Potteries. Even the gloomy religion of Wilden, where 'Aunt Louie and Mr Baldwin are struggling with the melancholy that seems to be settling on the latter', made a welcome change.[23] The invitation Rudyard extended to his father to accompany him and his family to South Africa in 1900 had regretfully to be turned down because Alice and Trix could not be left alone for so long. There were compensations for John, however, when he forged friendships with two prominent local families, the Wyndhams and the Morrisons. The famous Rudyard Kipling's father, with his artistic abilities and amusing store of tales, was a welcome guest at Clouds and frequently persuaded to stay for the weekend even though he lived nearby. Similarly the rich eccentric Morrisons, who were compulsive magpies collecting everything from autographs and gemstones to oriental carpets and exotic animals, were pleased to entertain an inveterate traveller at Fonthill. Their shooting parties and soirées were reminiscent of the glamorous days in Simla. On their healthier days, Alice and Trix also visited their upper-class neighbours, and in the company – albeit on the fringe – of aristocrats and intellectuals rediscovered the old Kipling spirits.

Health was naturally a concern of all the sisters as they grew older. In 1900 Louisa underwent an operation, the details of which are now lost, but with little effect on her overall condition. One outcome was the taking of annual cures at Bath, where she encountered Janey Morris again, whom she had known in her girlhood. Janey, now widowed and, like Louisa, nursing a permanent delicacy, spent her time touring the curative resorts of England and Europe. The opportunity to relive memories of Red House days and former friends delighted both, and meetings at Bath became a regular event.

is photograph of John Lockwood Kipling was taken at the time of his marriage to
ice in April 1865, two weeks before they departed for India.

A scene from an amateur dramatic production at the Gaiety Theatre, Simla in which Trix is sitting on the sofa and Alice, her mother, standing to the right of the picture.

John Lockwood Kipling accompanied by his pet dog and surrounded by Indian arti and craftsmen of all ages outside the Lahore School of Art. He was a dedicated teach who genuinely sought to encourage Indian art rather than smother it with European ideas.

yard Kipling, aged sixteen, during his
term at the United Services College
e Crom Price was headmaster. After
ummer Rudyard rejoined his parents
dia and began a career in journalism.

Trix Kipling earned the name 'Rose in
June' when she first entered Anglo-Indian
society, but this was changed to the less
attractive soubriquet, 'The Ice Maiden',
on account of her haughty manner.

om at Bikaner Lodge. The Kiplings thought themselves the arbitors of artistic taste
itish India. A bust of Trix sculpted by her father is visible on the left and a host
otographs, which were Alice's vital link with her sisters, on the right.

Rudyard Kipling with his mother in 1890, when Alice, at fifty-three, was still the m
important person in her son's life. 'Love is a scarce commodity and I hold the best
Mother's,' he told a cousin.

n Ruskin, known to Georgie by the
kname Saint Crumpet. He had an
barrassing affection for the young
st's wife, but his philosophy was her
pel.

An early woodcut by Georgie, which
eventually earned her a limited reputation
as an amateur engraver, but the lack of
encouragement from the male artists
caused her to lose heart.

salind and George Howard in the 1870s
he time of their great friendship with
Burne-Joneses. Georgie said that
salind was one of the few people she
ld be perfectly open with.

George Eliot, the novelist, who encouraged
Georgie to make a life for herself. It was a
friendship valued by both parties.

Philip Burne-Jones aged twenty-five. In the opinion of his cousin, Rudyard Kipling, he would never make a great painter unless he were stuck on a desert island with nothing but paint and canvas.

Margaret Burne-Jones Mackail aged twenty, said to look sweet though awfully sad, with the same build of brow, helmet-lidded eyes and vast space between lid and eye as her cousin Trix. To most she was the archetypal Burne-Jones maiden.

John William Mackail, a brilliant schola who married Margaret Burne-Jones. Georgie was delighted and said he was t one man on earth she would have liked l daughter to have chosen.

e older Lady Poynter, a society figure,
ved in circles which included the Prince
d Princess of Wales.

Edward Poynter 'whom some perhaps
might not call a pleasant man, when he
talks to himself always says yes most
amiably, and that's about the only time he
ever does say it,' declared his brother-in-
law, Burne-Jones, and most people agreed
with him.

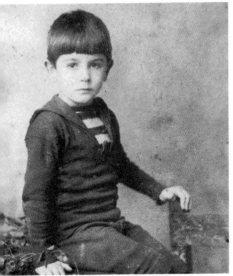

gh Poynter just before his fifth
rthday. His unexpected birth when
nes was thirty-nine was a great
barrassment. In adult life he rejected
e life of the artists in favour of a
ccessful business career with the
ldwin company.

Ambrose Poynter, although an architect,
joined the Royal Navy during the First
World War. He was a fun-loving person, a
childhood companion of Stanley
Baldwin's and an adult friend of Rudyard
Kipling.

Alfred Baldwin was undoubtedly an astute business man who increased the fortunes of the iron company he inherited to worth over a million pounds by the turn of the century.

Louisa Baldwin in middle age. She spent most of her married life nurturing a mysterious ailment which took her on expensive trips abroad and ensured that she survived into her eightieth year.

Edith Macdonald striking an aesthetic pose in the gardens of Wilden House where she lived with her sister Louisa Baldwin and helped bring up the young Stanley.

England's future Prime Minister, Stanley Baldwin, bribed by a biscuit to pose for the camera. He was aged three and taken out of skirts the following year.

All the sisters noticed how Agnes, who made less fuss about her health than Louisa, was gradually deteriorating in strength after 1900. Her husband, like most artists, alternated between intense activity and complete collapse, which Agnes said ground her down as a result. Sir Edward had little regard for his wife's condition or wishes and insisted she be towed round Europe, where he had spent much of his youth and now wanted to settle. Although the warmer weather suited her as much as Poynter, memories of an itinerant childhood made Agnes long to remain at home. Travels were brought to a halt in 1903, when doctors pronounced it necessary to perform a 'serious operation' on Lady Poynter. With Alice and Louie fully occupied with their own concerns, it fell to Georgie to care for her sister. This nursing continued at intervals for the next three years. Agnes tried to lead a normal life, insisting she go to Turkey in 1905 to attend the wedding of her favourite son Hugh, then working for the Ottoman Public Debt Administration and engaged to the United States Consul-General's daughter. The expedition proved too much for someone of sixty-one with a debilitating disease, and on her return Agnes became bedridden. Georgie was once more at her side, abandoning everything to nurse her sister. 'For two months I've been in constant attendance on her and have sometimes forgotten my own identity,' she wrote from Swanage, where they had gone to escape the London fogs.[24] In the quiet time spent reading and talking, they were able to rediscover the bond that had once existed between them, and Agnes pronounced Georgie to be the most blessed of sisters to her. Although they had seen little of each other during their married lives, both agreed that the more time they spent in each other's company, the better they liked each other. They were also aware that their time together was limited.

There were a brief improvement in Agnes's condition sufficient for her to return to London and spend the Christmas of 1905 with her husband, but early in the New Year Georgie told Sydney Cockerell: 'I wish you to know that I have a deep anxiety about my sister Lady Poynter. She seems fading out of life, yet the doctors can see no definite disease. The shock of her severe operation nearly two and a half years ago has never really passed.'[25] With Georgie and Louie by her bedside, Agnes died of cancer on 12 June 1906. 'The loss of my sister touches me very closely.' Georgie wrote two days after the event, 'but she has suffered so much and so long, I was thankful when the end came. She was really dying for three weeks and though unconscious for much of

173

the time, her state was deeply painful to us who loved her. Finally there came what looked like the most peaceful natural sleep and from it she never awoke.' Setting her sorrows aside temporarily, Georgie continued: 'I hope to get to Rottingdean next week, but first have to go round by Wiltshire to tell my sister there of what has been happening – for she was too unwell to come to London.'[26] This piece of sisterly duty was followed by another – that of caring for Louie for the next two months. The death of the sister who had been closest to her in childhood caused Louie to suffer a relapse, and she arrived in Rottingdean for Georgie to nurse, 'but she is a pleasant housemate and quite unexacting', the tired elder sister remarked.[27] In the garden of North End House, Louisa wrote her own memorial to Agnes, a poem distributed to various members of the family and published in 1911 in a collection of her work called *Afterglow*. The poem for Agnes, entitled 'Hail and Farewell', is an uninspiring piece of writing, beginning:

> Beloved one, how shall I bid thee farewell?
> Say will there be sign or token,
> A meaning fraught smile or caress, to tell
> What cannot be spoken.
> The day when we bid one another goodbye,
> When we must be parted, yea thou and I.

and contains little of the sparkle of the woman it commemorated.

What took everyone by surprise was the inconsolable grief displayed by Edward Poynter. But Alice was not taken in by it, remarking sardonically that it was a pity he could show his love so freely now his wife was dead, but had not been able to in her lifetime. Her death so completely overwhelmed him that even his business letters, usually cold and impersonal, were cut through with poignant references to his loss. He was isolated in his grief because both sons had felt the weight of their father's displeasure and gone their own way, retaining contact only with their mother. Poynter family life had not been of the happiest kind, as Georgie hinted when writing to Louie three years after their sister's death that the anniversary of Agnes's death still evoked painful memories, since it appeared rather more the last day of her great sorrows than the beginning of her peace. Nevertheless, in her usual stoical manner Georgie concluded that they would no doubt feel happier about it as time went, and both she and Louie had already given thanks to God that their sister left the world for a reason.

At Wilden Church two memorials were erected to her memory: a brass plaque on the wall donated by Alice, Georgie and Edith, and above it a richly coloured stained-glass window depicting Saint Agnes. The window was made up from a design by Burne-Jones conceived before his death, and was executed by Morris & Co. It was Louisa's personal tribute to the favourite sister of her childhood and is a fitting monument to one who was much in the company of artists.

Agnes's life is the least defined of the Macdonald sisters' and appears the saddest. She inherited the same intellectual abilities as the others and possessed an effervescent personality which could have been her salvation, if the dour character of Edward Poynter had not sapped her spirit. *The Times* report of her death the following day found nothing to say about her personal achievements and concentrated on the fact that she was 'one of the remarkable daughters of the late Reverend G. B. Macdonald whose house some forty years ago was a well-known centre of an artistic and literary circle'. It concluded simply that 'Lady Poynter was very widely known in society and her loss will be sincerely mourned'.[28]

Louisa's life seemed to hang by a thread after the death of Agnes, so that the family lavished extra care and attention on her. It came as a shock to everyone therefore, when it was Alfred Baldwin who suffered a heart attack in London in February 1908. He was returning from chairing a half-yearly meeting of the Great Western Railway Company and was taken ill in the cab, dying shortly after reaching his flat at Kensington Palace Gardens. Louisa returned twenty minutes afterwards to find herself a widow – a great shock, since there had not been the slightest forewarning of Alfred's impending demise. Louisa reacted in the predictable manner of one who has been long indulged and threw herself totally on the mercy of Georgie. She abdicated all responsibility, would not attend the funeral nor the subsequent memorial service and almost two years passed before she would visit her husband's grave.

Georgie shepherded Louisa down to Rottingdean and once again tended her younger sister for most of the year, which allowed little time for any other activities. Apologizing to a friend for her lack of correspondence, she explained: 'I have all the time been living another person's life and not my own.' This she did not resent: 'I am really thankful to be able to serve my sister in any way – and it is in a time of trouble many thoughts and feelings come to me that cannot be expressed, yet may be of help to oneself and others later on.' Caring for

Louie was assisted by 'a childlike streak in her character which is an immense help in times of life and death'.[29]

All watched the halting progress of Louisa, expecting one so frail to follow her husband into the grave at any moment, yet John Kipling remained sceptical: after visiting Rottingdean he wrote: 'I thought Louie was wonderfully well considering the burning fiery furnace into which she was so suddenly and cruelly plunged. And Georgie and Stan have held her up and carried her in their arms sharing her sorrow in the most marvellous way. At a great cost for Georgie, who I venture to think might have been a little spared. . . . But Lord! One comes back to the old saying – "it's easy to bury other people's darlings".'[30] Within two years he found himself similarly faced.

As the family watched Louisa, whose path through life was 'that of a fly on a window pane – six steps forward and five back', Alice gradually weakened.[31] Her continual weight loss worried John, though he put it down to anxiety about Trix, and as her father had done, Alice suffered increasingly from insomnia. In a vain attempt at light relief John said: 'I am thinking of suggesting cigarettes – I take a prodigious amount of smoke – how I sleep! But would she accept my suggestion? I hae ma doots.'[32] Recognizing that her health was poor, Alice tried the cure at Harrogate, where, according to Rudyard, 'they do such beastly things with mud', and Louie, never one to be denied such an opportunity, went with her.[33] But it was Trix that Alice really wanted by her side. Though the young woman was much improved and able to rejoin her husband for short spells, Alice was adamant that her daughter must always live with her parents.

In complete contrast to her sister Louisa, Alice was not one to give in to poor health and despite frequent severe pain struggled on. In a letter to their Anglo-Indian friend Edith Plowden in the autumn of 1910, John gave a graphic description:

Poor Alice has been going through a period of torment since she returned from Wilden about the end of October: which must be like the *sakht khench* . . . which your brother Chichele's myrmidons, in common with other native police-wallahs, are accused of using. This is a handkerchief twisted with a stick round the temples and head. I can think of nothing that more truthfully gives the agony of pain she has been enduring with scalp neuralgia. The last few days by dint of Trix's most kind and assiduous ministrations, and various tonics prescribed by Trix and the doctor, I think she has been a little better: but there's a wide-eyed demon of sleeplessness that torments her sorely. And why the Good God sends such pain to innocent women I cannot begin to understand. . . . Trixie has buttressed and supported her Mother for weeks, for indeed I don't know how she could have got on without her.[34]

John continually referred to Alice as suffering from 'neuralgia', but the cause of her pain was more deep-seated than that. At the end of 1909, Rudyard spoke with the doctor who was attending his mother and said, 'I was told for the first time of the nature of my mother's disease', continuing angrily: 'They should have consulted a competent London specialist long ago.'[35] Her death on 23 November 1910 was ostensibly of heart failure, but Rudyard's remarks and subsequent obsession that cancer was an inherited disease suggest otherwise.

John was heart-broken by his loss, but did his best to come to terms with an outcome he seems to have foreseen. The arrival of Captain Fleming for the funeral was untimely and induced a second nervous breakdown in Trix. Rudyard tried to arrange nursing for both his sister and father, but the Christmas they spent at the Gables in 1910 was a very sad one. So deranged was Trix that early in January Rudyard placed her in care, whilst the Wyndhams collected the tragic little figure of John Kipling to stay with them at Clouds, where he died in his sleep on 28 January 1911, two months after his wife.

Rudyard had the sad task of attending to his parents' possessions and will, and in compliance with their wishes all personal papers were burnt. In a pathetic attempt to appear younger than her true age, Alice had taken some time previously to wearing a grotesque ginger wig. She had also made it known that her age was not to be revealed on her death. As requested, the Kipling tombs were stark rectangles of granite, bare of any ornament and carrying the minimum inscription. Conscious of her family heritage to the last, Alice had insisted her epitaph should read: 'Alice Macdonald, wife of John Lockwood Kipling, 1910'. John's legend bore the dates 1837–1911 under his name and the letters C.I.E.

Intriguingly, many years later when her mental breakdowns had finished and she was able to lead a normal life, Trix wrote to Rudyard's wife:

To the best of my belief *the birthdate* on Father's tombstone is incorrect – he was born at Pickering July 6 1838 and Mother on April 15 1837. . . . *In 1878* – when I spent the first birthday I could remember with both my parents – Father said to me – 'You can easily remember my age – for I was thirty the year you were born and I shall always be thirty years older than

177

you are – however old you grow!' Mother laughed and said, 'Oh John, I wish I could say that.' She always told us she was born the year Princess Victoria was crowned. When people were inquisitive – at the time of the 'boom' – Father used to say – 'My birthday is in July and Mrs Kipling's in April' – and leave it at that.[36]

Trix remembered being with her father when he made some attempt at recording biographical facts about the family, but she observed how notoriously unreliable his notes were, saying he put the dates of both her and Rudyard's marriages down wrongly, whereas the dates of his early life were given him by Alice. Since John Lockwood Kipling may have been born before the compulsory registration of births, his correct age remains a secret exactly as Alice wished.[37]

The sudden removal in quick succession of both Kiplings caused the remaining members of the Macdonald family to think about recording their own views of their unusual family for posterity. With her *Memorials of Edward Burne-Jones*, Georgie felt her task was done, for she had ensured that the memory of the two great men in her life, her husband and William Morris, had been set down appropriately; in any case she believed her own life to be of no interest to others. Although aged seventy at the time of Alice's death, Georgie was still busy attending to the needs of others. In 1910 Crom Price, then in his mid-seventies, but with a young wife and family, turned to his old friend for help. He knew he was dying and brought his family to Rottingdean, confident that Georgie would care for them. Within a few weeks of his arrival in the village he was dead, and Georgie found herself looking after the Price family, who had very little money and no accommodation. Other figures from her early life concerned her: Philip Webb, unmarried and suffering from senile dementia, received her help, although distance prevented her from rendering much personal assistance. Janey Morris was more accessible, being at Kelmscott Manor in Oxfordshire, and Georgie did visit her and attempt to make her comfortable in her old age. Jenny, Morris's favourite daughter, who was tragically afflicted with epilepsy, was brought to Rottingdean for holidays along with her nurse, as much for Janey's benefit as Jenny's because the young woman's condition had deteriorated so much that fits occurred every day.

Fred Macdonald recorded the family's life and his career in the Methodist Church in an autobiography entitled *As a Tale That is Told*. In many ways his ministry was as successful as his famous grandfather's, for the Reverend Frederic Macdonald rose to the highest office in his Church in 1899, that of President of the Wesleyan Conference. His special interest in the Wesleyan Foreign Missionary Society ensured that he travelled widely in Europe, Ceylon, the Antipodes and the United States. By the time of his death in 1928 he had written ten books, including two biographies of religious figures, some theological essays, and the edited letters of his grandfather James Macdonald. Fred was probably the only one of his generation who managed to maintain contact with all the family. He was aware nevertheless that his vocation as a preacher set him apart from the artists and admitted: 'I used to wish sometimes that the two worlds did not lie so far apart, and that there was some little interchange between them, of the best that each had.'[38]

Louisa occupied her final years collecting memorabilia and writing childhood reminiscences. 'She liked nothing better than compiling albums of pictures of all sorts, and she left behind her cases of loose cut-out pictures of every kind, which would undoubtedly have found themselves mostly squared and pasted into volumes had she been spared,' Stanley mused.[39] She also concerned herself with writing down reminiscences of her childhood and the days spent at the edge of the Pre-Raphaelite circle as a much fussed and petted little girl. Those she regarded as her happiest days, when she was young, healthy and full of optimism. Her other literary efforts in those final years were sombre verses in commemoration of the dead, some of which appeared in newspapers. She was also responsible for the beautiful Burne-Jones windows which illuminate Wilden Church and are in the main memorials to members of the Baldwin family. The altar window is the only one designed and executed in Burne-Jones's lifetime and was given by Louisa and Alfred Baldwin as thanks for their family life. Alfred himself, greatly mourned by Louisa, received a Burne-Jones window depicting Joshua with his trumpeters passing over the Jordan, and a Burne-Jones cartoon of Margaret of Scotland was selected by Louisa as an appropriate saint for a Macdonald, to go in the space next to Joshua. Unfortunately the window Louisa planned for herself was the one which was never executed. It is said that by the time of her death in 1925 Morris and Co. were unable to get the necessary coloured glass, so instead of it being left as the one plain glass window in the church, the directors of Baldwin and Company arranged for another panel of Morris stained glass to go in its place. It is an unusual window inasmuch as there are no figures present, only a richly coloured design of intertwined briar roses.

Georgie died in 1920, before Louisa, and although Alice and John Kipling received a brass plaque commemorating their lives, Georgie, who had done far more for her younger sister, never received a mention, but her name along with Edith's appears on the tributes to Alice and Agnes. Georgie spent her last years travelling between her daughter in London and Rottingdean, and even paid a visit to France where she stood in the peace of Gothic cathedrals and read aloud from Ruskin, as Edward and Morris had done over fifty years before. Although her work on the Rottingdean Parish Council ceased in 1901, she maintained an active interest in socialism: 'How glad I am of the Labour party in this Parliament,' she wrote. 'I find myself turning eagerly to the Parliamentary reports now and am cheered so far now by the courage of the speech of the Labour members.'[40] To the end she looked after herself with only one maid to assist her and tried hard to put into practice her belief that 'one of the lessons of old age is to avoid being a nuisance'.[41] She continued administering to the needs of Louisa by calling regularly at Wilden and taking the invalid away on holiday. Edith, by then in her early seventies, was still treated as the younger sister and frequently overlooked by Georgie and Louisa. There was a brief time in 1917 when Fred joined his sisters at Wilden, and Georgie wrote: 'He came alone and we four who are the only ones of our generation of the family remaining had a particularly pleasant five days.'[42] That was their last family meeting, for in February 1920 Georgie was taken ill at her daughter's house and died. It was such a peaceful death that even Margaret was able to write a few days afterwards: 'Mother had the kindest little illness and gentlest departure and has left us comforted and satisfied and somewhere something is perfect.'[43]

With Georgie's death it seemed the old order had changed, yielding place to new, for though Louisa, Fred and Edith remained, the heart of that exceptional family of sisters had gone. Louie lived for a further five years, during which she read and prayed extensively, but was scarcely seen in Wilden village. A few can recall seeing a pasty-faced figure bundled up in furs being carried from Wilden House to the car, to be taken to Chequers for a weekend with her son, then Chancellor of the Exchequer. Edith Macdonald, however, was only rarely permitted that treat; instead the sprightly seventy-two-year-old continued to take sewing classes for the girls of the village, organize the Girls' Friendly Society and oversee church and school affairs on behalf of the Baldwin family. Georgie's death inspired Edith to write down her version of the Macdonald family history, as an interested bystander all her life. Her small volume, called *Annals of the Macdonald Family*, was published in 1923 for distribution amongst the surviving members of the family. The inscription on Stanley Baldwin's copy makes amusing reading, for she wrote: 'I hope you will not receive it, my dear, with that lack of enthusiasm which is not one of your most endearing qualities.' Edith went on to write another book entitled *Thoughts on Many Things*, which contained epigrams, witticisms and other snippets. In it she noted her impression that marriage was 'an ideal never lived up to' and an old maid was 'a woman who has missed much and escaped much'.[44] Having lived with two members of Parliament, Edith's wry comment on that fraternity was: 'To reply without answering, to expound without explaining, to keep words and facts as far as possible asunder, these seem to be the arts by which politicians too often attain success in parliamentary debate.'[45]

Louisa had the same fascination for politics as Georgie, though siding with quite the opposite side of the house to her sister, and it was with enormous pleasure that she watched how her son succeeded in that field of endeavour, almost in spite of himself. 'You have inflated your mother with pride of many kinds on your account, all of which I would hope and believe your Father knows about as well as myself.'[46] To her great delight she was with Stanley and his family at Chequers at Whitsun 1923 when the summons to London came. 'What does he want me for so early?' the Chancellor was heard to say. 'You don't think he would command you to be in town so early to discuss someone else's prospects of being Prime Minister,' was his mother's swift reply.[47] In a letter to Lady Lee, who had recently given Chequers to the nation as a place of refreshment for overworked ministers of state, Louisa spoke of her own astonishment that she who had for so many years lived apart from the world should have been the one to see great and unexpected events take place in front of her own eyes. Before her death in her eightieth year, Louisa was able to see her son returned to office by popular vote as well as through expediency. A short time after in May 1925 she died peacefully of old age.

Her death was followed by Frederic's in 1928, leaving Edith the sole survivor of her generation. Ignoring one of her own epigrams that 'being tired of living is far from being a sign that we are fit for dying', Edith decided her purpose in life was over following Louie's death and

181

took to her bed to await the end. As if bearing out her epigram to the letter, she lived on until 1937, a further twelve years. Edith's burial in Wilden churchyard beside her sister Louisa was the end of a unique sisterhood.

Epilogue

The children of the Macdonald sisters were surrounded by talented and successful relatives, which placed an unenviable pressure on the sons to make a name for themselves. The male offspring of Burne-Jones and Poynter suffered most, living from day to day in the shadow of famous fathers, so that their confidence was sapped and their careers and lives ruined, but with the reputations of the senior Baldwin and Kipling being more localized, their sons were able to extract any advantage from their fathers' positions without paying too great a price.

The Macdonald 'strain' could be a powerful creative force in some members of the family, but in others there appeared a dark destructive side which troubled the conscience to such an extent that the boundary between eccentricity and insanity became blurred. Angela Thirkell observed that in her uncle Philip Burne-Jones 'there was on his mother's side, coming from her mother's family, a strain of deep melancholy and self-distrust which in some of the family was almost a disease', and which John Kipling had recognized as that 'decided touch of the elegaic in their nature'.[1] This particular characteristic, allied with the family's high expectations of their children, made a dangerous amalgam. In their feminine role, the Macdonald sisters had escaped the worst of this, whereas their brother Harry had come under severe pressure. Fred was fortunate to be a younger son, because with all attention focused on Harry his performance received little notice, which enabled him to make his own way in life. He was also fortunate to be of different temperament; though ultimately becoming a Methodist minister, he was troubled far less by those 'dark nights of the soul' than most others in the family, but only he and Agnes shared this light-hearted side to their natures.

Most of the Macdonalds could be termed 'highly strung', but in the

183

younger generation only a small amount of pressure was necessary to break the strings. Trix Kipling was the obvious sufferer, having at least three complete mental breakdowns, which led to her being certified insane twice. She would have been certified a third time had not Rudyard intervened. Trusting that his sister's condition was only temporary, and knowing that after a third certification it would be almost impossible to have her ever declared sane again, he resisted Captain Fleming's pressure for an official verdict. Time ultimately vindicated Rudyard's decision, for in the late 1920s Trix emerged from her troubles and began to lead a normal life.

Rudyard himself suffered from great nervous strain in 1890 when he arrived in London to live in Villiers Street. He was working hard at his writing and receiving much public attention as a result. The loneliness of life in the capital without his adored parents and sister, added to a disregard for his own well-being, caused his breakdown in health and the dormant Indian fevers to reappear. Rudyard's description was that 'all my Indian microbes joined hands and sang for a month in the darkness of Villiers Street'.[2] The Athenaeum announced: 'We regret to hear that Mr Rudyard Kipling has broken down from overwork.' The reception given to his novel The Light That Failed had been excellent, but, like his uncle Harry, Rudyard was concerned that he might not be able to sustain such a high standard: 'Up like a rocket, down like a stick', was how he feared his popularity would go, and he worried about his mother's reaction.[3] 'If the success comes my father's delight will be greater than mine. If the money comes my mother will be more pleased than I,' but failure terrified him.[4] In the event, Rudyard Kipling of course more than fulfilled his early literary promise, and marriage to the powerful Carrie Balestier provided him with the necessary organization and protection for his talent to flourish.

Although Rudyard felt the force of both mother and later wife willing him to succeed, he was able to cope with this pressure, whereas Philip Burne-Jones never could. Georgie adored her son and made a conscious effort not to mar his life in the way her parents had Harry Macdonald's, and yet she failed. As a child, Philip experienced a large measure of freedom. When he expressed displeasure at his education at Marlborough School, his parents brought him home and employed a private tutor to prepare him for Oxford. His university career followed a similar path to his school one in that he left Oxford without taking a degree, despite Georgie's precaution of placing him under Faulkner's

184

eye at University College. In her disappointment, she took heart from the fact that neither Edward nor Morris had graduated but had still made successful careers. To Edward Burne-Jones's delight, Philip expressed a desire to be an artist, which gave both parents cause for optimism. Phil 'has a most true eye for colour. I find continual hope from him – more than I can ever give him back,' his father told the artist G. F. Watts in 1884.[5] But at the same time Rudyard Kipling commented that Phil 'would be greater if he were stuck on a desert island with nothing but paints and canvas and no society', and therein lay the truth, because the boy could not resist distractions.[6] Edward was heard to muse: 'Tis a funny life with Phil who thinks nothing matters and Georgie who thinks every little thing matters.'[7] However, it was then arranged for Philip to attend art school in London, and his own studio was set up at the Grange. His niece summed up the problem with Philip:

> He could have been a distinguished painter and would have been one under a luckier star, but two things told fatally against him. He never needed to work, and he was cursed with a sense of diffidence and a feeling that whatever he did would be contrasted unfavourably with his father's work. If he had had to depend on himself and had worked in his own way, I do not believe that what he feared would have happened. He had a genuine gift for landscapes and had made a style of portrait painting which was peculiarly his own, using canvas about 30 inches by 20 and painting his sitter in three-quarter length.[8]

Philip had the same sense of fun as his father and 'he was the most witty and amusing companion possible and reduced one to unquenchable and painful laughter that makes the whole body ache so that one longs for death to relieve one's agony'.[9] From his father also came the artistic temperament that could shower presents liberally on all and sundry or impulsively decide to vanish abroad. He might have survived fairly happily in this mode of life had he not his mother's acute sense of conscience which gave him no peace. 'Uncle Phil must have suffered under this all his life and could not control it enough to keep himself from making others suffer with him. He was quick to suspect an imagined slight or insult and would say or write something which would bring the unsuspecting offender to bewildered tears. Then he would fall into depths of repentance and self-accusation that shattered every one concerned.'[10] He also possessed the art of the 'cruel stinging word that annihilated one' – another Macdonald trait.[11]

Although Georgie always made it a point of honour to be realistic and honest in her dealings with everyone, with her son she could only be the indulgent parent. His first painting, exhibited at the Grosvenor Gallery in 1886, delighted her, and she preferred to concentrate her focus on this, rather than the extraordinary amount of money Philip was spending, little of which he had earned himself. Philip's early adulthood was dotted with bouts of lavish spending in the pursuit of a high life with some of the famous names who visited his father's studio. He made a fool of himself over the actress Mrs Pat Campbell by dashing round to escort her everywhere and lavishing diamonds, furs and a carriage on her. Philip also managed to create a scandal with one of his pictures in a manner reminiscent of his father, when in 1897 he exhibited *Vampire*. This painting showed a woman, readily recognizable as Mrs Campbell, in a clinging nightgown, astride a man who had collapsed on a bed. According to the *Illustrated London News* the whole subject was 'treated with no little passion but leaves an unpleasant impression'. There were other embarrassing instances of Philip chasing Lillie Langtry, even to the extent of following her to Monte Carlo. His life-style cost a fortune: in one attempt to raise some extra money he was indiscreet enough to write an autobiographical article and sell it to 'a disreputable publishing syndicate'. When he realized the full implications of his action, he had to rely on Rudyard to accompany him and prise the article away from them. Later on he disappeared to the Continent, got himself heavily in debt and then, on the verge of a complete breakdown, telegraphed his father to come and bail him out.

It was a great disappointment to Georgie, who had attempted to give her son the freedom which she considered essential to happiness. Freedom of action Philip Burne-Jones certainly did have, but he was always troubled by the judgement implicit in his mother's eyes, which W. Graham Robertson had also felt: 'Eyes like those of Georgiana Burne-Jones I have never seen before or since and, through all our long friendship, their direct gaze would always cost me little subconscious heart-searchings, not from fear of criticism or censure, but lest those eyes in their grave wisdom, their crystal purity, should rest upon anything unworthy.'[12] To her granddaughter those 'large eyes were clear blue and calculated to make a child stand abashed who had pricks of conscience', so that Philip with his ultra-sensitive conscience lived in perpetual torment.[13] He knew he had failed both parents, and after his father's death it troubled him greatly: 'I hold the memory of my father in the most loving reverence – and though I failed him at every turn, he never lost hope about me, nor despised me – but loved and forgave and comforted me to the end – I have never had such a friend since.'[14] Georgie never blamed him for his errant ways, believing instead that she was largely responsible, and admitted to a friend: 'I don't speak as one who has "managed" her children well.'[15]

Philip went off to America in 1902 in search of his fortune but his sister was less sure of the outcome: 'I have just come back from seeing Phil off at Euston,' she wrote. 'He starts for New York today: he appears to be travelling with a quite particularly shady set of people, most of them looking as if their only reason for going was to escape the strong arm of the law.'[16] However, out of this trip came an attempt at literature, a novel published under the title *Dollars and Democracy*. Unlike his uncle, Philip did not settle in America but drifted back home again to be near his mother, though not to live with her. Her death in 1920 left him dazed: 'I am quite alone now and don't think it much matters *where* one is – I prefer sunshine to fogs,' he ended, giving a hotel in the South of France as his next address.[17] Philip Burne-Jones never married, which was unfortunate, for a wife might have provided him with the necessary stability and happiness to develop his talents in the same way as his father had. He spent the remaining few years of his life drifting miserably between his cousins and his father's wealthy patrons until his death in 1926. He produced over sixty paintings in his lifetime, many of which demonstrate that Sir Philip Burne-Jones possessed much of his father's artistic ability, if none of his persistence.

Ambrose Poynter's progress through life was similarly aimless. When he died at the age of fifty-five, after a complete mental and physical breakdown, *The Times* tactfully noted: 'It is to be regretted that during an unusually busy career it was never his good fortune to leave a single work on such a scale as to leave permanent proof of his undoubted genius.' Despite this comparative failure, Ambrose Poynter displayed a more balanced personality than his cousin Philip and was a far more popular member of the family, combining much of the fun-loving nature of his mother with a modicum of his father's serious application to duty; but his father demanded complete dedication. Ambrose was the third generation in an established family of artists. His grandfather was the architect Ambrose Poynter, who had studied under Nash and been instrumental in founding the Royal Institute of

187

British Architects. Following this lead, his son Edward Poynter had attained international recognition for his classical subjects, and all then looked to Ambrose junior to bring even greater honours to the family. Unfortunately he did not possess the same ambition as his father, and neither did he have confidence in his work. If given the choice he would have preferred to spend his time enjoying life rather than painting. Much of his childhood was spent in the company of Stanley Baldwin, and though vastly different in character, the two cousins were firm friends: 'Ambo's beloved Stan', the politician was called. The two boys went through preparatory school together and would have stayed together at Eton had not Alfred Baldwin decided at the last minute that Stanley must be educated at Harrow. Ambrose had a reputation for being a dare-devil and getting into scrapes, but it came as a horrible shock to the 'holier-than-thou' Baldwin parents to learn that their son was the instigator of a piece of pornographic literature which was sent to Eton. Without doubt, Ambrose Poynter was behind the affair, but Stanley received the more severe punishment and had to live with the knowledge that he had failed his parents, which blighted his school and university career. Ambrose emerged unscathed and was directed along the path leading to the South Kensington School and then the Royal Academy schools. Quite early on he opted to follow in his grandfather's footsteps as an architect rather than copy his father. After training he was articled to G. Aitchison and began to practise on his own account at the age of twenty-six. Relations with his father were always strained, and whilst his mother was fond of him it was quite clear that she felt a stronger attachment to her younger son Hugh.

As Stanley followed a different path through Cambridge and into the family business, the former closeness between the two cousins diminished, and Rudyard Kipling became the companion of Ambrose's later life. In 1890, when Rudyard settled in London, the two were frequently to be found together; significantly, Ambrose Poynter was chosen as the sole relative at Rudyard's marriage (an event which was even quieter than his parents' had been). It was naturally the architect cousin who was asked to draw up plans for the alterations which the Kiplings wanted at their home, Batemans, but Carrie Kipling was very impatient at the easy-going pace Ambrose affected.

Little survives of Ambrose's architectural work bar a few monuments in churches, a clock-tower at Wilden Church in memory of Alfred Baldwin and the mansard roof of an oast house at Batemans. He did venture into print following his experiences in the Navy during the First World War, when, although almost fifty, he saw service as a lieutenant. In his book *The Coming of War* he predicted that Europe would be engulfed in a much larger conflict than it had recently gone through. He never lived long enough to see the fulfilment of his prediction, but it does vindicate his claim to have limited psychic powers. Although a close friend of Rudyard's, Ambrose never, for example, willingly slept at Batemans because he insisted the house was haunted.

Ambrose Poynter was a regular contributor to architectural journals and at the time of his death was engaged in a detailed study of the Italian Renaissance. He married in 1907 at the age of forty, but it has been claimed that this was not a happy union, and there were no children. He succeeded to his father's title twelve years later, but the middle years of his life were troubled by breakdowns, leading to his premature death in 1923.

His younger brother Hugh was probably the luckiest of the Macdonald cousins, being able to choose his own career, enjoy it and be successful. He benefited from the large age gap between himself and the other cousins, for the twenty-one years which separated him from Philip Burne-Jones, the eldest cousin, constituted a generation in which characters and attitudes had softened. Agnes exerted more influence on the upbringing of her 'ewe lamb' than she had on Ambrose, and consequently Hugh was permitted to attend a small prep school on the south coast and then St Paul's School rather than Eton. His career is interesting because he rejected art and literature completely. Business life intrigued him, and he showed a natural aptitude for languages which may have been attributable to his Macdonald grandfather or equally his Huguenot ancestors on the Poynter side. By his early twenties he was competent in five languages and obtained a post as secretary to the President of the Council of Administration of the Ottoman Public Debt. His first marriage to Mary Dickenson took place in Turkey and lasted twenty-five years until her death. With the outbreak of the First World War, the British presence was hastily removed from Turkey, and since Hugh Poynter had shown fine administrative powers, a similar post was found for him in the Army. After the war, Poynter was in his late thirties and, like many men, in need of a job. He turned to his cousin Stanley, Financial Secretary to the Treasury and owner of a metal industry firm which had boomed during the war years. Making use of Poynter's fluency in French, a post was found for him as Baldwin and Company's agent in Paris. After three years in that position demonstrating a surprising talent for business negotiations, in 1921 he was made President of Baldwin Steels in Canada and six years later became Chairman of their Australian enterprise, which he ran successfully until his retirement. He succeeded to the title in 1923 on the death of his brother and married for a second time in 1933, a widow, Mrs King. A widower again six years later, he married Irene Williams, a librarian at the Alliance Française of which he was President in Australia. Despite three marriages, there were no children and with his death in 1968 the Poynter line came to an end.

Stanley Baldwin probably endured the most difficult childhood of all the Macdonald cousins, yet survived it to become one of the best-known members of the family. It says much for his character that he was able to withstand the continual pressure his parents exerted both to do well in business and lead a devout life. His father managed to combine these things successfully, for under Alfred Baldwin's direction the company expanded at an impressive rate, and at the same time his religious beliefs found expression in paternalistic good deeds in the village of Wilden, yet none of this brought Alfred true happiness. Louisa, already endowed with her full measure of Macdonald melancholy and hypochondria, was hardly a cheerful mother. Yet it was Georgie's opinion that the Baldwins made the best set of parents amongst the family, and she jokingly suggested they should receive a medal engraved 'First Prize to Parents' – this verdict would hardly accord with late twentieth-century opinion. Stanley's childhood was overshadowed by duty and hard work, with opportunities for pleasure or independence severely curtailed and his life mapped out for him without any regard to his wishes or abilities. It was his parents' intention he should combine the family ironmastery business with a little gentlemanly politics.

Rudyard Kipling thought Stanley was a prig, with no experience of life but an enviable inheritance. The differences of opinion which led to schoolboy fights in the library at Wilden House persisted throughout their lives, and letters to Margaret Burne-Jones show Rudyard could never resist sly attacks on this Baldwin cousin with whom neither had any sympathy. John Kipling understood his nephew's position better and attempted to get Stanley to widen his vision by travel: 'Pater has

190

been writing sheaves to Aunt Louie,' Rudyard told Margaret. 'It seems he has a notion that Stan ought to come out to India – he seems as keen on Stan's travels as I am on Phil's. I don't for an instant suppose that Aunt Louie would let that paragon with a horror of fast girls go away for a year, but . . . 'twould be a grand thing for the boy – I beg his pardon – varsity man,' he ended, displaying envy of the university education he lacked.[18] Time healed many differences, and Rudyard could not but admire the way his cousin coped with the high offices forced upon him. For a brief period the two shared similar political views, and after a two-hour discussion with Kipling in the early 1920s Baldwin noted: 'I was highly pleased to find that he had come to the same conclusion about the Government that I had, and by the same road, after almost as long and anxious a cogitation. We have common puritan blood and he said a thing I have so often said and acted on. "When you have two courses open to you and you thoroughly dislike one of them, that is the one you must choose, for it is sure to be the right one." '[19] There was some measure of familiarity in subsequent years: in 1923 the families met up at Aix-les-Bains where Mrs Stanley Baldwin always went to take the cure. In later years differing opinions over the administration of India ended their association, and Kipling was heard to accuse Baldwin of being a socialist in disguise.

One of Stanley's greatest family admirers did indeed come from the socialist camp, although Philip Burne-Jones's politics tended to change as quickly as his company. In 1923, when his mother had been dead three years, Sir Philip was an ardent supporter of the new Conservative Prime Minister. He wrote to Gladstone's daughter:

> It is all very interesting about the new P M whom I greatly admire as a man and a politician. I have known him intimately since childhood and he is one of the very best men that ever lived. It was all very unexpected – and quite unsought and undesired by my cousin – but I think they have got the right man in the right place this time . . . what a blow his adopting Dizzy as his model, the farthest I fancy from his modest nature.[20]

Stanley Baldwin's success in politics surprised all the Macdonald relatives, for though it was well-known he would take his father's seat in due course, few anticipated dynamic results from the intense young man. The key to Stanley's rise was undoubtedly a very strong-willed wife, for as his daughter said later, 'If it hadn't been for my Mother, my Father would have remained quite happily where he was in Worcester-

191

shire, going daily to the office and back. He had no ambition, push or drive. My Mother supplied them all: he was her first concern, and she always saw he had every comfort in his library, especially in his *London* library as *she* preferred London to the country.'[21] It was yet another instance of one of the men linked to the Macdonalds achieving success through the powerful support of a woman.

Stanley's sombre upbringing affected his personality and his own family life. He was a quiet individual whom few people could claim to know well and whose children regarded as a stranger. His daughter Margaret admitted that she was terrified of him, and although she had heard he was good with other people's children, decided he must be nervous of his own because he was impatient when little legs could not keep up on country walks, had a hatred of noise and was annoyed by childish questions, so the children learned to keep out of his way and not to speak to the great man. This sort of upbringing allied with the malaise which sometimes affected Macdonald males had a bad effect on Stanley's elder son and heir, Oliver. He had an aimless life which led him through various careers from Labour MP during one of his father's administrations to being a chicken farmer in Wales, creating scandals as he went.

Mrs Stanley Baldwin was a completely different character from her husband, being a robust extrovert woman who reputedly caught Stanley's eye when she scored an amazing number of runs for the women's cricket team at Rottingdean. Essentially a cheerful person who enjoyed entertaining and good living, she was able to protect Stanley from the Macdonald melancholy which would surely have overcome him. Although Mrs Baldwin endeavoured to enjoy a standard of living commensurate with her husband's rank, involving a large town house in Eaton Square, a country house at Astley Hall and regular receptions at Number Ten Downing Street, Stanley was essentially a frugal non-conformist at heart. It amused the locals at Wilden to see the chauffeur from Astley Hall go every week to the railway station to collect the dirty washing, which was sent from London to be laundered in Worcestershire because it saved money. Stanley's daughter Margaret also watched rather sadly after her father's death, as his bed, an old single one with springs that sagged to the floor, was put out as rubbish, for despite his fortune he never troubled about his own comfort.

Like his father, Stanley too was a good employer with a conscience about the conditions his employees lived and worked in. His conscience

192

extended further: seeing that he had made a large profit out of the First World War, he arranged an anonymous donation of much of this gain back into the country's coffers. His time in government subjected him to far greater daily strain than other members of the family experienced, but Stanley Baldwin survived well. It has been said that the facial twitch and odd mannerisms he exhibited were symptoms of stress, and in 1936 and again in 1937 he suffered mental breakdowns, although these could as well have been the effect of Edward VIII's abdication crisis as much as his Macdonald blood. At the end of his political career Baldwin was offered an earldom, and according to his biographer Montgomery Hyde, Mrs Baldwin was responsible for its acceptance, because Stanley was as reticent about taking an honour as his uncle Burne-Jones had been.

The exceptional abilities of the Macdonald sisters never passed to their daughters. Margaret Burne-Jones seemed to be a younger version of her mother in looks and temperament. John Kipling described her in 1899 as 'looking very sweet but at times awfully sad – it is part of her style of beauty. She and Trix have the same build of brow, helmet lidded eyes, and vast space between lid and eyebrows,' in fact the epitome of the maidens in a Burne-Jones painting.[22] Georgie cherished secret hopes of a vicarious academic success through her daughter, but in the end it came through her son-in-law, for Margaret had no aspirations. She was an average, conscientious pupil at school, but not the sort of girl to pioneer women's education at Oxford, and so her mother agreed that she could study music with a private tutor at home. She willingly sat for her father who adored her, but the world of the theatre held more fascination for her than the art world in which she had grown up. With her mother's reluctance to enter the limelight, Margaret contented herself with being a quiet observer of life. She formed a close and lasting friendship with the actress Mrs Pat Campbell (for whom her brother had displayed such embarrassing attachment) and was more than happy to be available to provide warm affection and domestic assistance to the flamboyant actress. Any hope of a career for Margaret was dashed early on when at the age of twenty she married Jack Mackail. The influence of her mother can be seen in her choice of husband, although Georgie played no part in encouraging the romance. Jack Mackail was nine years Margaret's senior and a rising star in the literary scene at Oxford. Not only was his chosen subject close to his mother-in-law's heart, but so were his politics, and the two were in total accord from the start. Mackail's career brought him two professorships and many other academic honours, and was punctuated with a score of publications. Throughout, Margaret remained in the background as a supporter of her husband and a contented mother of his children, without displaying any of the burning idealism which had motivated her mother and correspondingly little of the melancholy either. Her daughter, Angela Thirkell, became a celebrated novelist in the thirties, and Angela's son Colin MacInnes made his name as a writer and broadcaster. It was only through Georgie's branch of the family that any of the Macdonald talent continued to flourish.

As the daughter of such a determined personality as Alice Kipling, Trix stood little chance of the peaceful domestic life Margaret Mackail enjoyed. Back with the family in India in her late teens, Trix took to writing naturally and happily. She did have her poetry, novels and short stories published, but these are not easy to trace because of her use of pseudonyms: Beatrice Kipling was one and Beatrice Grange another. Her earliest published poetry appeared in *Echoes*, when at the age of sixteen she added eight poems to Rudyard's thirty-nine, and seven years later she published the first of two novels dealing with marriage in Anglo-India. Her writing was severely restricted by her mental state, yet it was also one of the things that finally aided her return to normality. Much of her work still exists in manuscript form, amongst it an enlightening parody of one of her brother's poems:

IF

'O God, why ain't it a man?' – R.K.
(To a young C.O. now enjoying complete exemption)

If you can keep your job when all about you
Are losing theirs, because they're soldiers now;
If no Tribunal of C.O.s can flout you,
Or tilt the self-set halo from your brow;
If you hold forth, demand your soul's pre-emption,
And play up conscience more than it is worth,
You'll win your case, enjoy 'complete exemption',
And – at the usual price – possess the earth.

If you can take from college and from city
Culture and comfort all your conscious days,
Take all and render nothing, more's the pity,
But cunning preachments of self-love, self-praise;
Exempt you are, forsooth, and safely nested,

194

Above your priceless pate a plume of white,
Protected by this symbol all detested,
Your worst foe – self – is all you need to fight.

If you can claim to follow Christ as Master
(Tell us when he shirked service or grim death),
How dare you plead for freedom from disaster,
And, wrapped in cotton-wool, draw easy breath?
If you evade – not touching with a finger –
The heavy burdens other young men bear,
We dare not breathe the ugly word 'malinger',
For fear, perchance, your craven soul we scare.

If girls in uniform do not distress you,
If you can smile at verbal sneers made plain,
If you don't wince when soldier friends address you,
Proffer bath chairs, and greet you as 'Aunt Jane',
Then rhino hide is nothing to the human,
Holier than they are, grudge ye not their fun,
But, laddie, realise the average woman
Gives heartfelt thanks that you are not her son.

(With due apologies to my brother, who wrote the original 'If', and who did not love shirkers.)

Alice Macdonald Fleming.[23]

After her parents' death, Rudyard took over the care of his sister, much of which had to be in a private nursing home. With husband Captain Fleming conspicuous by his absence, Rudyard paid the bills and visited his sister. He detested Fleming, whom he held responsible for Trix's problems, commenting: 'My experience of him has always been that he is hardly a man calculated to make any sort of life pleasant for those about him.'[24] However, Trix disagreed and once in command of her senses returned to her husband in Edinburgh.

Her mind was restored to her, but those who saw her talking to elephants in the zoo had their doubts. What observers did not realize was that after their years in India, both Rudyard and Trix knew enough Hindi to speak to elephants in the language they had been trained in. An article appeared in a magazine in 1930 about a dangerous elephant called Bozo, who was condemned to death because he had attacked his keeper. Before the sentence could be carried out, a little man with glasses emerged from the crowd and, disregarding everyone's warnings, insisted on being let into the cage with the wild beast. After a few quiet words the terrified animal calmed down and caused no further problem: he was simply homesick, Rudyard Kipling explained to the amazed onlookers. No such dramatic reports appeared about Trix's exploits, but her notebook of elephant talk and some photographs of her with the animals have been handed down the family.

Rudyard died in 1936, some twelve years before his sister, and in the intervening time she wrote, talked and broadcast extensively about her brother's early life, much of which material provides a useful insight into the Kiplings' life in India. There were no children of Trix Fleming's marriage, and with the death of Rudyard's daughter Elsie in 1976, the Kipling line died out completely.

The Macdonald sisters and their progeny, brought up to admire a 'galaxy of brilliant kinsfolk', added more to the sparkle of that galaxy through their lives than any of those distant ancestors could have imagined.

Notes and References

Chapter One: Venerated Ancestors

1 *Kipling Society Journal*, No. 46, 1938, p. 47.
2 K. Middlemass and J. Barnes, *Baldwin: A Biography*, p. 8.
3 F. W. Macdonald, *As a Tale That is Told*, p. 3.
4 Advice to George Browne Macdonald, 1824, Thirkell Papers.
5 Edith Macdonald, *Annals of the Macdonald Family*, Thirkell Papers.
6 Ibid.
7 Ibid.
8 Ibid., p. 26.
9 Ibid., p. 27.
10 F. W. Macdonald, p. 60.
11 Ibid., p. 59.
12 Lady Burne-Jones to S. C. Cockerell, 3 Sept. 1900, Victoria and Albert Museum.
13 Edith Macdonald's Pocket Book, a manuscript book of notes used in the writing of *Annals of the Macdonald Family*, Thirkell Papers.
14 F. W. Macdonald, p. 15 and G. Burne-Jones, *Memorials of Edward Burne-Jones*, Vol. 1, p. 56.
15 Edith Macdonald's Pocket Book.

Chapter Two: An Introspective Childhood

1 Quoted in John Sanders' *Birmingham* (Longman 1969), p. 86.
2 William Dodd's description of Leeds in 1841, quoted in J. F. C. Harrison's *Early Victorian Britain 1832–51* (Fontana 1981), p. 40.
3 F. W. Macdonald, p. 3.
4 Edith Macdonald's Pocket Book.
5 J. L. Kipling to E. Macdonald, 12 Dec 1866, Kipling Papers.
6 J. L. Kipling to Edith Plowden, 17 July 1908.
7 G. Burne-Jones, Vol. 1, p. 133.
8 F. W. Macdonald, p. 34.
9 Ibid., p. 38.

10   Ibid., p. 36.
11   Ibid., p. 43.
12   Edith Macdonald's Pocket Book.

Chapter Three: Widening Horizons

1   G. Burne-Jones, Vol. 1, p. 55.
2   F. W. Macdonald, p. 114: here there is a discreet dash for the family's surname, but it can be identified from the entry in Hannah Macdonald's diary.
3   G. Burne-Jones, Vol. 1, p. 55.
4   Ibid., p. 67.
5   Ibid., p. 105.
6   Ibid., p. 67.
7   Ibid., p. 134.
8   Edith Macdonald's Pocket Book.
9   G. Burne-Jones, Vol. 1, p. 94.
10   Ibid., p. 93.
11   Ibid., p. 67.
12   Ibid., p. 65.
13   Ibid., p. 87
14   F. W. Macdonald, p. 48.
15   G. Burne-Jones, Vol. 1, p. 105.
16   Ibid., p. 123.
17   Ibid., p. 142.
18   Ibid., p. 134.
19   Ibid.

Chapter Four: Pre-Raphaelite Experience

1   Edith Macdonald's Pocket Book.
2   G. Burne-Jones, Vol. 1, p. 169
3   Ibid.
4   G. Burne-Jones, Vol. 1, p. 169.
5   Rooke's Notes in a manuscript book copied out by G. Burne-Jones, Thirkell Papers. Rooke was Burne-Joneses' studio assistant.
6   G. Burne-Jones, Vol. 1, p. 169
7   G. Burne-Jones to Rosalind Howard, 18 August 1867, J22/27 Castle Howard archives.
8   William Morris, 'Sir Peter Harpdon's End', in *Defence of Guenevere*.
9   G. Burne-Jones, Vol. 1, p. 297.
10   William Morris, 'The Blue Closet', in *Defence of Guenevere*.
11   F. W. Macdonald, p. 67.
12   J. W. Mackail, *The Life of William Morris*, Vol. 1, p. 113.
13   G. Burne-Jones, Vol 1, p. 188
14   Manuscript book of Alice Macdonald's poetry, Macdonald Papers.
15   G. Burne-Jones, Vol. 1, p. 176.
16   Ibid. p. 97.

17 E. Macdonald, *Annals of the Macdonald Family*, p. 37
18 G. Burne-Jones, Vol. 1, p. 203.

Chapter Five: The Marriage Stakes

1   F. W. Macdonald, p. 68.
2   Manuscript book of Alice Macdonald's poetry.
3   Ibid.
4   Ibid.
5   G. Burne-Jones, Vol. 1, p. 250
6   F. W. Macdonald, p. 104.
7   Ibid., p. 115.
8   Ibid., p. 335.
9   Ibid., p. 334.
10 Ibid., p. 108.
11 E. H. Fowler, *The Life of Henry Hartley Fowler – First Viscount Wolverhampton*, p. 552.
12 Ibid.
13 Ibid.
14 George Du Maurier, *Trilby*, p. 104.
15 H. Montgomery Hyde, *Baldwin – The Unexpected Prime Minister*, p. 6.

Chapter Six: A Courtly Love?

1   Bodleian MS., quoted in *The Pre-Raphaelites*, Tate Gallery 1984, p. 65.
2   Undated letter of late 1856 from Edward Jones and Georgie Macdonald to F. W. Macdonald, at school in Jersey, Macdonald Papers.
3   G. Burne-Jones, Vol. 1, p. 200.
4   Rooke's Notes.
5   G. Burne-Jones, Vol. 1, p. 217.
6   Rooke's Notes.
7   G. Burne-Jones, Vol. 1, p. 218.
8   Rooke's Notes.
9   Ibid.
10 G. Burne-Jones, Vol. 1, p. 215
11 *The Young George Du Maurier: A Selection of his Letters 1860–67*, ed. Daphne Du Maurier, p. 235.
12 G. Burne-Jones, Vol. 1, p. 218.
13 Ibid., p. 213.
14 G. Burne-Jones, Vol. 1, p. 236, and the same words occur in a letter of G. Burne-Jones to S. C. Cockerell, 27 June 1914.
15 G. Burne-Jones, Vol. 1, p. 213.
16 Letter of John Ruskin to Pauline Trevelyan, 20 July 1862, quoted by Jan Marsh in *Pre-Raphaelite Sisterhood*, p. 266.
17 Ibid.

18   G. Burne-Jones, Vol. 1, p. 307.
19   G. Burne-Jones to S. C. Cockerell, 17 Dec. 1916.
20   Edward Burne-Jones to George Howard, undated.
21   G. Burne-Jones, Vol. 1, p. 287.
22   G. Burne-Jones to R. Howard, 5 Sept. 1868.
23   Daphne Du Maurier, p. 31.
24   G. Burne-Jones, Vol. 1, p. 309.
25   G. Burne-Jones to L. Baldwin, 5 Jan. 1869, Thirkell Papers.
26   G. Burne-Jones to S. C. Cockerell, 20 Aug. 1907.
27   G. Burne-Jones to Rosalind Howard, dated only Wednesday, but probably written at the end of Jan. 1869.
28   Ibid.
29   Ibid., 18 Feb. 1869.
30   Ibid., 24 Feb. 1869.
31   Ibid., 2 March 1869.

Chapter Seven: The Memsahib

1   Trix Fleming to Carrie Kipling, 29 Nov. 1936.
2   Alice Kipling to Edith Plowden, 26 Nov. 1880.
3   J. L. Kipling to Edith Macdonald, 12 Dec. 1866.
4   'Some Childhood Memories of Rudyard Kipling', by his sister (Mrs A. M. Fleming), *Chambers's Journal*, March 1939, p. 168.
5   R. Kipling, *Something of Myself*, p. 2.
6   Quoted in Birkenhead, *Rudyard Kipling*, p. 8.
7   Alice Kipling to Edith Plowden, 18 Dec. 1881.
8   Ibid., 20 Nov. 1880.
9   Undated cartoon drawn by J. L. Kipling, Kipling Papers.
10   *Pioneer* article by J. L. Kipling, 1878.
11   R. Kipling, p. 90.
12   J. L. Kipling to Edith Plowden, 30 June 1882.
13   Trix Fleming to Stanley Baldwin, 11 April 1945.
14   J. L. Kipling to Edith Plowden, 21 Dec 1880.
15   *Chambers's Journal*, March 1939, p. 171.
16   Trix Fleming to Stanley Baldwin, 27 March 1945.
17   *Chambers's Journal*, March 1939, p. 168.
18   Trix Fleming to Stanley Baldwin, 11 April 1945.
19   Alice Kipling to Edith Plowden, 26 Nov. 1880.
20   Alice Kipling to G. Burne-Jones, 17 March 1899.
21   Alice Kipling to Edith Plowden, 18 Nov. 1880.
22   *Pioneer* article by J. L. Kipling, 1878.
23   Ibid.
24   Trix Fleming to Stanley Baldwin, 11 April 1945.
25   Quoted in Angus Wilson, *The Strange Ride of Rudyard Kipling*, p. 60.

Chapter Eight: The Rivals

1   J. L. Kipling to Edith Plowden, 17 July 1908.
2   Ibid., 4 July 1879.
3   *Pioneer* article, 1878.
4   R. Kipling to Margaret Burne-Jones, 2 June 1884.
5   Letter of G. Burne-Jones to L. Baldwin, 29 Aug. 1869, Thirkell Papers.
6   Ormond, *Du Maurier*, p. 62.
7   Quoted in New South Wales Art Gallery, Project Five Leaflet, p. 1.
8   W. Graham Robertson, *Time Was*, p. 51.
9   William Morris to L. Baldwin, 30 Sept. 1871, N. Kelvin, *Collected Letters of William Morris*, Vol. 1, p. 150.
10 R. Kipling to Louisa Baldwin, 1895.
11 J. L. Kipling to Edith Plowden, 17 July 1908.
12 R. Kipling to Margaret Mackail, 4 Dec. 1903.
13 R. Kipling, p. 12.
14 W. Graham Robertson, p. 51.
15 *Kipling Society Journal*, No. 84, Dec. 1947, pp. 3–5.

Chapter Nine: Dear Little Epigram

1   P. Henderson, *Letters of William Morris to his Family and Friends*, p. 98.
2   G. Burne-Jones to George Eliot, 2 August 1870, Yale.
3   Quoted in P. Fitzgerald, *Burne-Jones: a biography*, p. 125, letter in Colbeck Collection, British Columbia.
4   Rooke's Notes.
5   *Times* Obituary, 8 Feb. 1920, written by J. W. Mackail.
6   J. W. Mackail, Vol. 1, p. 210, quoted in P. Fitzgerald, p. 123.
7   BM Add. MSS 45298.
8   Volume in the Fitzwilliam Library.
9   J. W. Mackail, Vol. 1, p. 287, letter 22 June 1872.
10 Quoted by Henderson, p. 328.
11 G. Burne-Jones to May Morris, 6 Sept. 1910, BM Add. MSS 45347.
12 J. Ruskin to C. E. Norton, 2 June 1861.
13 John Ruskin to G. Burne-Jones, 16 Aug. 1863, Fitzwilliam.
14 Ibid., 22 Nov. 1861.
15 Ibid., letters of 1863, 1864, 1865.
16 M. Strickland, *Angela Thirkell – Portrait of a Lady Novelist*, p. 159.
17 G. Burne-Jones to S. C. Cockerell, 19 April 1915.
18 A. Thirkell, *Three Houses*, p. 79.
19 C. E. Norton to G. W. Curtis, 26 Jan. 1869, Harvard.
20 D. Henley, *Rosalind Howard, Countess of Carlisle*, p. 25.
21 Ibid., p. 38.
22 G. Burne-Jones to R. Howard, July 1870.
23 G. Burne-Jones to R. Howard, 28 Sept. 1869.
24 Ibid., 1 April 1870.
25 Ibid., 12 Jan. 1875.
26 Ibid., 1 Nov. 1879.

27 George Eliot to G. Burne-Jones, 3 Aug. 1874, Yale.
28 Edward Burne-Jones to George Howard, 7 May 1875.
29 G. Burne-Jones, Vol. 2, p. 4.
30 G. Burne-Jones to George Eliot, 2 August 1870, Yale.
31 George Eliot to G. Burne-Jones, 26 June 1870.
32 Ibid., 22 July 1879
33 Ibid., 11 May 1875.
34 G. Burne-Jones, Vol. 2, p. 4.
35 George Eliot to G. Burne-Jones, 3 Dec. 1877, Yale.
36 Ibid., 6/7 May 1880.
37 G. Burne-Jones to R. Howard, 11 August 1870.
38 Rooke's Notes.
39 G. Burne-Jones to R. Howard, 22 Jan. 1878.
40 Reminiscences of Sara Anderson, BM Add. MSS 52703. Sara Anderson was Burne-Joneses' secretary.

Chapter Ten: The Family Square

1   Alice Kipling to Edith Plowden, 18 Dec. 1881.
2   Ibid.
3   Kipling Society Journal, No. 84, 1947, pp. 3–5.
4   Alice Kipling to Edith Plowden, 26 Nov. 1880.
5   R. Kipling, p. 207.
6   J. H. Rivett-Carnac, Many Memories, p. 164.
7   Alice Kipling to Edith Plowden, 18 Dec. 1881.
8   Ibid.
9   Alice Kipling to Edith Plowden, 8 March 1882.
10 Ibid., 8 March 1882.
11 Ibid., 28 April 1882.
12 Ibid., 1 May 1882.
13 Ibid., 28 April 1882.
14 Trix Kipling to Rudyard Kipling, 18 March 1882.
15 R. Kipling, p. 40.
16 Kipling Society Journal, No. 84, 1947, pp. 3–5.
17 Ibid., No. 44, 1937, p. 16.
18 Rivett-Carnac, p. 164.
19 Birkenhead, p. 84.
20 Rudyard Kipling to Margaret Burne-Jones, 1885.
21 R. Kipling, p. 206.
22 J. L. Kipling to Margaret Burne-Jones, 31 Jan. 1886.
23 Kipling Society Journal, No. 85, April 1948, pp. 7–8.
24 R. Kipling to Mrs Hill, 1 May 1888, quoted in Carrington, p. 135.
25 Quoted in A. Wilson, p. 154.
26 R. Kipling to Edith Macdonald, Feb. 1884.
27 Ibid., 30 July 1885.
28 R. Kipling to Edith Macdonald, 14 Aug. 1883.
29 J. L. Kipling to M. Burne-Jones, 10 Oct. 1885.

30   A. Kipling to Edith Plowden, 1881.
31   R. Kipling to M. Burne-Jones, 14 Aug. 1885.
32   J. L. Kipling to M. Burne-Jones, 16 March 1885.
33   Trix Fleming to Stanley Baldwin, 27 March 1945.
34   J. L. Kipling to Edith Plowden, 27 July 1886.
35   Ibid.
36   Ibid.
37   *Civil & Military Gazette*, 1888.
38   Birkenhead, p. 83.
39   Kipling Papers, a selection of remarks from letters of Alice Kipling to Edith
     Plowden in the early 1880s.
40   Kipling Papers.
41   R. Kipling to Margaret Burne-Jones, 3 May 1886.
42   Ibid., 28 Nov. 1885 and 11 Feb. 1889.
43   Ibid., 25 Jan. 1888.
44   R. Kipling, p. 58.
45   R. Kipling to Margaret Mackail, 1927.
46   J. L. Kipling to Edith Plowden, 28 Aug. 1888.
47   R. Kipling to M. Burne-Jones, 11 Feb. 1889.
48   R. Kipling to Mrs Hill, quoted in Carrington, p. 154.
49   R. Kipling to Mrs Hill, 2 June 1888.
50   Carrington, p. 175.
51   J. Kipling to Edith Plowden, 8 Aug. 1892.

Chapter Eleven: Middle Age

1   Bodleian MS Don. E. 62, June 1885.
2   Sara Anderson's Reminiscences.
3   Ibid.
4   Ibid.
5   Quoted in P. Fitzgerald, p. 217.
6   G. Burne-Jones to George Howard, 17 Feb. 1894.
7   R. Kipling to L. Baldwin, 24 Sept. 1901.
8   G. Burne-Jones to S. C. Cockerell, 22 Dec. 1897.
9   G. Burne-Jones to R. Howard, 18 Oct. 1867.
10   Ibid., 20 March 1908.
11   *A Summary of the History of the South London Art Gallery*, 1893, p. 5 (Southwark
     Collection).
12   E. Burne-Jones to G. F. Watts, Nov. 1894, Fitzwilliam.
13   Ibid.
14   G. Burne-Jones to George Howard, 28 Sept. 1897.
15   E. Burne-Jones to Mrs G. F. Watts, 1894, Fitzwilliam.
16   Reminiscences of Sara Anderson.
17   Open Letter to the Electors of Rottingdean, 15 July 1897: Rottingdean
     Preservation Society.
18   Ibid.
19   Ibid.

20 R. Kipling to M. Burne-Jones, 1895.
21 A. Kipling to Edith Plowden, 25 Nov. 1897.
22 J. L. Kipling to Edith Plowden, 17 July 1908.
23 G. Burne-Jones, Vol. 2, p. 284.
24 Ibid., p. 288.
25 G. Burne-Jones to S. C. Cockerell, 7 Oct. 1896.
26 Ibid., 30 May 1897.
27 S. C. Cockerell's note in his own hand in Collected Letters of Lady Burne-Jones, June 1898.
28 G. Burne-Jones to S. C. Cockerell, 26 July 1898.

Chapter Twelve: The End of a Generation

1 F. W. Macdonald, p. 199.
2 Ibid., p. 155.
3 G. Burne-Jones, Vol. 2, p. 1.
4 Ibid., p. 1.
5 Bodleian MS Don. E. 62, 12 Dec. 1898.
6 Ibid., 19 June 1899.
7 Ibid.
8 G. Burne-Jones to Mary Drew, 16 Dec. 1898, BM Add. MSS 46246.
9 G. Burne-Jones to Jenny Morris, 26 Sept. 1897, BM Add. MSS 45347.
10 G. Burne-Jones to Mary Drew, 6 July 1899.
11 A. Thirkell, p. 86.
12 G. Burne-Jones to Carrie Kipling, 1 March 1899.
13 G. Burne-Jones to Carrie Kipling, 7 March 1899.
14 G. Burne-Jones to S. C. Cockerell, 5 Aug. 1906.
15 J. L. Kipling to Edith Plowden, 22 July 1899.
16 J. L. Kipling to Miss Norton, 5 Feb. 1900.
17 A. Thirkell, p. 80.
18 Ibid., p. 78.
19 R. Kipling to M. Mackail, 4 Dec. 1903, and R. Kipling, p. 177.
20 Robert Colenzo to Capt. Fleming, 15 Nov. 1899, Macdonald Papers.
21 R. Kipling to Alfred Baldwin, 18 Nov. 1898.
22 J. L. Kipling to Miss Norton, 21 Nov. 1899.
23 J. L. Kipling to Edith Plowden, 4 July 1899.
24 G. Burne-Jones to S. C. Cockerell, 10 Dec. 1905.
25 Ibid., 29 March 1906.
26 Ibid., 14 June 1906.
27 Ibid., 27 July 1906.
28 Times Obituary, 13 June 1906.
29 G. Burne-Jones to S. C. Cockerell, 22 Aug. 1908 and 22 Dec. 1908.
30 J. L. Kipling to Edith Plowden, 17 July 1908.
31 G. Burne-Jones to S. C. Cockerell, 15 Oct. 1916.
32 J. L. Kipling to Edith Plowden, 3 Nov. 1910.
33 R. Kipling to Louisa Baldwin, 8 July 1909.

34 J. L. Kipling to Edith Plowden, 28 Jan. 1909.
35 R. Kipling to Louisa Baldwin, 27 Oct. 1909.
36 Trix Fleming to Carrie Kipling, 29 Nov. 1936.
37 Compulsory registration of births, deaths and marriages began on 1 July 1837, but the early entries are very unreliable.
38 F. W. Macdonald, p. 120.
39 Stanley Baldwin to F. W. Macdonald, 18 June 1925 (Mrs Macdonald Bendle).
40 G. Burne-Jones to S. C. Cockerell, 1 March 1906.
41 Ibid., 31 Jan. 1907.
42 Ibid., 1917.
43 Margaret Mackail to Lady Mary Murray, 14 Feb. 1920, Bodleian MSS Gilbert Murray.
44 Edith Macdonald, *Thoughts on Many Things*, p. 25 and p. 10.
45 Ibid., p. 71.
46 Montgomery Hyde, p. 148.
47 E. Macdonald, p. 18.

Epilogue

1 A. Thirkell, p. 67, and Kipling Papers, J. L. Kipling to Edith Plowden, 17 July 1908.
2 R. Kipling, p. 93.
3 Birkenhead, p. 125.
4 Ibid., p. 126.
5 E. Burne-Jones to G. F. Watts, 1884.
6 R. Kipling to M. Mackail, 11 Feb. 1889.
7 Sara Anderson's Reminiscences.
8 A. Thirkell, p. 66.
9 Ibid., p. 67.
10 Ibid., p. 67.
11 Ibid., p. 68.
12 W. Graham Robertson, p. 75.
13 A. Thirkell, p. 50.
14 Philip Burne-Jones to Mary Drew, BM Add. MS 46246, 18 Dec. 1917.
15 G. Burne-Jones to S. C. Cockerell, 22 July 1908.
16 Bodleian MSS Gilbert Murray, 156 and 552, 19 Feb. 1902.
17 Philip Burne-Jones to Mary Drew, BM Add. MSS 46246, 24 Feb. 1920.
18 R. Kipling to M. Burne-Jones, 28 Nov. 1885.
19 K. Middlemass and J. Barnes, p. 58.
20 Philip Burne-Jones to Mary Drew, 28 May 1923, BM Add. MSS 46246.
21 Montgomery Hyde, p. 43.
22 J. L. Kipling to Edith Plowden, 22 July 1899.
23 From an unpublished collection of Trix Fleming's work, Macdonald Papers.
24 R. Kipling to M. Mackail, 1927.

Bibliography

PUBLISHED SOURCES

Abdy, Jane, and Gere, Charlotte, *The Souls*, Sidgwick & Jackson, 1984.

Allen, Charles (ed.), *Plain Tales from the Raj*, André Deutsch, 1975.

Allingham, Helen (ed.), *William Allingham: a diary*, Longman, 1911.

Baldwin, A. W., *My Father: The True Story*, Allen & Unwin, 1955; *The Macdonald Sisters*, Peter Davies, 1960.

Baldwin, Oliver, *The Questing Beast*, Grayson & Grayson, 1932.

Benge-Jones, Mark, *The Viceroys of India*, Constable & Co, 1982.

Birkenhead, Lord, *Rudyard Kipling*, Weidenfeld & Nicolson, 1978.

Bough, James, *The Prince and the Lily*, Hodder & Stoughton, 1975.

Burne-Jones, G., *Memorials of Edward Burne-Jones*, 2 vols., Macmillan, 1904.

Carrington, Charles, *Rudyard Kipling*, Macmillan, 1955.

Chambers's Journal.

Colvin, Sir S., *Some Personal Recollections*, Scribner's Magazine, Vol. 67, 1920.

Cornell, Louis L., *Kipling in India*, Macmillan, 1966.

Davies, R., George A. R., and Rupp, G., *A History of the Methodist Church in Great Britain*, Vol. 2, Epworth, 1978.

Dudley, Ernest, *The Gilded Lily: The Life and Loves of the Fabulous Lillie Langtry*, Odhams, 1958.

Du Maurier, Daphne (ed.), *The Young George Du Maurier: A Selection of his Letters 1860–67*, Peter Davis, 1951.

Du Maurier, George, *Trilby: a novel*, Osgood, McIlvaine & Co., 1895.

Fitzgerald, Penelope, *Burne-Jones: a biography*, Michael Joseph, 1975.

Fowler, Edith H., *The Life of Henry Hartley Fowler – First Viscount Wolverhampton*, Hutchinson, 1912.

Gross, John (ed.), *Rudyard Kipling, the Man, his Work and his World*, Weidenfeld & Nicolson, 1972.

Haight, Gordon S., *George Eliot, a biography*, OUP, 1968; (ed.) *Letters of George Eliot* (7 vols.), OUP, 1956.

Henderson, Philip, *William Morris: His Life, Work and Friends*, Thames & Hudson, 1967; *Swinburne*, Routledge & Kegan Paul, 1974; (ed.) *Letters of William Morris to his Family and Friends*, Longman, 1950.

Henley, Dorothy, *Rosalind Howard, Countess of Carlisle*, Hogarth Press, 1958.
Horner, Frances, *Time Remembered*, Heinemann, 1933.
Ionides, Alexander, *Ion: a Grandfather's Tale*, Cuala Press, 1927.
Ionides, Luke, *Memories*, Herbert Press, Paris, 1925.
Kelvin, Norman (ed.), *Collected Letters of William Morris*, Vol. I 1848–1880, Princeton University Press, 1984.
Kipling, Rudyard, *Something of Myself*, Macmillan, 1937.
Kipling Society Journals
Lago, Mary (ed.), *Burne-Jones Talking*, John Murray, 1981.
Macdonald, F. W., *As a Tale That is Told*, Cassell, 1919.
Mackail, J. W., *The Life of William Morris*, 2 vols, Longman, 1899.
Marsh, Jan, *Pre-Raphaelite Sisterhood*, Quartet, 1985.
Middlemass, Keith, and Barnes, John, *Baldwin: A Biography*, Weidenfeld & Nicolson, 1967.
Montgomery Hyde, H., *Baldwin – The Unexpected Prime Minister*, Hart-Davis, 1973.
Ormond, L., *George Du Maurier*, Pittsburg University Press, 1969.
Peters, Margot, *Mrs Pat*, The Bodley Head, 1984.
Rivett-Carnac, J. H. *Many Memories*, Blackwood, 1910.
Roberts, Charles, *The Radical Countess*, Steel Brothers, 1962.
Robertson, W. Graham, *Time Was*, Hamish Hamilton, 1931.
Stewart, J. M., *Rudyard Kipling*, Gollancz, 1966.
Strickland, Margot, *Angela Thirkell – Portrait of a Lady Novelist*, Duckworth, 1977.
Surtees, Virginia (ed.), *The Diaries of George Boyce*, Yale University Press, 1980; *The Diary of Ford Madox Brown*, Yale University Press, 1981.
Thirkell, Angela, *Three Houses*, OUP, 1932.
Thornton, T. H., and Kipling, J. L., *Lahore*, Government Civil Secretariat Press, 1876.
Victorian Olympians, catalogue of exhibition in Art Gallery of New South Wales, Australia, 1975.
Waters, B., and Harrison, Martin, *Burne-Jones*, Barrie & Jenkins, 1973.
Wilson, Angus, *The Strange Ride of Rudyard Kipling*, Secker & Warburg, 1977.
Young, G. H., *Stanley Baldwin*, Rupert Hart-Davis, 1952.
Young, Kenneth, *British Prime Ministers – Baldwin*, Weidenfeld & Nicolson, 1976.

UNPUBLISHED SOURCES IN PUBLIC COLLECTIONS

Bodleian Library, Oxford: Letters of F. G. Stephens; letters of Gilbert Murray which include those written by Georgie Burne-Jones and by Margaret Mackail.
British Library: various Morris and Burne-Jones papers.
East Sussex Record Office: Minutes of the Rottingdean Parish Council; letters of Lady Burne-Jones and Mrs Stanley Baldwin to Mrs Elizabeth Beard; draft letter of Steyning Beard to the Parish Council concerning Philip Burne-Jones's interference in Parish Council matters.
Fitzwilliam Museum, Cambridge: Burne-Jones papers deposited by Lady Burne-Jones after writing *Memorials of Edward Burne-Jones*; Ruskin letters.

BIBLIOGRAPHY

Sheffield Library: Wharncliffe papers containing letters of Edward Poynter.
University of Sussex Library: Kipling papers, property of the National Trust; Baldwin papers.
Victoria and Albert Museum: Letters of Sir Edward Poynter; letters of Lady Burne-Jones to Sir Sydney Cockerell.
Worcester Record Office: Baldwin papers; papers of Canon Cory who was the vicar of Wilden in Louisa Baldwin's time there.

UNPUBLISHED SOURCES IN PRIVATE COLLECTIONS

Mrs Meryl Macdonald Bendle: papers of the Macdonald family.
Castle Howard archives: correspondence between Edward and Georgiana Burne-Jones and George and Rosalind Howard, 9th Earl and Countess of Carlisle.
Misses Helen and Margaret Macdonald: papers of the Macdonald and Kipling families.
Mr Lance Thirkell: papers of the Burne-Jones and Macdonald families.

Index